SORRY . . . NO GOVERNMENT TODAY
UNIONS *vs.* CITY HALL

SORRY...
NO GOVERNMENT
TODAY
UNIONS
vs.
CITY HALL

An Anthology Edited by
Robert E. Walsh

BEACON PRESS   BOSTON

To Sallie

Copyright © 1969 by Beacon Press
Library of Congress catalog card number: 79–84798
Beacon Press books are published under the auspices
of the Unitarian Universalist Association.

Published simultaneously in Canada
by Saunders of Toronto, Ltd.

Printed in the United States of America

CONTENTS

ACKNOWLEDGMENTS

When the idea for this book was initiated, it was agreed by the publisher and editors that an anthology which included pieces by many persons involved in collective bargaining in the field of public employment would carry more credibility than the views of a single writer. It has certainly proved true. I should like to express my sincere appreciation to those contributors of articles and speeches who have made this book possible. Its purpose was to arouse interest in some of the basic questions and to acquaint the public with some of the diverse views on these issues.

I should also like to express my appreciation for the help received from Howard V. Doyle, president of Massachusetts Public Employees Council 41 of the American Federation of State, County and Municipal Employees; Alfonso D'Apuzzo, executive secretary, and James J. Cody, attorney, of the Massachusetts Labor Relations Commission; Rose Claffey, the voice of the American Federation of Teachers on the Massachusetts State Labor Council; Frank Lavigne, research and education director of the Massachusetts State Labor Council; Francis E. Sweeney of the Massachusetts Legislative Research Bureau; and the always helpful staff of the Ventress Memorial Library in Marshfield, Massachusetts.

SORRY . . . NO GOVERNMENT TODAY
UNIONS *vs.* CITY HALL

1

BACKGROUND OF AN ISSUE

THE QUESTION
by Robert E. Walsh

It was prophetic that the strike of 35,000 transit workers which paralyzed New York City for twelve days began on New Year's Day, 1966. It marked the beginning of a year in which many strikes by public employees occurred across the nation. There were strikes by policemen in Detroit, firefighters in Atlanta, and teachers in New Orleans, Philadelphia, and Newark. Elsewhere, other city employees who worked on golf courses, in tax and public works departments, in sewer disposal plants, on ferry boats, and in public zoos also went on strike.

This pattern was to continue throughout 1967. Once again the nation focused its attention on New York City in September of that year when 50,000 school teachers went on strike and postponed the opening of the schools. Some six months later 10,000 sanitation men in New York walked off their jobs, leaving mounds of garbage to pile up in the city. The garbage accumulation reached an estimated 190 million pounds, causing a public health emergency which prompted Mayor John Lindsay to request the National Guard's aid. Governor Nelson Rockefeller, knowing the danger of sending troops into a highly unionized city in a strike situation and realizing that even the militia could not effectively collect garbage in a modern urban area, decided the strike should be settled by a third party.

While New York City was grappling with its garbage problem, sanitation workers were also striking in Memphis. The problems there seemed small in February compared to those in New York City, yet two months later the Memphis strike was to hold the attention of the entire nation.

1

The strike in Memphis began on February 12, when twenty-two black workers, members of Local 1733 of the American Federation of State, County and Municipal Employees AFL–CIO, walked out over an issue involving racial discrimination. Black workers had been sent home after working two hours on a rainy day while white workers were retained and sent back to work when the rain stopped, thus earning a full day's pay. The strikers refused to return to work until the discrimination issue and others were resolved, and the mayor in turn refused to talk to them until they returned to work. The strike turned into a civil rights crusade which was climaxed by the assassination of Dr. Martin Luther King, Jr.

The Memphis local won wage increases and other benefits, but they also won a promotional system that could lead to the appointment of a black man as a supervisor. Two other facts about the Memphis strike stand out. First, the sanitation men were members of the American Federation of State, County and Municipal Employees Union, which is the fastest growing union in the AFL–CIO today, and a union with a 30 per cent black membership. Second, the low wages of $1.60 per hour indicate the gap between the wages of many public employees and their counterparts in private industry.

The events in Memphis made it quite apparent that in many cases there was a connection between the increasing militancy of public employees and the civil rights movement. In other instances, however, such as teachers' strikes, the public employee militancy was bringing the unions into conflict with the civil rights movement. The new militant teachers in ghetto areas frequently found themselves involved in controversy with minority groups who held the teachers partly responsible for the poor education of their children.

New York City with its 300,000 employees provides the most dramatic example of what is happening in the field of public employee-labor relations. But people in other cities are becoming increasingly aware of the problems and frustrations of the urban dweller. Whether he lives in New York or San Francisco, the urban resident reacts the same way when he must battle his way home during a transit strike. The feeling is equivalent in New Haven and Los Angeles when garbage piles up in front of the house. The urban resident often feels as though he is a helpless hostage in a fight between public officials and union leaders; he is left wondering where and when it will all end and how much it is going to cost him. If the city dweller is pressed hard enough, he is likely to feel that "The whole damned business ought to be stopped and stopped right now." He probably remarks to his wife or neighbor that anyone involved in providing a vital service for a city or town has absolutely no right to go out on strike. He might be surprised to learn that, at this writing, there is no law on the books of any town, city, or state which gives public employees the right to strike.

Yet, as we have seen, when conditions become intolerable public employees do go on strike. What should a community do—put 10,000 sanitation men, 35,000 transit men, or 50,000 teachers in jail? If the community elects to jail its leaders, this only serves to make them martyrs and deepens the loyalty of their followers. However, the most important thing is that as a nation we have given the right to strike to employees in private industry. Thus we should think twice before passing punitive laws applying to people in the public sector.

Former Secretary of Labor W. Willard Wirtz proved himself a true prophet in 1965 when he told a conference of mayors in New York City,

> In most of the cities of the nations there is today a wavering between new confidence and new concern. A strong and thriving economy is going from month to month from record to record. There is unprecedented agreement on major issues of public policy among a majority of the American voters and of those in effective control of Congress and the Executive Branch. It is nonetheless generally expected that the months ahead will be troubled, turbulent, perhaps even dangerous.

What the Secretary then said about the civil rights movement has become even clearer with the passage of time.

> The occasion of this mixture of high hopes and deep anxieties is, of course, the civil rights movement. The great question about the civil rights movement has been too little asked. The question is not whether this movement will

continue. It will. Neither is there any question whether it will prevail in most of the essential demands now being made. It will, as it must. The great question is what institutional form the civil rights movement will assume on a permanent basis. And the answer to this question depends on the nation's response to this movement.

It is possible that what will develop here is another well-organized, disciplined, special interest group representing one particular segment of the population. We are entitled to a higher hope: that the current civil rights movement will become a broadly-based, integrated and creative force for the advancement of human rights and the improvement of the human condition throughout the United States, and for the rebuilding of America's cities.

The Secretary went on to warn the mayors that they would be seriously misjudging the civil rights movement if they believed it was solely concerned with such matters as formal segregation or overt, calculated discrimination. Wirtz explained that the civil rights movement had shown itself to be profoundly concerned with the entire complex of economic, cultural, and sociological forces that are precisely those forces that have turned American cities into slums: the forces of poverty, unemployment, ignorance, and alienation. He said, "The civil rights movement has developed as a massive, militant force demanding that something be done, not just about racial discrimination, but about conditions which include the worst of urban life in America."

Thus the increasing militancy of the public employees can be attributed in part to the civil rights movement. Another aspect is the emergence of unionism in a new sector of the American economy which will write a new chapter in the history of American labor. The issue of public employee unionism in the broader context of urban society as described by Secretary Wirtz was probably best summarized by Walter Lippmann in a recent *Newsweek* column when he said, "Modern living is dangerous. We are confronted with a fateful question—can we remain a free society and still provide the great urban masses with the vital services they must have?"

Although the issue is simply stated, it is not a simple one. It is not an issue which we can put aside but one which must be faced and discussed because it involves our health and safety, the education of our children, and the hard-won freedoms gained by working people during years of strife.

Also contained in Lippmann's question are a host of other issues which must be dealt with. Some of these questions are:

Will Civil Service survive public employee collective bargaining?

Should public employee bargaining be done in public?

Can elected officials allow outside parties to become involved in helping to make decisions which bind government at various levels?

Can procedures which have worked successfully in labor relations in the private sector be transferred to the public sector without drastic change?

Should public employees not involved in providing vital services be given the right to strike?

LABOR IN PRIVATE INDUSTRY

In order to understand the militancy of today's public employees, it is helpful to know something about the development of organized labor and its function in the private sector.

In the early years of our national history, skilled labor was in such short supply that it was necessary to pass laws setting a maximum on the wages of craftsmen. Around 1780, the first associations of workingmen were formed along craft lines in the large population centers. By 1790 the shoemakers and the printers had organizations which can be considered the forerunners of our modern labor unions.

The process which has developed into contract negotiations started at the beginning of the nineteenth century. One of the first instances of its use occurred in New York City in 1809 when a group of journeyman printers drew up a price list for their work and submitted it to their employers. After studying the list, the employers formed a committee to compose a counterproposal. The printers then formed their own committee and the two groups worked out a compromise list agreeable to both sides. Essentially this procedure is still the basis for labor relations today and is called collective bargaining.

The concern of the New York printers with wages has a modern ring, but it was not typical of the main interests of early labor groups. The early unions tried to improve social conditions, and fought for such goals as the public education of their children. Other major union interests were the improvement of sanitary conditions in their places of employment, shorter working hours, prevention of imprisonment for debt, and public land for settlers in the West.

In the early 1800s these unions were organized on a local level, and in many cases did not survive for even a decade. But strikes did occur. For example, the women weavers of Pawtucket, Rhode Island, went out on strike to improve their working conditions in 1824. By 1825, unions of carpenters, weavers, tailors, masons, cabinetmakers, hatters, and stevedores had become established in the cities, and by 1827 Philadelphia had a citywide council of unions.

A financial panic in 1837 created widespread unemployment, and many unions lost ground. But a boom period followed, topped off by the California gold rush in 1848, and the year 1850 found labor unions again on the rise. In this period some of our modern unions emerged, such as the International Typographical Union.

During this phase of union development, labor's attempts to organize and bargain collectively were fought by employers in the courts. Business argued that employees acting in concert were actually engaging in a conspiracy against the public good. One of the first judicial opinions challenging this idea was handed down in 1842 by Massachusetts Chief Justice Lemuel Shaw, who said, in the case of the *Commonwealth* v. *Hunt,* that employees had the right to form unions and bargain with their employers.

The Civil War brought new problems for the unions. Unions in New York City supported some of the Irish who refused to be called in the draft. Other unions such as the stonecutters, hat finishers, and molders were unable to hold themselves together and passed out of existence. In 1861 the president of the Machinists' Union did not even attend the convention of his union because he was positive that no delegates would be there.

At about this time, also, numerous groups that were formed

to fight for specific labor reforms—notably the Grand Eight Hour Day League and the Labor Reform League—attracted large followings of workingmen and farmers. In 1866 an attempt was made to organize a national labor union concerned with the issues of prison labor and the national debt. This movement, like others of its kind, died as its members moved to political parties or organizations such as the Greenbacks, who were then campaigning for legislation to make greenbacks the national currency.

In 1868 the shoemakers formed a secret society called the Knights of St. Crispin, which was dedicated to fighting the advances of the industrial revolution, especially the pegging machine which brought widespread unemployment in their trade. A series of strike victories boosted the membership of the Crispins to 50,000 until a combine of shoe manufacturers fought back and quickly destroyed their power. By 1878 they were no longer functioning as an effective union. Other craftsmen such as skilled steelworkers and locomotive engineers also formed secret societies during the post-Civil War period, going under such names as the Sons of Vulcan and the Brotherhood of the Footboard.

The panic of 1873 caused huge layoffs which took a toll of union membership, and employers' demands for longer hours and pay cuts led to numerous clashes between workers and the police and militia. One of the groups which benefited from the unrest was the Knights of Labor, founded as a secret society in 1869 by a group of Philadelphia garment cutters. By 1886 the Knights— no longer secret—had grown to a membership of 700,000 by accepting everyone except doctors, lawyers, stockbrokers, gamblers, and saloonkeepers. The Knights of Labor supported the eight-hour day and the graduated income tax, and waged campaigns against the growing power of the railroads and banks. In the latter part of the 1880s, the Knights successfully supported some western railroad strikes but lost eventually to the Texas and Pacific Railroad. This defeat, combined with antilabor sentiment which arose over the Haymarket Riot in Chicago in which seven policemen were killed by a bomb, caused the Knights to fall into public disfavor.

A conflict was beginning to develop over the question of whether labor unions should concern themselves with the improvement of social conditions in general or whether they should take the narrower view and dedicate themselves only to improving the lot of the workingman within his own craft. The latter view prevailed and became known as the new unionism.

In 1881 a group of men who believed in the new unionism formed the Federation of Organized Trades in Pittsburgh. Among the group were Peter McGuire of the Carpenters and Samuel Gompers of the Cigar Makers. In 1886 the Federation of Organized Trades was restructured as the American Federation of Labor. It was set up as a loosely knit federation of unions that would each handle its own affairs in its own trade but that would act together on matters of general political and economic welfare through labor councils organized in central cities and through federations at the state level.

Eugene V. Debs, who in 1893 became president of the American Railway Union, disagreed with the leadership of the A.F. of L. and felt that unions should be organized along industrial rather than craft lines. His American Railway Union consisted of workers who were not skilled tradesmen and consequently not eligible for membership in other railroad brotherhoods.

In the spring of 1894, employees of the Pullman Company in Chicago went on strike to protest wage cuts which left them little or no money after rent was taken from their pay for their company-owned homes. As a result of this strike, which was supported by Debs's Union, the Attorney General in the administration of President Grover Cleveland went into Federal court and obtained an injunction—a court order to stop the strike—because the delivery of mail was impeded. Violence followed and Debs, who ignored the injunction, was sentenced to prison for contempt of court. This injunction was the start of the use of the biggest weapon against striking workers.

Judicial opinion continued to go against labor in the hatters strike in Danbury, Connecticut, in 1902. The union members boycotted the products of nonunion employers which led to a 1909 U.S. Supreme Court decision ruling the boycott illegal and awarding the Danbury company triple damages.

Encouraged by the more sympathetic attitude of the Wilson administration which took office in 1913, labor tried to change various laws in order to enable workers to organize and bargain with the employers. President Woodrow Wilson made Gompers a labor adviser and addressed a convention of the A.F. of L. During World War I, labor made some gains under decisions of the War Labor Board. However, the war ended before the National Committee for Organizing the Iron and Steel Workers could get a foothold in the steel industry.

The year 1919 set a new high in both strikes and antilabor sentiment. John L. Lewis called his workers out of the mines and the Attorney General broke the strike with a Federal injunction. The Boston police strike further intensified the bitterness against labor unions and made many think of unionism as the "Red Menace."

Against this background the confrontation between the steel industry and the A.F. of L. first took place. It became increasingly apparent in labor circles that the unions would have to establish a beachhead in the steel industry before they could go on to organize the other growing mass-production industries such as automobiles and rubber. The management of the steel companies, led by Judge Elbert Gary of the United States Steel Corporation, decided to take a firm stand against labor unions. This resulted in one of the most explosive strikes in a strike-filled year. The steelworkers left their jobs before their leadership was ready, and this resulted in a crushing defeat for organized labor.

The prosperity of the 1920s coupled with a management campaign urging workers to join company unions generally stalled the growth of the labor unions. During this period the leadership of the A.F. of L. was convinced that they had to move into the political arena in order to obtain basic changes in the law of the land.

The Depression with its widespread unemployment and the election of President Franklin D. Roosevelt set the stage for these legal changes. One of the first of the new laws was the Norris-LaGuardia Act, which prohibited the Federal courts from issuing injunctions against unions involved in labor disputes unless there was evidence of fraud or violence. In 1935, Congress encouraged organized labor even further by passing the Wagner Act, whose three main provisions gave workers new rights and protections: (1) it made certain acts by employers unfair labor practices; (2) it established an election system through which employees could select labor unions of their choice; and (3) it established the

National Labor Relations Board (the NLRB) to handle elections
and to administer the regulations against unfair labor practices.
For example, an unfair labor practice is an attempt by an employer to prevent an election among his employees after they have
decided they want a union.

Armed with the legal backing of the Federal Government,
the unions began massive organizing drives, and within three years
after the passage of the Wagner Act organized labor had swelled
its ranks by more than a million workers.

Now an old issue surfaced once again to split the union
ranks. Since 1886 the American Federation of Labor had become
a solid bloc of craft unions such as the plumbers, bricklayers, carpenters, and so forth. This meant that unskilled workers employed
in the mass-production industries would be left unorganized unless
the structure of the A.F. of L. were changed. A group of labor
leaders led by John L. Lewis of the United Mine Workers insisted
that the unskilled workers be organized. In 1935 the officers of
eight big unions with nearly a million members formed the
Committee for Industrial Organization to encourage the idea of
forming unions by industry rather than by crafts. At first the Committee's leaders planned to work within the framework of the A.F.
of L., but clashes developed and the Executive Council of the
A.F. of L. suspended the Committee's leaders. Late in 1939 the
Committee formed the Congress of Industrial Organizations with
John L. Lewis as its first president. Lewis was succeeded subsequently by Philip Murray of the Steelworkers' Union.

In 1937, just as the Steelworkers' Organizing Committee was
about to move against the big steel companies, Myron C. Taylor
of U.S. Steel sat down with John L. Lewis and agreed to recognize
the right of his company's employees to bargain collectively through
representatives of their own choosing. Labor had established the
beachhead in steel without a strike, and the entry of the union
into the steel companies had come to pass in less than two decades.

Through the use of the sit-down strike in the thirties, the
CIO succeeded in gaining recognition from General Motors and
the Chrysler Corporation. Finally in 1941 the Ford Motor Company agreed to bargain with the United Auto Workers. Thus, by
the time the United States entered World War II, the United
Auto Workers Union claimed a membership of 300,000 and the

Steelworkers 600,000. During this same period other labor organizers were making big membership gains in the rubber, textile, electrical, and maritime industries.

The postwar period was marked by the regulation and reorganization of unions. The action of John L. Lewis in leading his mineworkers out on strike during the war and the postwar inflationary period both helped to swing public opinion to an antilabor position. This sentiment mounted until Congress placed restrictions on the labor unions. In 1947, Congress passed the Taft-Hartley Act to try to bring about a balance between labor and management at the bargaining table. Under this law certain union practices were made unfair labor practices and certain sections of the Wagner Act were amended.

The deaths of William Green, president of the A.F. of L. and Philip Murray, president of the CIO, within weeks of each other in 1952 facilitated the merger of the two labor federations which took effect in 1955. George Meany, president of the A.F. of L., became president of the combined AFL–CIO.

In 1959, after 2½ years of investigations, a congressional committee headed by Senator John L. McClellan of Arkansas made public a disturbing record of fiscal corruption and coercion of employees and small employers by several labor unions. These disclosures led to still another Federal law, the Labor Management Reporting and Disclosure Act. This law set up a code of conduct for unions and their officers as well as for consultants used in labor relations by employers. Under this law labor unions must have a constitution and bylaws, an annual financial report must be made to the Secretary of Labor, and these reports must be disclosed to union members.

At this time certain amendments were also made to the Taft-Hartley Act which gave to state labor relations boards and state courts the jurisdiction over certain areas not covered by the National Labor Relations Board. Thus a small manufacturer who does not handle a volume of $50,000 in shipments to or from another state would be governed by state regulation rather than by Federal law.

On July 1, 1968, a new schism developed when Walter Reuther, president of the United Auto Workers and former president of the CIO, led his union out of the AFL–CIO. Reuther and

Meany had long disagreed over policy matters such as the social goals of the federation and the AFL–CIO's position on foreign policy. Soon after leaving the AFL–CIO, the United Auto Workers and the International Brotherhood of Teamsters, who had been expelled from the federation in 1957, joined forces to form the Alliance for Labor Action (ALA).

Then in April 1969, District 65 of the Retail Wholesale and Department Store International Union, claiming a membership of 30,000 in the New York City area, left the AFL–CIO for the ALA. This union, with a membership of 30 per cent black and twenty-five per cent Puerto Rican gave as its reason dissatisfaction with the AFL–CIO's attitude toward civil rights and minority groups.

One of the goals of the ALA is supposedly a more liberal stand on social issues and civil rights than that taken by the AFL–CIO. Whether or not the ALA will move into the public employee field remains an unanswered question. However, there have been some predictions that one or two leaders of the big public employees union might be added to the Executive Council of the AFL–CIO in 1969.

THE GROWTH OF THE AFL–CIO
by Nathaniel Goldfinger

The official voice of the AFL–CIO is its 75-year-old magazine the American Federationist. *In the following article which appeared in the December 1967 issue of the* Federationist, *Mr. Goldfinger, director of the AFL–CIO Department of Research, discusses the recent growth of the labor federation.*

Union membership gains have been in an upsurge since 1963. The past four years have been a period of expansion of organized labor, following a small membership decline in the previous six years. And the growth of trade union membership is continuing.

In 1966–1967, the average paid membership of AFL–CIO affiliates rose to 13.8 million. By the first six months of 1967, per capita dues payments of unions affiliated to the AFL–CIO were up to 14.3 million—representing 18.6 per cent of the civilian labor force. This was a gain of 1.8 million since the 1962–1963 low point, when the AFL–CIO's paid membership represented 17.6 per cent of a much smaller labor force.

Reflecting steady membership growth during the course of 1966 and 1967, the per capita dues payments of affiliated national and international unions to the AFL–CIO are continuing to rise.

Organized labor's actual strength is greater than these figures indicate. The U.S. Department of Labor's estimates of the civilian labor force, for example, include many people who are not eligible for union membership—such as executives, managers and self-employed businessmen, professionals, and farmers. In addition, national and international union per capita payments to the AFL–CIO tend to understate the actual membership of the federation's affiliates for a number of reasons, including less than full payment or nonpayment by many unions for members on strike or unemployed. And there are several unions that are not affiliated with the AFL–CIO.

In the past year, the number of trade union members in the United States has represented somewhere about 35 per cent of those eligible for membership.

In some industries, trades, and occupations, the membership of organized labor represents 80 per cent or more of the people who are eligible. And in others, the membership represents 20 per cent or less. But in most parts of the economy since 1963, trade union membership has been advancing as rapidly or faster than employment.

AFL–CIO unions represent wage and salary earners in hundreds of different industries, occupations, trades, and labor markets across the length and breadth of the country. Membership trends of each union are affected by a host of factors—including employment, economic and technological changes within its jurisdiction, national and regional economic and political developments, and its own resources and efforts. The expansion or decline of total membership reported to the AFL–CIO is the net result of these and other factors on the membership of affiliated unions.

AFL–CIO MEMBERSHIP, 1955–1963

When the AFL–CIO was established in 1955, the combined per capita dues payments of affiliated unions to the AFL and the CIO represented 12,486,000 members or 19.2 per cent of the civilian labor force. These figures exclude per capita payments from the four international unions expelled from the AFL–CIO at its second constitutional convention in December 1957.

Per capita dues payments to the AFL–CIO increased in 1956–57 to 12,883,000. This rise in paid membership of the federation was somewhat faster than the slow increase of the civilian labor force in those two years. As a result, the AFL–CIO's paid membership of affiliated unions represented 19.3 per cent of the labor force in 1956–1957.

After 1957, the membership reflected in per capita payments to the AFL–CIO declined slowly. By 1962–1963, this paid membership was down to 12,469,000 members, representing 17.6 per cent of a greater civilian labor force.

Between 1957 and 1963, some unions continued to expand, as reported in per capita payments to the AFL–CIO. Among them were the Building Service Employees, International Brotherhood of Electrical Workers, Operating Engineers, Government Employees, Retail Clerks and State, County and Municipal Employees.

However, such membership gains in 1957–1963 were more than offset by substantial membership declines of many unions— particularly among railroad employees and workers in manufacturing industries. The membership of many other unions remained about the same.

This situation in 1957–1963 largely reflected economic and political conditions during most of those years.

There was a deep recession in 1958 and another recession in 1960–1961. Unemployment was in a rising trend—from 4.3 per cent of the labor force in 1957 to 5.7 per cent in 1963. The impact of spreading automation in a relatively stagnant economy, with recurring recessions, was frequent layoffs, part-time work, shifts in industry location, plant shutdowns, and declining employment in many industries.

In several key parts of the economy and areas of traditional union strength, employment either dropped or failed to grow. Between 1957 and 1963, the number of production and maintenance workers in manufacturing industries, for example, dropped 600,-000; jobs on Class I railroads fell 200,000, and the number of workers in contract construction remained about the same.

The small employment increases of those years were mainly in state and local government, the services, retail trade and among executives, supervisors, clerical workers, sales and service workers, professionals, and technicians. Many of the new jobs in private business were part time.

In the latter 1950s and into 1960, there was a mounting political attack on organized labor. From many Republicans and conservative Democrats, there was a continuing outcry about corruption, with the finger of blame pointed at all of organized labor. Conservative politicians also hammered away at organized labor as the source of inflation, while similar charges were made at frequent intervals by business leaders and some university economists, including self-proclaimed liberals. Hardly a week passed during those years without a public attack on trade unions and collective bargaining, loudly proclaimed through television, radio, the newspapers, and magazines.

The AFL–CIO's early and strong support of civil rights legislation and programs also made organizing gains more difficult, especially in the South.

The combination of these economic and political trends placed trade unions increasingly on the defensive—particularly in industries whose employment was declining. Yet, despite these difficulties, organizing gains were made—not only by the unions that expanded their memberships but also by unions whose memberships declined.

Large-scale turnover of employment in many industries required continuing organizing efforts to keep the overall membership stable. During 1957–1963—with plant shutdowns, changes in industry location, and frequent layoffs—unions in such industries as auto, steel, and machinery had to gain new organizational victories in order to prevent their overall memberships from dropping even more than they did.

Some unions, such as those on the railroads, already represented close to 100 per cent of eligible employees and could hardly gain new organizational victories. For them, declining employment meant declining memberships, while they continued to represent close to 100 per cent of the work force in such industries.

Despite these difficulties, organized labor made strides in collective bargaining. Wages and salaries increased moderately. Significant forward advances were made in fringe benefits—such as pension plans, medical insurance, vacations, and holidays. And the unions began to develop numerous job security measures, adjustment procedures, and protective machinery against the impact of automation on the work force.

These complex and varied factors help to explain the 414,000 net decline in the membership of AFL–CIO affiliated unions between 1956–1957 and 1962–1963, as well as the decline from 19.3 per cent of the civilian labor force to 17.6 per cent in those years.

MEMBERSHIP GAINS, 1963–1967

The political situation changed considerably in 1961, after the inauguration of President John F. Kennedy. Public attacks on organized labor began to ease off. It was much more possible for trade union representatives to obtain a fair hearing in most government agencies instead of the usual cold shoulder of previous years.

On January 17, 1962, President Kennedy issued an Executive order which directed federal agencies to recognize and bargain with unions representing their employees. While this executive order dealt directly with Federal employees, it provided an atmosphere of support for union organization and collective bargaining in public employment generally—state and local government as well as Federal. Moreover, it reflected the Administration's general acceptance of trade unions and collective bargaining as important American institutions.

These policies and attitudes toward unions and collective bargaining as institutions have been carried on generally by the Administration of President Lyndon B. Johnson.

While the national political situation began to improve in 1961, it was not until 1963 that economic conditions started to pick up significantly. The real volume of national production increased at a yearly rate of 5.5 per cent between 1963 and the first half of 1967—two-thirds faster than in 1957–1963. Moreover, this more rapid rise of sales and production was partly concentrated in heavy goods manufacturing, industrial and commercial construction, and related activities.

As a result, factory employment and jobs in construction bounced up, while employment in government, the services, and retail and wholesale trade continued to move forward strongly.

In the three and one-half years from 1963 to the first half of 1967, nonfarm employment (including executives, supervisors, and part-time) increased 7 million, 40 per cent more than in the previous six years. Unemployment declined from 5.7 per cent of the labor force in 1963 to 3.8 per cent in the first half of 1967.

The number of factory production and maintenance workers shot up 1.6 million in those three and one-half years—bringing the total slightly above the Korean war peak in 1953. In the same period, the number of jobs in contract construction rose 300,000.

These changes in economic conditions and the national political environment provided the framework for a resurgence of trade union growth since 1963.

The increasing number of young entrants into the labor force responded much more favorably to union organization and collective bargaining than the dire predictions of the late 1950s and early 1960s would have led people to believe.

Unions continued to make significant collective bargaining gains in wages, working conditions, and fringe benefits. Pension and health insurance plans were expanded and improved. Job security measures and supplemental unemployment benefit plans were gained. And the AFL–CIO's national leadership, in seeking progressive economic and social legislation, bore fruit in the adoption of such measures as Medicare, federal aid to education, substantial expansion of coverage of the federal minimum wage and an increase in the minimum wage, civil rights legislation, and expanded aid for housing and community facilities.

The AFL–CIO's internal jurisdictional disputes machinery, which became effective in January 1962, sharply reduced jurisdictional disputes among affiliated unions. Although this internal federation machinery did not deal directly with organizing, its successful operation eased the way for cooperative efforts.

Organizing activities expanded. And these efforts were increasingly successful.

The unions that had been growing in the previous six years, when the AFL–CIO membership declined, continued to make substantial forward strides—such as the Retail Clerks, Building Service, IBEW, State-County and Operating Engineers.

But the continued membership growth of these unions in 1963–1967 was not offset by large membership declines of many other unions, as occurred in 1957–1963. As industrial production and employment rose, the memberships of most unions of manufacturing workers increased, exceeding membership figures of 1955–1957 or restoring much of the losses of earlier years—such as Auto, Steel, IUE, and Rubber.

Added to this membership expansion has been the growth of the Government Employees, the Teachers, and Postal Unions. The majority of affiliated national and international unions, in various different types of industries and occupations, have moved forward—the Machinists and the Meatcutters, the Seafarers and the Actors, the Airline Pilots, Communications Workers, and Sheet Metal Workers.

From 12.5 million or 17.6 per cent of the labor force in 1962–1963, the AFL–CIO's paid membership rose to 13.8 million in 1966–1967. And it was at 14.3 million or 18.6 per cent of the labor force in the first half of 1967.

By the first half of 1967, the membership of AFL–CIO affiliated unions, as reported by per capita dues payments to the federation, was substantially greater than in 1955. And the percentage of the civilian labor force represented by the AFL–CIO's paid membership was rapidly returning to what it had been in 1955–1957—and it was continuing to advance.

MAJOR GROWTH UNIONS

The adaptability of the organized labor movement to changes in the work force and economic conditions can be seen in the resurgence of membership growth since 1963.

This adaptability of an organized labor movement that is broadly representative of a varied work force can be seen also in the list of the AFL–CIO affiliated national and international unions that have grown substantially since 1955. These unions expanded their memberships through the period that covered major national economic and political changes. They represent a wide variety of occupations and industries—professionals and technicians, as well as government employees, retail sales clerks, service and production workers, skilled workers, and the unskilled.

Between 1955 and the first half of 1967, per capita dues payments to the AFL–CIO from the following nine affiliates increased by 100,000 or more: United Auto Workers, Building Service Employees, International Brotherhood of Electrical Workers, Operating Engineers, American Federation of Government Employees, Retail Clerks, International Association of Machinists, Meatcutters and Butcher Workmen, and State, County and Municipal Employees. The American Federation of Teachers narrowly missed this list.

In that same period, per capita dues payments from the following 12 affiliates increased 50 per cent or more: Actors and Artistes, Airline Pilots, Building Service Employees, Doll and Toy Workers, International Brotherhood of Electrical Workers, Operating Engineers, American Federation of Government Employees, Retail Clerks, Seafarers International Union, Sheet Metal Workers, State, County and Municipal Employees, and the American Federation of Teachers. (Unions with less than 10,000 members are not included.)

Other unions that were significantly greater in per capita dues payments to the AFL–CIO in the first half of 1967 than in 1955 include the Postal Unions, the Clothing Workers, the Communications Workers, the International Union of Electrical Workers, the Glass Bottle Blowers, the Laborers, the Plumbers and Pipe Fitters, and the Retail, Wholesale and Department Store Union. And dramatic organizing activities by the United Farm Workers Organizing Committee have been proceeding among agricultural workers.

These gains considerably outstripped declines in membership among a number of unions, including the railroad and textile unions, whose memberships declined mainly because of technological changes, reduced production and service, shifts in industry location, and strong employer and political opposition in areas of industry expansion.

By the first half of 1967 there were 15 affiliated unions which reported memberships of 300,000 and more—up from eight in 1955. These 15 large unions represent wage and salary earners in a wide variety of occupations, industries, and skills: Auto Workers, Steelworkers, Machinists, Carpenters, International Brotherhood of Electrical Workers, Retail Clerks, Laborers, Meatcutters, Ladies' Garment Workers Union, Communications Workers, Building Service Employees, State, County and Municipal Employees, International Union of Electrical Workers, Operating Engineers, and Hotel and Restaurant Workers.

Since 1963, membership gains have been reported by AFL–CIO affiliates in various occupations and economic activities. There still are difficulties which have not been entirely overcome—changes in technology, the composition of the work force, and the location of industry. Moreover, strong opposition to organized labor persists in some industries, communities and areas of the country, and several unions, such as those on the railroads, continue to be confronted by declining employment in their jurisdictions. In addition, despite some pickup of union membership among office workers, union strength remains very weak in that group, as well as among scientists and engineers. But union membership generally is continuing to advance and gains are widespread across most of the broad spectrum of employment in the nation.

PUBLIC EMPLOYEES: AN EMERGING FORCE
by David L. Perlman

> *The following article by David L. Perlman, an assistant editor of the* AFL–CIO News, *a newspaper published by the labor federation, discusses the growth of the public employee unions. He reports on this growth as of July 1967, when this article appeared in the* American Federationist.

A decade ago, the public employee field—Federal, state, and local —was labeled the "growth stock" of the labor movement.

That's just what it has been and the boom shows no sign of petering out. The curve of membership, bargaining units, and con-

Reprinted with permission from the *AFL–CIO American Federationist*.

tracts points sharply upward and may go a long way before reaching a plateau.

There have been unions in the government service since the nineteenth century. And there have been examples of success to cite.

The postal unions, after surviving a bitter quarter century of management union-busting attacks, demonstrated that a muscular, politically potent union could flourish even in the midst of a bureaucracy.

The coalition of craft unions in the Tennessee Valley Authority proved thirty years ago that collective bargaining could work successfully when an agency was given leeway to negotiate and make binding agreements. The Government Printing Office and some U.S. Department of Interior installations verified this experience, as did a scattering of cities.

Nevertheless, the surge of union growth in the private sector during the 1930s and 1940s had no parallel in government employment.

By the mid-1950s, union organization in the Federal service still drifted up and down in a narrow range. There was a measurable expansion of union membership in city, county, and state employment—but only when measured from its low starting point. And this in the nation's most rapidly expanding field of employment.

It would have been hard to quarrel with one commentator's description of public employee unionism of yesteryear as "the 97-pound weakling" of the labor movement.

The era of explosive growth dates from the late 1950s in the nonfederal field and to the advent of the Kennedy administration in the Federal Civil Service.

In both areas, election of labor-backed candidates to public office helped bring about new ground rules which opened the door to large-scale organization.

The key was and is the trade union fundamentals of exclusive bargaining rights for the union which represents a majority and a written contract enabling unions to do the basic day-to-day job of representing workers on grievances as well as negotiating basic conditions of employment. Along with a dues checkoff—now common at all levels of government—this has provided both the organizing impetus and the stability necessary to retain and expand on an initial organizing success.

The first sign of a massive breakthrough came when big cities like Philadelphia and New York demonstrated that a labor relations policy based on collective bargaining worked with a large, diverse work force which included laborers and tax collectors, hospital attendants and typists, zookeepers and draftsmen, mechanics and street cleaners.

The pillars of city halls did not topple nor did civil service commissions crumble when conditions of employment were negotiated instead of being set unilaterally.

It took a bit of adjustment, to be sure. There were personnel directors whose ingrained reaction to union contract proposals was along the lines of, "We can't agree to this. It's against civil service regulations." Then the union reply. A shrug, "So let's negotiate a change in the regulations. Why not?" And, indeed, why not?

The example of the cities made it easier for President Kennedy's task force to draw up a labor relations code for the Federal Government. And the Federal Executive order in turn spurred additional state, county, and city laws and policies.

There are weaknesses in the Federal policy and further steps toward meaningful collective bargaining are overdue. But critics of the policy agree the impact of Kennedy's Executive order has been comparable to that of the Wagner Act in the private sector.

The other indispensable ingredient in the surge of public employee unionism has been the growing militancy of public employees.

Perhaps, as one union president suggests, it is the change from the Depression generation, when a civil service job and pension represented security—insulation against breadlines and the factory scrap heap.

Before World War II, both pay and fringe benefits in public employment were generally superior to those in private industry.

But during and after the war, pay scales in government lagged far behind the private sector and the catchup raises at two- or four-year intervals seldom closed the gap. Unions in private industry were catching up and starting to surpass government fringe benefits.

In recent years, public employees have been regaining some

of the lost ground. And the lesson has not been lost that militant unions have gotten the best settlements.

To the general public, the visible phase has been strikes and picket line demonstrations by local public employees, including teachers. Strikes of city and county workers are not new, but there have been more of them—despite the prevalence of "no strike" laws.

And it would be hard to convince negotiators who bargain with local governments that the willingness of workers to strike if necessary hasn't been a major factor in reaching good settlements without a strike.

A news item from Gary, Indiana, makes the point: "The highest salaries in the nation for beginning teachers were won by negotiators for the Gary Teachers Union in a marathon bargaining session that ended only 30 minutes before a scheduled strike."

It was, incidentally, a first contract—made possible through a representation election in which the Teachers' local defeated the local affiliate of the National Education Association by a 1,529 to 267 margin.

There are unions which do not seek the right to strike, including the solidly organized Fire Fighters and Federal employee unions whose leaders recognize that strike talk might boomerang in Congress. But there are incidents such as the limited strike threat by New York City firefighters and the reaction of rank-and-file delegates to a speech by AFL–CIO President George Meany at a big Postal Clerks pay rally.

Meany had the current railroad dispute in mind when he told the delegates that workers "don't like to strike, but sure like to have the right to strike." The prolonged applause which interrupted the speech at that point was dramatic evidence that workers who think they are not getting a fair share react the same, whether in public or private employment.

A great many unions have some public employee membership and contracts with government agencies. Virtually every trade is represented either in separate contracts or in joint bargaining such as the metal trades agreements. But as a quick benchmark of growth, let's take a look at unions made up almost entirely of public workers or with a large percentage of such workers.

In 1959, the American Federation of Teachers had fewer

than 50,000 members. Currently the AFT reports over 140,000.

The American Federation of State, County and Municipal Employees had already grown to a respectable 174,000 membership. But its latest report shows 330,000 members.

From 60,000 in 1959, the American Federation of Government Employees has passed the 235,000 mark.

There has been a comparable growth in the public employee membership of unions whose major strength is in private industry.

The Machinists, which for many years had an active Federal employee district, more than doubled its government employee membership since the advent of Federal collective bargaining.

Unions bargaining through metal trades councils quickly won exclusive recognition in most naval shipyards, although the closing of several big shipyards cut the growth rate in recent years.

The Building Service Employees showed a 35 per cent increase in the public employee sector—both local and state and in the Federal government.

The Laborers, barely represented in the public employee field before 1960, jumped from 7,500 to nearly 30,000 and are now actively organizing.

All the AFL–CIO maritime unions have contracts covering government vessels—another byproduct of the Presidential executive order.

In the Federal field, unions now have exclusive bargaining rights covering well over one million workers—with AFL–CIO affiliates accounting for 90 per cent of the total. More than half of these—600,000—are in the postal service, where union membership long has been the norm.

Outside the postal service, however, the growth is keyed to the new era of collective bargaining.

By the spring of 1963, 15 months after the Presidential order, unions had won exclusive bargaining rights for 94,000 nonpostal Federal employees.

By mid-1965, the number had grown to 300,000. The latest official tally was in August 1966 and the current figures certainly are higher. But at that time the total had reached 445,000. Of these, 252,000 were blue-collar wage board workers and 194,000 were classified salaried employees.

It should be noted that the classified group includes such

occupations as hospital attendants and guards as well as white-collar jobs. And, in all areas of public employment, the bulk of union members are manual workers. But in both the Federal and nonfederal fields, the proportion of organized white-collar workers is moving up—slowly but apparently steadily.

It has not been easy to stake out clear-cut lines in public employee unionism.

In the era of no contracts, several unions often had conclaves of membership and old arguments over industrial versus craft bargaining units echoed at all levels of government. The possibility of meaningful bargaining also brought additional unions into the field. Adding to the complications was the presence of a number of unaffiliated organizations actively competing for membership. Some of these carved out an ultra-militant stance, with a shriller appeal to workers. Others shunned the word union and basked in the approving smiles of old-line supervisors.

AFL–CIO affiliates, however, have more than held their own and, as bargaining units are determined and contracts negotiated, the area of conflict has shrunken.

At the same time that unions have moved to take advantage of the opportunities for organizing, they also have faced the problem of leadership training from the shop steward to the negotiating committee level—and the problem of translating votes in bargaining elections into membership.

The AFL–CIO Department of Education has helped supply this training, especially in the Federal field, with individual unions, the Metal Trades Department, and the Government Employees Council.

One problem, still to be fully resolved, is to sign up all the workers in a unit after winning representation elections overwhelmingly. The long-established unions, such as postal groups and the Fire Fighters, do not have this problem because a new worker is made aware that the union is something everyone belongs to.

Part of the problem, perhaps, is the more limited area of bargaining in most government agencies. In many cases, as in the Federal service, wages are set by legislative action for white-collar workers and on the basis of prevailing wage scales for blue-collar workers. One of the chief goals of AFL–CIO unions in the federal service is to achieve a much greater degree of union participation in determining wage scales.

The union shop exists in some city and county jurisdictions, although it is still the exception. In the Federal service, it appears a long way off, although concepts can change quickly. This writer remembers sitting in on a panel discussion at a conference of Federal personnel officials in the mid-1950s. Bill Ryan of Machinists' District 44 shocked the audience—and perhaps some of the panelists from other unions—by insisting that collective bargaining must be the basis of government employee-management relations. It seemed then a more distant possibility in the Federal service than the union shop does now.

There has been a changed attitude, too, towards the role of civil service commissions. Once they saw themselves, and to an extent were viewed by the embryo public employee unions, as avenues of appeal and arbiters between the worker and his agency. Now union negotiators tend to view them as arms of management and seek independent arbitration, factfinding, and mediation as a substitute for a paternalistic personnel agency.

Attitudes towards the Hatch Act and the little Hatch Acts that have sprung up at the state and local levels have changed also. Government workers want and need protection against political kickbacks and the mass patronage turnover when a new administration takes office. But they see no reason why this requires them to give up their own citizenship rights, including the right to support their friends and oppose their enemies.

Postal workers have long been one of Washington's most powerful lobbies and other government employee unions are taking a leaf from the same book.

At the state and city level, public employee unions work hard at lobbying, usually in close cooperation with AFL–CIO central bodies. One of New York's biggest union demonstrations recently overflowed Madison Square Garden into nearby streets as members of the AFSCME, the Transit Workers, and the Teachers bitterly protested a punitive state antistrike law.

What will the future bring? The potential for organizing remains great. About 40 per cent of the Federal government's 2.5 million civilian workers are organized and the figure probably will pass the 50 per cent mark within a few years.

In the nonfederal sector of public employment, a smaller

percentage are union members or work under a union contract. A 1964 Labor Department estimate was 544,000 members of AFL–CIO unions—about 7.5 per cent of total government employment. The number is considerably higher today and state and local employment is expected to soar from 7.7 million in 1965 to 11.4 million by 1975.

Some localities still bitterly resist union organization; a few have even made union recognition illegal. But in the Federal government and in a growing number of states and cities, the union organizer's greatest foe is apathy, not management intimidation.

The potential for meaningful collective bargaining also is great. Some of the frustrations which limit bargaining today will be swept away and that, in turn, will make union membership more meaningful and valuable to the public worker.

In vigor of leadership, in acceptance of a more realistic dues structure than the "bargain basement" rates of a few years back, unions representing government employees are becoming a more significant factor in the American labor movement.

The past decade has been bright. The future looks even brighter.

THE ROLE OF THE AFL–CIO
IN THE GROWTH OF PUBLIC SECTOR
COLLECTIVE BARGAINING
by Harvey L. Friedman

In this article a former union official, now a professor of government, discusses the role of the AFL–CIO in the growth of public sector collective bargaining. Mr. Friedman is the assistant professor of government and assistant director of the Labor Relations and Research Center at the University of Massachusetts at Amherst. Formerly the New England Education Director of the Amalgamated Clothing Workers of America, AFL–CIO, he is presently teaching classes in public-sector collective bargaining, trade union structure, and administration and politics.

Used by permission of the author.

The great leap forward in public sector collective bargaining which came in the middle and late 1960s was the direct result of the promulgation of Executive Order 10988, the Magna Carta of Federal collective bargaining. It was issued by President John F. Kennedy on January 17, 1962, partially in response to the requests of the government worker unions backed up at least nominally by the AFL–CIO and partially to head off the passage of the tougher and less flexible Rhodes bill. It guaranteed the right of Federal employees to join employee organizations of their own choice (not called unions). It also provided a rudimentary process for securing collective bargaining rights and for the development of collective bargaining agreements.

Despite the fact that this Order involved only Federal employee collective bargaining, the development of state and municipal employee collective bargaining stemmed directly from its issuance. Prior to 1962, isolated municipal collective bargaining existed only in New York City, Philadelphia, and a few other isolated locations. Bargaining was based on labor's political muscle, some collective action by the unions involved, and some foresight by government administrators. The power of the unions was almost nil since it was dependent on a grudging, bare tolerance of their existence. Limited consultation rather than extensive negotiation was the watchword. But what are the roots of real public sector collective bargaining?

The American labor movement developed as a result of the revolt of craft workers against the emerging industrial society and the role assigned to workers in the economic and social life of the country. In order to attain their long-range goals, unions were first forced to develop immediate economic goals to improve the lives of the workers at home as well as at the place of work. In the 1930s, the craft workers were joined in trade union organization by the relatively unskilled mass-production workers of the industrial unions. The immediate economic goals were combined with a new goal—economic security—as a result of the Depression and the ensuing unemployment. Eventually, some social goals for the entire country became a part of labor's program.

During the first 140 years of organized labor in the United States, most government workers—except for the postal service employees—were considered unable to be organized. They were more interested in developing and maintaining the prestige of their jobs than in banding together to improve their economic lot. They felt that their economic goals and security had already been secured forever by Civil Service and the merit system. The white-collar government employee felt that he was a part of the middle class. He did not view himself as being a "wage" worker.

The craft and industrial worker resented this attitude. He looked upon government unions as being weak, lacking in class consciousness (however he might have phrased this) and dependent on the false security of a Civil Service law which could be changed and destroyed whenever government officials wished. (It is interesting to note that this security has been taken away by statute and legal interpretation in many states where punitive public sector collective bargaining laws have been passed or where differentiated staffing of public institutions has been accepted.) The craft and industrial unions mirrored the views of their members in their attitude and approach to the government workers' unions.

In the 1960s this began to change. Suddenly, the government worker looked around and found that his craft or industrial worker neighbor had climbed into the middle class and was comfortably secure there. A one-family house instead of a multi-family tenement, paid vacations and holidays, the security of pension, health, and welfare programs, two television sets and one car (or two cars and one color-television set), and the desire and appreciation for education had become common attributes of the life of the blue-collar worker. The government worker discovered that the industrial worker had indeed caught up with and in many cases passed him on the ladder of success.

Despite the fact that the postal workers and some government shipyard workers had been organized for many years, the thrust toward trade union organization by the bulk of government workers was at first a painful experience. First organizing small, weak unions and then combining into larger ones, they moved slowly to secure the collective bargaining rights that their blue-collar, nongovernmental workers had won from their employers years before. The job was made more difficult because of the general prohibition against organizational strikes based on the doctrine of sovereignty.

At the same time, these *unions* were being challenged by large, well-financed employee *associations* whose original purposes had been expanded to include collective bargaining. Such organizations as the National Education Association, the National Association of Government Employees (formerly the Federal Employee Veterans Association), the American Nurses Association, and uncountable, independent, unaffiliated municipal associations provided an alternative choice for the AFL–CIO unions—the Government Employee Union, the Teachers, the State, County and Municipal Employees, the Fire Fighters, the Letter Carriers, the Postal Clerks, and others—while at the same time taking on most of the coloration of the trade unions.

The AFL–CIO responded with caution. There were some real problems. Members of the traditional unions viewed the demands of the government workers from their newly acquired perch in the middle class. For the first time, manual workers considered themselves both as consumers of government services and also as employers of government workers. They were now affected to a significant degree by taxes. The rather loose personnel practices of the government groups which did not place much value on productivity could easily be compared to the management approach to productivity in the industrial plant. And the blue-collar workers objected to the lack of industrial know-how in the government service.

Other pressures were produced by the rapid expansion of the services that government was expected to provide and by the expansion of the government work force itself. The growth of the government's role in education and its role in public welfare produced an almost geometrical jump in employment. Where total government employment was 10.6 million people in October 1965, by March 1969 it had grown to 12.7 million. It has been widely predicted that public employment will reach the 16 million mark by the end of 1975.

The AFL–CIO, in the forefront of the fight to provide more and better public services, suddenly realized that the public service industry had become the largest industry in the country. At the same time, many of the nongovernmental AFL–CIO unions decided to set up public sector divisions based in some cases on traditional craft jurisdictions and in other cases without regard for tradition.

The Laborers, the Technical Engineers, the Communication Workers, the Building Service Employees, and other groups joined the AFSCME, the AFT, the AFGE, the postal unions, and the Metal Trades Department in organizing government workers. The Building Service Employees dropped the word "Building" from their title in order to expand their jurisdiction and expedite organization. The Teamsters—not affiliated with the AFL–CIO— also expanded their activities in the public sector.

The AFL–CIO in its corporate structure moved in several directions at the same time. On one hand, they testified for changes in Executive Order 10988 to make it more palatable to the traditional trade union approach to collective bargaining. At the state and local level, the AFL–CIO assisted unions in pushing for collective bargaining statutes and in organizing government workers.

In early 1969, the AFL–CIO agreed to pay the fine levied on the New York Teachers Union as a result of their 1968 strike. This was to indicate the AFL–CIO's unhappiness with the punitive provisions of the New York collective bargaining statute. In addition, some grants and loans have been made to public sector unions while the AFL–CIO's organization department is assisting in organizational drives in many parts of the country.

On the other hand, despite the fact that the number of organized government workers as a percentage of the total AFL–CIO membership grew from 5.1 per cent in 1963 to 8.1 per cent in 1966 to approximately 12 per cent in early 1969, there was by that time no representative of a public sector trade union on the 29-member Executive Council of the AFL–CIO. (In early 1969, there were rumors that the AFL–CIO at its 1969 convention would expand the Council in order to bring in one or more representatives of the public sector unions.)

The Government Employee Council of the AFL–CIO is a council, not a department, as are the Metal Trades, Construction Trades, Maritime Trades and Industrial Unions groupings. And although the AFL–CIO testified in favor of the amendment of the Executive order, it did not use its considerable political strength to force the report of the interdepartmental committee—generally forward-looking—from the limbo of lost causes.

The dichotomy of protecting the traditional trades while at the same time encouraging the growth of new all-government unions has found the AFL–CIO in awkward and conflicting positions. The public-sector unions have not helped the situation themselves. Traditionally weak, they have depended too much on political action rather than on direct job action to win their demands. This may work in terms of short run gains, such as wage demands, but it is detrimental in the long-range attainment of their goals, such as building unions and the passage, expansion, and improvement of collective bargaining statutes, laws, ordinances, and orders. In addition, they have failed to utilize the traditional political action processes to develop administrative strength in enforcing the statutes. They, as well as the other elements of organized labor, still look on appointments to labor boards and civil service commissions as rewards for deserving labor leaders rather than as sources of strength in building the public sector labor movement.

The public sector unions are not in the same mold as the traditional trade unions; in fact, they were until recently quite indistinguishable from professional associations, civil service organizations, and company unions. The concept of conflict rather than reason which had produced the great craft and industrial unions was really not considered important until after 1962. And until 1962, none of the unions was willing to confront the doctrine of sovereignty and its stifling of legitimate trade union activity.

The structure of the public sector unions, with its emphasis on narrow political action, was itself more dictatorial than democratic, more political than dynamic. The dues of the unions generally reflect the "penny wise, pound foolish" techniques of fraternal organizations rather than the "musclebuilding by sacrifice" concepts of the trade unions. Even the most downtrodden workers in traditional trade unions were willing to make some sacrifice, while the very concept of sacrifice has been, for the most part, lost upon the government workers.

The use of the strike as an economic weapon by the Teachers and the State, County and Municipal Employees, among others, in the mid-1960s certified the end of this "hat in hand" attitude and the beginning of the development of true trade unionism. Though almost always against the law, this revolt awakened the conscience of many legislative bodies and permitted the growth of collective bargaining for many segments of the public sector.

Yet even here there was a germ of trouble within the AFL–CIO. Many leaders of craft and industrial unions really did not want to encourage strikes in the public sector, feeling that a public backlash would limit strikes in the private sector as well. They did not want the legitimation of compulsory arbitration or labor courts, both proposals for resolving public sector strikes. Once placed in operation, it might be a simple step to extend these proposals to the private sector. Hence there appears to have been a subtle discouragement of public sector strikes. Offers of mediation on the part of private sector union leaders and the drying up of strike funds which have been traditionally extended to new and expanding unions prevented many strikes and limited the duration of many more. In all fairness, this tendency toward discouragement also has its roots in the traditional leaders' unhappiness with the low dues structure of the new unions.

The future looks rosier for the public sector unions. The AFL–CIO has absorbed the new unions and they are preparing for their inevitable growth. Just as the A.F. of L. absorbed the CIO and modified its approach to industrial unionism, it is doing the same thing with public sector trade unionism.

The generation gap in trade unionism has been recognized and is beginning to narrow. While the trade union leadership in the public sector is just barely changing at the top levels of the unions, more and more second-level leadership is coming from the ranks of the younger employees in the government in recent years. This is also happening with the traditional craft and industrial unions, and should encourage cooperation and agreement on techniques and goals.

The traditional business unionism is once again adapting to the new scene. As it does, public-sector trade unions will continue to grow, collective bargaining will produce mildly innovative solutions to the problems of the governmental office or workroom, and the public sector unions will be absorbed into the mainstream of American trade unionism.

2

MANAGEMENT AT THE
BARGAINING TABLE

Officials representing their governmental units, or agencies such as school boards or city-operated hospitals, hammer out contracts with labor representatives at the bargaining table. The voice of these public administrators is often carried in the *Nation's Cities,* a magazine published by the National League of Cities.

Kenneth O. Warner, who authored the first article in this section, is an outstanding example of a public administrator. Over a period of thirty years he has served at every level of government, and since 1949 has been the executive director of the Public Personnel Association. His duties over the years have included teaching and writing.

Today collective bargaining in the public sector is moving so rapidly that members of small town personnel boards and town counsels are also finding themselves involved. The second and third selections offer an insight into what is happening in many towns on the eastern seaboard.

In the final article, Arthur J. Flamm, a labor lawyer, gives us an inside look at collective-bargaining negotiations in a small city-owned hospital and states his views on what happens when the bargaining is carried on before the public and the press.

CITIES AT THE BARGAINING TABLE
by Kenneth O. Warner

Current headlines clearly indicate that: municipal officials in many of the nation's cities will spend long hours at the bargaining

Reprinted with permission of *Nation's Cities, The Magazine of the National League of Cities.*

table . . . they will face tougher public policy problems than ever before . . . they will repackage the content of municipal personnel administration.

The reason? The likely expansion of public employee organizations—unions and associations—will enable them to exert even greater influence on determining conditions of work, benefits, and more important, salaries and wages of municipal employees.

The impact of collective bargaining is already certain. While its ultimate significance remains speculative, in all probability the practice will cut more deeply into the fabric of public administration.

Its importance cannot be overstressed. In the judgment of Frank P. Zeidler, former mayor of Milwaukee, only civil rights ranks higher than management relations with organized public employees as an issue facing public administrators. *The heart of the subject is collective bargaining, its nature and scope.*

Municipal labor relations pose a tremendous challenge. Because many employee groups have gained the legal right to bargain, city fathers must now develop a sound philosophy of government labor relations. Then they must fashion practical methods for carrying out that philosophy.

City officials at the bargaining table often discover that the conduct of management's relations with organized employees is profoundly influenced by state law.

Just look at some of the questions lawmakers must answer.

Should cities follow the lead of the private sector in setting up industry-type methods of recognition and negotiation? Will matters subject to bargaining be limited by state law, or will everything be "up for grabs" to be decided at the municipal bargaining table? What can or will be done about public service strikes?

Answers to these questions and hundreds more are being mulled over in state legislatures, and to a lesser degree in city councils. But many councilmen, mayors, and city managers are unaware of how the answers affect them and their communities. That's not surprising because municipal collective bargaining is a relatively new phenomenon. The movement gained momentum in 1958 when New York City adopted a system of labor relations designed to promote the type of "collective bargaining prevailing in industry." Large and small cities followed New York's lead.

Today's developments have been so swift that they defy comprehensive analysis. The current status of labor relations in state and local governments is reflected in these facts:

About 7 per cent of these employees are union members.

Over half of the states have granted public employees the right to organize.

One-third of the states grant some type of bargaining right to various classes of public employees. In municipalities alone, approximately 1,000,000 employees have the legal right to representation at the bargaining table.

Since 1959, at least eight states have enacted comprehensive labor relations laws affecting public employees (Connecticut, Delaware, Rhode Island, Massachusetts, Michigan, Minnesota, Oregon, and Wisconsin).

In 1965, state legislatures considered 153 bills on labor relations in public employment.

By 1966, state and local governments had entered into more than 1,000 separate agreements with employee organizations.

Employee organizations expanded among white-collar workers and professionals: nurses, social workers, teachers, etc.

Collective bargaining is now a fact of administrative life in many cities. Although no common pattern of operation has emerged, current trends and future developments are discernible.

A VARIED PATTERN

Variety typifies the present pattern. Bargaining for most municipal employees is mandatory in several states, including Connecticut, Massachusetts, Michigan, Oregon, and Wisconsin. Others, such as Delaware, authorize bargaining at the option of local governing boards.

In several instances the same state agency that handles labor relations in the private sector also performs services for local governments. This is true in Connecticut, Michigan, and Delaware. In Wisconsin, a separate state agency known as the Wisconsin Employee Relations Board, serves units in state and local governments exclusively. These central state agencies, among other things, provide mediation, arbitration, and factfinding services. All operate under laws that deal exclusively with public employers.

Generally, local governments are free to decide "who does what" in the actual conduct of negotiations. Thus the council determines its own role, fixes bargaining responsibilities of the mayor, manager, personnel officer, and other officials. A danger is that municipalities often do not clearly define the bargaining duties of their official family. Neglect of this cardinal principle is one sure road to the "house-divided" syndrome: it's an open invitation for the other side to exploit a muddled situation to its own advantage.

THE STRIKE BUGABOO

Strikes against governments in the United States are widely outlawed—but they continue to occur.

The position of public employee organizations on strikes is both interesting and pertinent. Unaffiliated employee associations oppose strikes; most unions pay lip service to antistrike laws, but some union spokesmen still use the strike threat as a bargaining weapon. The American Federation of State, County and Municipal Employees now openly espouses strikes; they say in effect, "except in fire and police departments, strikes are a last resort right of all workers."

One conclusion seems tenable in the strike dilemma. State antistrike laws with *automatic heavy penalties* against striking public employees have proved unenforceable. Employees cannot be deterred from striking if they believe their employer cannot or will not penalize the strikers.

Probably no single device will end strikes either in the private or public sector. Ida Klaus, an experienced public service negotiator, suggests reasonable, enforceable laws and a solid collective bargaining program as possible solutions. Greater emphasis might also be given to discipline and limitation of sanctions to those who lead employees into illegal strikes.

Public service strikes may be illegal or justified, depending upon which side of the bargaining table you represent. But they should be viewed in perspective.

The Bureau of Labor Statistics points out that "public employee strikes in general show no rising trend," and strikes in governments fall in the lowest category of all industries.

COMPULSORY ARBITRATION

Collective bargaining theory holds that differences will be settled by compromise. Mediation, conciliation, factfinding and arbitration—all provided for in the comprehensive state laws mentioned earlier—are means of dispute settlement.

In some respects the most controversial is compulsory arbitration. This prospect is viewed with suspicion by both management and labor. Management sees it as an infringement of its right to manage. Labor sees it as taking away its prerogative to accept or reject management proposals. Jerry Wurf, president of the American Federation of State, County and Municipal Employees, says: "There is no freedom at the bargaining table on either side when the gun of compulsory arbitration is pointed at the heads of the negotiators."

Both sides believe that an outside third party lacks the background to understand the complicated issues involved in a dispute. They also believe that it diminishes the effectiveness of the collective bargaining process because bargaining teams may rest on their oars if a third party can step in and make a final decision.

MERIT SYSTEM CONFLICT

Collective bargaining can pose threats to "traditional" merit system concepts. Conflicts between collective bargaining and merit system tenets include: *Open competition* and equal opportunity to compete for public jobs versus the union shop; *equal pay for equal work* versus the principle of salary setting on the basis of prevailing wage rates; *promotion on merit through competition* versus seniority.

These threats may be removed in one of three ways:

1. Accommodate the merit system to collective bargaining. An arrangement like this is proposed by Arvid Anderson, a member of the Wisconsin Employee Relations Board. Accordingly, the closed shop would be prohibited; selection and examination would be completely reserved to the personnel agency; straight seniority as a basis for promotion would be tempered by giving some credit for seniority and some for other qualifications.

2. Limit the merit system agency responsibility to recruitment and career development. This plan is proposed by AFSCME's Jerry Wurf who favors "dehydrating" the merit system. Except

for limited recruitment-career development functions, he believes all other aspects of management's relations with organized employees "must be handled as part of the contractual relationship between the employer and the union."

3. Improve and extend merit systems. Many administrators hold the traditional view that more and better merit systems will meet the needs of management and employees, and, moreover, will provide a more satisfactory arrangement than collective bargaining. On this point the position of unions varies from the position of unaffiliated employee associations.

Within the merit system framework, proponents believe they can develop procedures short of bargaining which will assure a viable personnel program involving greater cooperation and joint participation between management and employee groups.

These three methods of resolving conflicts between merit system and collective bargaining ideologies illustrate one important public policy issue confronting all public officials.

If certain collective bargaining practices and merit system concepts are on a collision course, then public officials need to gird themselves with facts on the scope and operation of both merit systems and collective bargaining—facts that will enable them to make solid judgments about what they should do.

POLITICS AND PUBLIC INTEREST

Traditionally, organized employees have sought many of their objectives through political action. When bargaining fails, they still have access to the legislative body. At national, state, and local levels, officers and members of employee organizations exercise their civic responsibility by holding elective and appointive public office. They also support active lobbies to gain commitments from political parties on specific issues and to win support on broad programs.

These are facts of political life in America. The quest for political power through regular democratic processes is neither sinister nor illegal. What really matters is whether the nature of the bargaining process encourages a runaway type of power politics that fails to protect the public interest.

The issue raises ethical questions of the first order. Answers may go in any of three directions:

1. The personal integrity of political and union leaders assures adequate protection of the public interest.

2. The political system, of which collective bargaining is an inherent part, contains checks and balances that automatically protect the public.

James A. Belasco, author of the case study, *Collective Bargaining in City X,** reached two important conclusions: (1) The balance of power assets between unions and the city administration tend to limit union activity and demands which may be detrimental to the public interest; (2) "The essence of the collective bargaining relationship is swapping of political power assets."

3. Political activities of unions, like those of the individual employee, could be regulated and restricted. In the light of recent liberalized political activity provisions, such a proposal would likely attract little support. But, if the tempo of employee organization activities continues at its present rate, then the issue of union political activities may develop into a vexing problem of public policy.

SCOPE OF BARGAINING

What should be open to negotiation is a moot question. The federal government severely limits bargaining, putting such matters as classified pay rates, pensions, and basic merit system concepts off limits. Laws on municipal bargaining tend to widen the area of negotiation and narrow management prerogatives.

However the bargaining area may be defined, municipal officials need to be alert to the possible inroads on home rule to be made by extending the scope of bargaining.

SOME STARTLING POSSIBILITIES

As the nation's city officials sit down at the bargaining table they may face some unexpected developments. Briefly stated, each of the following emerges as an established fact or a clear prospect:

Changed fiscal practices. If bargaining becomes a year-round activity, pressure will mount to maintain a continuing budget appropriation system to meet employee demands and needs quickly.

Higher taxes. Cities may be forced to levy taxes to meet

* From *Government Labor Relations in Transition,* Keith Ocheltree, Ed., Public Personnel Association, Chicago, 1966.

salaries set through bargaining. A factfinding recommendation in one Wisconsin càse said that in effect the inability of a county to increase wage rates without raising taxes "is hardly a persuasive reason" for substandard wages.

Regional bargaining. Activities of national unions, with their strong research and education units and their growing political power, could conceivably force regional bargaining on a cooperative basis, at least among local governments in metropolitan areas. This is now done among some Canadian cities.

Bargaining expertise. Municipal officials will devote more time to the *man* part of management-employee relations. To keep abreast of informed, skillful, and experienced representatives of employee organizations, public officials will be forced to study labor relations at seminars sponsored by municipal leagues, universities, and associations of government officials. Only in this way can public officials make up for the head start of organized employees who draw substantially on their industrial compatriots for leadership and financial assistance.

Expansion of personnel functions. Cities will beef up the agency responsible for the personnel program and increasingly cast the personnel director as an adviser to top management.

The bargaining table presents a monumental challenge to cities and their officials. If they take their seats well prepared in advance, they can uphold their end of the bargaining process. If they come as reluctant last-minute guests, the result could be disastrous.

CITIES AND TOWNS—WHAT ARE THEY?
by Joseph M. Harvey

In the private sector, management is usually a small company or a large corporation controlling many firms which are frequently responsible to stockholders. In the public sector, management takes the form of a governmental unit such as a city, town, or even a state. Instead of being responsible to stockholders, the agents and managers of these governmental units are respon-

sible to the taxpayers. In the following article, a town counsel defines the term "Municipal Corporation" and compares it to the private corporation.

Joseph M. Harvey is an attorney and newspaperman. He was a member of a reportorial team that won a Pulitzer Prize for the Boston Globe. *He is the town counsel of Winthrop, Massachusetts, a suburb of Boston, and the president of the City Solicitors and Town Counsel Association of Massachusetts.*

Cities and towns are often referred to as "municipal corporations." That is the general heading under which the law books lump the law relative to those local units of government. But cities and towns are not corporations like General Motors, General Electric, or United States Steel; and he who would engage in municipal collective bargaining with such governmental units had better keep their differences clearly in mind.

On the surface similarities do exist between the municipal or public corporation and the private business or industrial corporation. A dictionary definition of "corporation" includes both a municipal corporation as "the municipal authorities of a town or city," and the private corporation as "a body formed by law to act as a single person although constituted by one or more persons and legally endowed with various rights and duties."

The municipal and private corporations are alike in that both are the creatures of a state legislature. That is the general rule, and as with any general rule, there is always an exception. In the older parts of the country, especially along the Atlantic seaboard and particularly in the New England area, there are towns that were never formally incorporated. Yet they are legal entities.

The administrative managements of the municipal and private corporations are organized along similar lines. Somewhat akin to the corporation president, chairman of the board, and board of directors are the offices of mayor, Board of Selectmen, City Council, Board of Aldermen, and comparable county and district officers. A New England-style town meeting is about as close as the municipal corporation comes to the private corporation's stockholders meeting.

The powers and duties of the municipal and private corporations are derived from a charter granted by a state legislature subject to special and general statutes also enacted by the legislature. Once again, the statement of that general principle requires a reminder that there are exceptions. While the private corporation may be held rather strictly to its conferred powers and duties, the law admits that there are instances where the municipal corporation can be said to have implied powers, or powers arising out of long established custom and usage, necessary for the municipality to accomplish its basic purpose.

This point is illustrated in a decision of the Massachusetts Supreme Judicial Court—a court which claims to be the oldest court of its kind of continuous existence in the nation—in an 1859 case discussing the duties of town selectmen:

> Many of the acts usually performed by them in behalf of towns, and which are recognized as within their appropriate sphere, have origin and foundation in long continued usage. The management of the prudential affairs of towns necessarily requires the exercise of a large discretion, and it would be quite impossible by positive enactment to place definite limits to the powers and duties of selectmen to whom the discretion and control of such affairs are entrusted.—*Smith* v. *Cheshire,* 13 Gray (79 Mass.) 318, 319.

Over the intervening years, statutes have to some extent more clearly delineated the powers and duties of the traditional and unique office of town selectman, but he still retains a measure of discretionary power not always enjoyed by his private corporation counterpart.

The private and municipal corporations exist for the purposes usually spelled out in their respective charters obtained from the legislature. The usual private corporation is commercial in nature and operated, hopefully, for business profit. The municipal corporation is basically a service corporation. The very name "municipal" derives from two Latin words and connotes one who undertakes to perform a duty or a service. The performance of this service or services for the citizens within its boundaries falls into two broad categories. One is described as "governmental" and the second as "proprietary."

Generally speaking, a city or town engages in a governmental function—its primary purpose for existence—when it provides police and fire protection and operates schools. Municipalities are generally considered to be engaging in "proprietary" functions when they operate undertakings such as water supply systems and similar revenue-producing services.

The general principle is that the private corporation is liable legally for the wrongs it does in the course of conducting its business. That rule usually does not apply to the municipal corporation for damages arising out of performance of its governmental services. This doctrine of "municipal immunity" does not apply, however, to the accidents and mishaps caused by a city or town in carrying out proprietary functions. With that note of difference, the listing of similarities between private and municipal corporations—a listing that, of course, is only an outline and not all-inclusive—comes to an end.

It is here that the person, individual, or union, who undertakes collective bargaining with a municipal corporation, be it city, town, county, or district, should be informed and alert. The representative of the municipality should also know definitely the limits and limitations of his authority to negotiate a contract. The powers of the private corporation and of the municipal corporation to make contracts are quite different.

Comparatively speaking, a person might undertake to negotiate a contract, be it a business or labor contract, with a private corporation quite secure in his belief or information that the representatives with whom he was dealing had full power to agree upon a binding document. Not so with the city or town. Once again, the general rule is that a person dealing with a municipal corporation has an extra added burden.

The Massachusetts Supreme Judicial Court put this into a few, blunt words: "A person who enters into a contract with a public officer is bound at his peril to ascertain the extent of the authority of such an officer with whom he deals" (*Meader* v. *West Newbury* [256 Mass.], 37, 39). In other words, the bargainer with a municipality should first be certain of the powers and authority of the man who sits across the table from him.

Those powers and duties may not always be clearly ascertainable from a mere reading of the state statute establishing collective bargaining covering municipal employees. Frequently, such statutes have reservation clauses that make agreements subordinate or subject to local city and town charters, bylaws, ordinances and, most important, to the availability of an appropriation —money—to carry the agreement into effect.

For example, consider the wording of the Massachusetts municipal collective bargaining statute:

> In the event that any part or provision of any such agreement is in conflict with any law, ordinance or by-law, such law, ordinance or by-law shall prevail so long as such conflict remains.—Massachusetts General Laws, Chapter 149, Section 178 I.

This same section provides further that if the city or town appropriating body refuses the good faith request of its authorized negotiator to raise the money necessary to implement the agreed-upon bargaining contract, "the matter shall be returned to the parties for further bargaining." In short: no money, no contract.

Statutory schemes prescribing governmental activity in broad areas such as medical and automobile insurance and collective bargaining are often the product of one or more political, business, or educational persons or groups. Once promulgated and incorporated into the statutes of one state, such schemes have a way of spreading out across the nation so that the statutory language frequently is virtually copied from state to state. While there are differences, there are enough similarities so that one can learn from what happens in one state what may be expected in a neighboring state under municipal collective bargaining or similar programs.

With that in mind, the municipal bargainer on both sides of the table, employee and employer, might profitably acquaint himself with proceedings not only in the nearby cities and towns, but also in other states. Collective bargaining in the field of public employees negotiating directly with the local units of government is relatively new. But this new activity carries over in the background some of the legal principles governing the conduct of public officers and public affairs that were laid down by the courts as long as a century ago.

It is still pretty much the law that such public officers as mayors and selectmen are not general agents of their municipalities with comprehensive powers to make binding contracts. They have such power only if some law, some statute, or in some instances, if some ordinance or bylaw says so. And, by way of further caution, any such local ordinance or bylaw must be one that is not contrary to a state statute, a town or city charter, or the state or United States constitutions.

To minimize difficulties and disappointments, the collective bargainers should understand at the outset the nature of that city or town whose name they propose to get on a binding contract. The power and authority to negotiate and sign such a contract must be clearly granted by law and the authority must be exercised only by the officer to whom the power is given. And he must exercise that power within the limits prescribed. It is the job of the employee's negotiator to find out the source and extent of those powers and limits. Unless he does so, the employees' negotiator may wind up with a contract which his union members will pull down over his ears and the city or town negotiator may wind up with the screams of irate taxpayers in his ears.

COLLECTIVE BARGAINING IN WELLESLEY, MASSACHUSETTS

During 1968 and the first two months of 1969 the Town has been engaged in collective bargaining with labor organizations representing certain employees of the Department of Public Works, and School custodians, including storemen and grounds and maintenance crews employed by the Schools. The School Committee has been and is bargaining with the Wellesley Teachers' Association. Steps are underway which may lead to collective bargaining with certain employees of the Fire Department and the Trustees of the Wellesley Free Library (petitions are pending before the

Reprinted from the Wellesley, Massachusetts, Town Report.

State Labor Relations Commission which, in due course, may lead to the designation of labor organizations as bargaining representatives of the employees involved). This activity is governed by the Municipal Employee Relations Act which became effective in February 1966.

Collective bargaining involving the Town is conducted for the most part during the evening and, where engaged in by members of the Personnel Board and/or the School Committee, requires an inordinate amount of time. The process is essentially one of give and take, and when an agreement is arrived at by the parties, it is always the result of compromise. What the labor organization does not obtain among the several proposals submitted for bargaining in previous negotiations is frequently resubmitted for further bargaining in a succeeding negotiation. Long and arduous preparation is engaged in by the Town's Personnel Director and members of the Personnel Board prior to the commencement of and during the negotiations. Consultations also take place with Town Counsel and Special Counsel for Labor Relations because of the complexity of the bargaining process today.

In the nature of the case, a definite timetable cannot be established for the commencement and conclusion of collective bargaining negotiations. The parties to such negotiations may attempt in good faith to comply with the mandate of the statute and the Resolution of last year's Town Meeting. However, techniques may be employed by the parties in an effort to arrive at an agreement that is incompatible with a strict timetable, and such techniques, although exasperating at times, are utilized in the utmost of good faith. Again this year, as in the previous year, it is doubtful that either the Personnel Board or the School Committee will have concluded negotiations prior to the date of the Town Meeting.

We understand that the parties involved have met at reasonable times and have conferred in good faith, a mutual obligation imposed by the statute. A good deal of learning is going on in this area, both on the part of the Towns which are involved in collective bargaining for the first time, and on the part of the employees involved. This has led to protracted conferences, in an effort to understand the bargaining processes as well as to conclude agreements. Sometimes negotiations require the intervention of mediators and factfinders. Such procedures create additional uncertainties insofar as following timetables are concerned. While the Advisory Committee is conscious of the underlying feeling of frustration which led to the passage of last year's Resolution urging the completion of pay schedules sufficiently in advance of the Town Meeting so that the Committee would be in a position to make its recommendations, it does feel that much progress has been made in the collective bargaining area, and that the Town will recognize the need to adapt its processes to the realities of the collective bargaining process.

RX: COMPETENCE AND GOOD FAITH
by Arthur J. Flamm

> *Mr. Flamm is an attorney in the Boston firm of Segal & Flamm, which represents many labor organizations in the New England area. A graduate of the School of Industrial and Labor Relations at Cornell University and the Harvard Law School, Mr. Flamm is now counsel for the Massachusetts Nurses' Association and has also been active with other labor organizations. In the following article he relates what happened in one bargaining session between a city-owned hospital in Massachusetts and the Nurses' Association.*

Collective bargaining for nurses in Massachusetts became a reality in January 1965 with the adoption of amendments to the State Labor Relations Act extending its coverage to registered and licensed practical nurses employed in health care facilities. In addition to the usual representation and unfair labor practice procedures, the amendments prohibited nurses from striking but provided for compulsory arbitration of all disputes in nongovernmental facilities. No provision was made for resolving disputes in municipal or state hospitals. A subsequent statute did establish factfinding procedures in municipal disputes, but the factfinder's recommendations were only advisory.

The Massachusetts Nurses' Association, which had sponsored

Used by permission of the author.

the amendments, immediately became active in seeking to represent registered nurses. The association, an affiliate of the American Nurses Association, was well established in the state as a professional organization. Its first contact with the city of Haverhill involved some seven public health nurses who voted in July 1966 to be represented by the association. The city demonstrated a completely adamant attitude in the subsequent negotiations and refused to make any changes in salaries or benefits. At the association's request, a factfinder was appointed by the Massachusetts Board of Conciliation and Arbitration. The factfinder recommended a modest adjustment in salaries, but the city refused to change its position.

In the spring of 1967, the association negotiated an agreement with the Lawrence General Hospital, the largest and most prestigious hospital in the Merrimac Valley area. The agreement increased the weekly starting rate for staff nurses from $90 to $110, with comparable increases for all classifications, and contained many other improvements in benefits and conditions. Other hospitals in the area tended to follow the pattern set in Lawrence. However, the Hale Hospital, which is operated by the city of Haverhill, ignored this development. Nurses at Hale requested the association to assist them, and it petitioned for an election. In the subsequent election, the nurses voted 120 to 24 to be represented by the association.

On June 6, 1967, the association submitted its proposals in contract form and requested a meeting which was finally scheduled for July 26. At the negotiating table, the city was represented by its Director of Public Works, who was serving as Acting City Manager, the City Solicitor, and the hospital Director. The association was represented by its counsel, an Assistant Director and a bargaining committee of nurses from the hospital. The tenor of the parties' relationship was established at the opening of the meeting when the City Solicitor stated that the city representatives had not read the association's proposals and were in no position to comment on them. The meeting abruptly came to an end. The request for another meeting date was met with the response that the City Solicitor did not have his appointment book with him. The following day, the City Solicitor informed the association counsel that he was leaving for California and would be gone for several weeks during which no meetings could be held.

Under Massachusetts law, a municipality may not increase salaries in the last three months of any election year. Since 1967 was an election year in Haverhill, any adjustment in salaries for the nurses would have to be negotiated before September 30. Moreover, assuming that an agreement was reached with the City Manager, the subsequent legislative process is time consuming; and therefore any agreement, if it were to be effective in 1967, would have to be reached sometime prior to September 30. The association concluded that the city was deliberately stalling with the objective of relying on the Massachusetts statute to preclude any salary adjustment in 1967.

After the breakdown in negotiations, a meeting of the nurses was held on August 3. Association representatives and the members of the Nurses Committee reported what had transpired and their conclusions with respect to the city's motivations in stalling. The speakers also discussed the various options available to the nurses. Factfinding was not feasible since it could not be completed before the September 30 deadline and the city had previously ignored a factfinder's recommendation. It was pointed out that, although the law precluded strikes, those nurses who were dissatisfied with the status quo could resign and find other employment since there were many available positions for nurses in the area. It was explained that the decision to resign would have to be made on an individual basis, and that no group action could be taken at the meeting. The nurses formally voted to request the association to impose sanctions against the hospital. Many individual nurses took the floor and stated that they intended to submit their resignations. The headline in the following day's *Haverhill Gazette* was "Nurses Ask Sanctions Against Hospital," and the lead story was a report of the meeting.

During the following week, nurses began to submit individual resignations with the usual two- to four-weeks' notice. The hospital responded by restricting the admission of new patients to emergency cases and referring other patients to hospitals in the area. The *Haverhill Gazette* story of August 10 quoted the hospital Director to the effect that fifty-nine nurses had submitted resignations. A meeting between the parties was scheduled for August 16.

When the nurses' negotiating team arrived at City Hall on

August 16, they were ushered into the Council Chambers, where the City Manager publicly inquired whether the association had any objection to the presence of reporters and the broadcasting of the negotiations over the local radio station. Under the circumstances, the association did not object, although its counsel privately advised the city representatives that these procedures were absurd. In the two hours that followed, the citizens of Haverhill were afforded the opportunity to listen to the "negotiations," which largely consisted of counsel for the respective parties engaging in a heated debate. Although debating points were made, little was actually accomplished toward arriving at a settlement. When the spokesmen had exhausted themselves, the negotiations were adjourned until August 18. Prior to the opening of the meeting, the City Manager indicated to the association counsel that, if the association requested the exclusion of press and radio, the city would be agreeable. The association responded that it would not unilaterally make such a request but would join the city in doing so. Initially, this meeting was a repetition of the first with the two attorneys engaging in debate. However, at the end of the meeting, counsel for the parties and the City Manager met privately and, for the first time, began to discuss the issues in an attempt to arrive at some resolution.

The association was essentially seeking an agreement the terms of which would be comparable with those of Lawrence General Hospital. Since the Lawrence agreement was to expire on March 1, 1968, the association would accept either an interim agreement until March 1, 1968, or a fifteen-month agreement with a wage reopener in 1968. The city rejected the Lawrence rates, insisted on a firm fifteen-month agreement with no reopener, objected to any grievance arbitration provisions, and, in general, resisted the inclusion of provisions that the association had in its standard hospital agreement. However, as a result of the informal discussion, it was agreed that the next meeting, which was scheduled for August 22, would be closed to the press and radio by joint agreement and that the city would present a salary proposal.

The agreement to bar the press from the August 22 meeting fell apart when the City Manager, under pressure from reporters, disclaimed any such understanding. However, the parties did make some effort to discuss the issues and the city proposed a new salary schedule which was lower than that in effect at the Lawrence General Hospital. The negotiating committee rejected the proposal, but the city insisted it be submitted to the entire unit. The association then agreed to present the proposal to the nurses on August 25.

More than one hundred nurses were present at the meeting, and the city's proposal was discussed in detail. The nurses voted unanimously to reject the proposal. Following the rejection, three physicians representing the Hale Hospital's medical staff requested an opportunity to appear before the group and were admitted. The physicians, while expressing sympathy for the nurses' position, equivocated when various nurses requested that the medical staff openly support their position, and repeatedly stated that they could take no sides during the dispute. By this time, some 78 out of 180 nurses had submitted resignations, and the hospital was in the process of closing down several wards. The patients, however, were adequately cared for, and there was no reduction in the quality of patient care during this period.

Negotiations resumed on August 28, and the city representatives took an even harder position than before. Charges and countercharges were made, and much of the time was devoted to ancillary issues having no relationship to the basic dispute. The city representatives challenged the right of certain nurses to serve on the negotiating committee since they had previously resigned from the hospital. The response by the association—that the nurses had a right to select their bargaining committee and, moreover, that the nurses were not overly delighted with the city's bargaining committee—is indicative of the discussions that day. The *Haverhill Gazette*'s headline the following morning was "Faraci [City Solicitor] Calls Nurses 'Unfit,' Would Ban Them."

On August 28, the City Solicitor and the City Manager met privately with the association counsel and made some progress toward resolving the issues. The parties agreed to refrain from making any statements to the press other than that progress had been made. On August 30, a meeting of the full committees was held together with a conciliator from the State Board of Conciliation. The parties were together at times and at other times were separated with the conciliator moving between them in the usual pattern. The city finally made a salary proposal which was substantially equivalent to the rates at Lawrence General Hospital. However, it was for a fifteen-month period with no reopener, and other provisions of the contract proposal were still short of the Lawrence agreement. The committee agreed to submit the matter to a vote of the nurses on September 1.

The membership meeting was well attended. The proposed agreement was discussed by association representatives as well as by members of the negotiating committee. It became evident that there was a substantial difference of opinion among the nurses with respect to the action to be taken. At the request of the nurses, the hospital Director appeared and was asked whether the hospital would reemploy all of the nurses who had previously resigned. He responded in the affirmative. The results of a secret ballot vote were 68 to 42 to accept the proposed contract. Subsequently, all of the nurses who had resigned and desired to return to work were reemployed by the city without any interruption in their continuity of service.

This controversy is an example of the oft-repeated observation that collective bargaining can only succeed if both parties approach the bargaining table with a desire to arrive at an agreement. It also illustrates the point that the failure of a party to have competent representation is of no advantage to the other but only contributes to a breakdown of the process. In short, good will and a reasonable degree of competence are essential ingredients for a successful bargaining relationship. The difficulties in Haverhill are not the exception in the public sector. Unfortunately, many communities are represented by individuals whose only qualification for their positions are political connections, and who submerge their inadequacies in a sea of bombast and arrogance. The existing factfinding procedure for resolving disputes is not adequate. In Haverhill, the city representatives simply ignored the factfinder's recommendations; this practice is all too frequent in the public sector in Massachusetts. The Massachusetts Nurses' Association has had four such proceedings, and in each case the municipality has refused to comply with the recommendations. It is interesting to note that in January 1968, a new administration took office in Haverhill, and the picture has completely changed. In June 1968, the city voluntarily reopened the agreement and established salaries on a par with the new Lawrence General Hospital schedule. In March 1969, a new two-year agreement was reached with salaries and most benefits in accord with area conditions.

3

THE PUBLIC SAFETY AND THE STRIKE

Public employee strikes always make headlines, but when the public safety is at stake the headlines loom larger and blacker. In September 1966, public employees made news when 500 firefighters in Atlanta went out on strike. The striking firefighters were quickly suspended without pay, shifts of those remaining on the job were lengthened and policemen were brought in to fill the nonfirefighting jobs.

In 1967 a strange sort of "strike" hit the city of Detroit when policemen in that city called in sick after city officials refused to meet their pay demands.

These two strikes were reported in the following selections from Labor Week (September 19, 1966, and July 3, 1967, respectively), a feature of *U.S. News & World Report*.

WHAT DOES A CITY DO WHEN FIREMEN GO ON STRIKE?

ATLANTA

Two-thirds of the firemen in this major southern city walked off their jobs on September 2 in a strike for immediate pay raises. They went out in violation of a Georgia state law, and they stayed out in defiance of a court order to return to work.

All of the nearly 500 striking firemen were suspended without pay. Mayor Ivan Allen, Jr., refused to negotiate with the strikers. Instead, he ordered a recruiting drive for new firemen to fill the vacant jobs.

The suspended firemen were given 10 days to show why they should not be fired.

Mayor Allen says that most of the strikers will be fired. Thus, a major city is left with its defense against fires seriously weakened. So what happens now? Is Atlanta burning?

Fire Chief C. H. Hildebrand, Jr., supplies the answers. By regrouping the more than 250 firefighters who stayed on the job, Chief Hildebrand was able to get 19 of the city's 32 fire stations in full operation within four days after the strike began.

All available firemen were put on long shifts, and 89 policemen were assigned to the fire department—most of them to fill nonfirefighting jobs.

As a final step, the city of Atlanta called into effect a mutual assistance pact with the fire departments of surrounding municipalities.

Atlanta's fire chief says that this opens the "possibility" of calling in 10 firefighting units "reasonably quickly" in the event of a major fire, and an additional half dozen or more from more distant points.

Chief is confident. The 19 stations reopened in Atlanta operate 27 firefighting units. Adding to these the 16 additional units that might be called in for an extreme emergency would bring Atlanta's fire defenses back up to more than three-quarters of normal strength, Mr. Hildebrand estimates. That, he believes, should be enough to handle anything.

Fire insurance underwriters appear to agree. Jason Woodall, manager of the Southeastern Underwriters Association, says there are no plans to boost Atlanta's fire insurance rates.

Mr. Woodall says the association "feels that protection for ordinary homes is reasonable."

"Our concern," he adds, "lies in the possibility of fires in the congested downtown areas."

Mr. Woodall notes that the fire underwriters "prefer to give the city an opportunity to work this thing out." Whether or not there are to be increases in fire insurance rates, he indicates, depends on how long it takes to get the fire department back to normal.

The trouble began last spring. At that time the only union

representing Atlanta firemen was the International Association of Fire Fighters, affiliated with the AFL–CIO. This union has a no-strike clause in its constitution. The union asked the city to reduce the firemen's work week from 60 to 56 hours.

City officials rejected that request on the ground that such a move would amount to a pay boost that would be illegal at that time of year under the city charter.

The Atlanta charter prohibits pay raises after March 31 of each year until the beginning of the next year. City officials, however, promised to consider the shorter work week at the end of the year.

A change of unions. Dissident firemen then broke away from the AFL–CIO union and organized an independent local called the Atlanta Fire Fighters Union. Its constitution does not contain a no-strike clause.

In June the independent union went on strike to enforce the firemen's demands. The striking firemen agreed to mediation without binding themselves to the findings and went back to work. The mediator recommended an increase in firemen's wages or a reduction in working hours.

City officials accepted both suggestions—not just one—but said both would have to wait until January 1, in keeping with the law.

The city's offer amounted to an 8.66 per cent pay increase in cash, plus the equivalent of a 7.14 per cent raise in the form of a shorter work week—in all, a total of 15.8 per cent.

Under existing pay scales, beginning firemen get $403 a month. On January 1, the starting rate is to rise to $438 a month. The top pay for privates is to go to $638 a month on January 1, from the present $563.

Still not enough. The independent union again struck on September 2, demanding that the pay raises be granted immediately.

Within hours after the strike began, Judge Luther Alverson of the Fulton County Superior Court ordered the strikers back to work.

State law provides that "no person holding a position by appointment or employment in the government of the State of

Georgia or any agency, authority, board, commission or public institution thereof, shall promote, encourage or participate in any strike."

The Georgia state government grants charters to cities, and this is interpreted as making the cities political institutions of the state, and their employees subject to state law.

Immediately after the order was issued, Fire Chief Hildebrand served notice that all firemen absent without authorization should report at their next regular shift or be suspended. A few firemen returned.

Mayor calls strike illegal. Mayor Allen refused to negotiate with the strikers on the ground that they were using illegal means in an effort to force the city to grant an illegal pay raise.

Firemen's wives began sporadic picketing of city hall and of the operating fire stations. Firemen kept their children out of school, on the ground that the schools were not safe because of inadequate fire protection.

The hiring of new men to replace the strikers went steadily ahead. By September 8, the city had applications from 117 men. Of these, 51—32 whites and 19 Negroes—had passed written examinations and were eligible to be hired if they passed physical examinations.

A handful of the strikers sought to go back to work, saying they would like to forget the whole thing. Officials refused to take them back.

The replacements must undergo rigorous training for three weeks before being assigned to active duty. Fire officials estimate that it will take at least a year to rebuild the Atlanta fire department to full strength.

City officials and officials of the AFL–CIO Fire Fighters Union, meanwhile, claim that it is the Teamsters Union that is really behind the fire department's troubles. They note that the striking firemen have their headquarters in the Atlanta Teamsters Union hall.

"This is a power grab." Officials note, too, that Tony Zivalich, a Teamsters organizer, sits in on all of the strikers' strategy meetings, and that Robert L. Mitchell, attorney for the local Teamsters, is the striking firemen's lawyer.

"This is a power grab," snaps an official of the AFL–CIO firemen's union. "The reasons they give for striking don't make sense. They say they've got to have their pay raise right now instead of four months from now, when the city has agreed to give it to them. And for that they are jeopardizing the safety of this whole city.

"They want to put the AFL–CIO out of business here and take over the whole fire department. Then the Teamsters will take them over and the Teamsters will run the fire department."

Since the strike started, at least two fires have been started by Molotov cocktails. Whether these were thrown by strikers, rioters, or others has not been established.

A large warehouse and a sales office of a tire company were destroyed by one of the Molotov cocktail fires. Damage was estimated at several hundred thousand dollars.

Another Molotov cocktail was tossed onto the roof of a one-story home, but the blaze did little damage. False alarms have been numerous.

WHEN POLICEMEN STRIKE
IN A BIG CITY—

DETROIT

How far can policemen go to support their demands for wage increases?

This question is being asked in the wake of five weeks of less-than-normal law enforcement in Detroit, climaxed by what amounted to the first general strike by police in any major U.S. city since 1919. That was the year of Boston's famous police strike.

Michigan law, and that of many other states, bans strikes by public employees, although it permits public workers to organize and bargain collectively.

Unionized teachers and municipal workers in Michigan have ignored this strike ban frequently in the two years since the law was adopted, but this was the state's first major work stoppage by law enforcement officers.

Detroit's police problems surfaced in mid-May during city council hearings on next year's municipal budget. Mayor Jerome P. Cavanagh said no funds were available for pay increases for any city employees.

Traffic ticket slowdown. On May 17, Detroit police began a slowdown in writing traffic tickets. The number of tickets issued dropped 50 per cent the first day and even more in subsequent days, despite demands by the city administration that the slowdown end.

The Detroit Police Officers Association, which says it represents the patrolmen but is not a union, began a $20,000 advertising campaign urging higher wages. The DPOA asked that patrolmen's pay be increased from $8,335 a year to $10,000 for men having at least five years of service.

As the slowdown continued, men from scout cars assigned to traffic details were switched to patrolling beats. On June 13, Police Commissioner Ray Girardin suspended 61 patrolmen for failure to enforce traffic laws.

"Blue flu." These suspensions triggered an epidemic of "blue flu." Officers by the hundreds called in sick. A temporary injunction against the "sick boycott" brought a switch in tactics. Officers sought emergency leaves, claiming members of their families were ill.

The city ordered policemen to be examined by city doctors when they reported in sick. Such action could not be extended to the families.

Officers found to be fit for duty were ordered back to work. If they refused, they were suspended. When the situation appeared to improve slightly, Mayor Cavanagh left for a convention of the U.S. Conference of Mayors in Honolulu. He is president of that organization.

The mayor's departure set off another wave of absenteeism. By June 20, one third of Detroit's 2,668 patrolmen were off duty. Mr. Cavanagh hurried home.

Wives and children of policemen joined in the protest, forming picket lines around police headquarters and police stations.

Throughout the dispute, the president of DPOA—Carl Parsell—maintained that the wave of illnesses was not a concerted action by the officers. He denied that any strike call had been issued by the association and said officers were protesting "on their own."

Suits filed. City officials thought otherwise. They filed a million-dollar damage suit against the DPOA. The association countered with a million-dollar suit against the city, alleging harassment and intimidation of association members.

Settlement efforts by the state mediation service failed, and the city asked for a factfinding board, as provided in the state law covering municipal-employee disputes. A truce was arranged June 20 by an independent citizens' committee headed by the Rt. Rev. Richard S. Emrich, Episcopal bishop of Michigan.

The DPOA agreed to resume "normal police operations." The city lifted suspensions of officers who had been disciplined, the lawsuits were postponed, and the citizens' group set up a panel to negotiate. Police strength returned to near normal June 21.

Mayor Cavanagh, repeating that the city faces a deficit of 14 million dollars in the fiscal year starting July 1, said money is not available for pay raises.

While Detroit policemen were returning to work, the idea of "sickness strikes" spread to Salem, Ohio. Nearly all of that city's 40-man force of police and firemen reported sick and began staying home on June 21. This was after the city council had rejected demands for pay raises of $34 a month.

"Crossed our fingers." How does a city the size of Detroit operate with more than 1,000 police off duty?

"We crossed our fingers and hoped," said one high police official. "At times it was touch and go."

Scout cars were juggled between precincts. Officers on duty worked 12-hour shifts. Furloughs and emergency leaves were canceled.

The National Guard and the Michigan State Police were alerted.

Crime normally reaches a peak during the afternoon shift—from 3 P.M. to 11 P.M. City officials said that police manpower during this shift June 19 was at its lowest point during the strike.

Yet an unofficial check of police records showed no reports of any major crime during that eight-hour period.

Major crimes generally were down during the height of the dispute. For five days, the total number of robberies, rapes, and murders was 48, compared with 56 in a comparable period a week earlier and 57 in the five days of May just prior to the start of the dispute.

Total arrests also dropped, to 673 from 760 one week earlier and 705 in the May week.

In addition to an immediate increase in wages, the police association is seeking guarantees of a further raise next year. In reply, Mayor Cavanagh said: "This is nothing more than a shakedown, and, if I give in to the police, I would be helping those who have acted most irresponsibly."

Mayor Cavanagh said that Pittsburgh's Mayor Joseph M. Barr had told him: "If you don't win this fight in Detroit, then every major American city is going to have to fight this same type of police and firemen's maneuvering."

The outcome was in doubt when the truce began. The plan called for 10 days of negotiations, with unsettled issues to go to a special panel of citizens. Neither the city nor the police association committed itself immediately to abide by the findings.

POLICEMEN AND FIREFIGHTERS
by Robert E. Walsh

Policemen and firefighters are in most instances the government after dark. To the students and black militants who are challenging the establishment in this period of social upheaval, these two departments symbolize a hated authority. In attacking the police and firefighters, these groups are protesting the representatives of a government they feel is responsible for unemployment, poor housing, poor education, and all the other factors that create and maintain a ghetto.

A police officer making a lawful arrest often finds himself harassed, or firefighters are pelted with bricks and bottles and even shot at while fighting a fire. The angry student or black militant doesn't hate the individual police officer or firefighter; he hates what he represents—authority.

In city after city, police have met force with force. Many people have reacted angrily against them. In turn, the police and some firefighters have become disillusioned, frustrated, and angry. They feel they are underpaid for performing a duty which has become increasingly hazardous, and in many states they are still treated as unskilled laborers.

To be honest, the public really hasn't paid any more attention to the plight of policemen and firefighters than to that of the poor. During the depression, a policeman's or fireman's job was coveted because it offered more security than other forms of employment. But since the arrival of the affluent society, these two occupations have become progressively looked down upon by the public.

Many people regard the police as a necessary evil. Yet, they want the law enforced until they happen to break it. Too many also see the firefighters as men who sleep all night and get paid for it and who carry an axe because they like to chop up buildings. But an arrest means additional paperwork and a court appearance for the policeman, and urban firefighters seldom get a night's sleep and carry an axe only because it is a tool of entry.

Are policemen and firefighters skilled workers?

Today's policeman must be part lawyer, part sociologist, and part sleuth. He also must be a technician in weapons and knowledgeable in the area of drugs, evidence, identification, and investigation. He should understand something about crowd and riot control, and he is sometimes called upon to be an ambulance driver with a working knowledge of first aid. Actually, a policeman spends 70 per cent of his time performing public services and only 30 per cent preventing and fighting crime. Recent decisions of the U.S. Supreme Court make it evident that today's policeman will have to become even more of a technician if he is to continue as a crime fighter and still not deprive a citizen of his constitutional rights.

A firefighter must have a working knowledge of fire control, fire prevention, and rescue techniques. Each of these areas requires a certain amount of specialized skill, including the use of a variety of power tools, the manipulation of hydraulic controls in complex pumping equipment, the operation of gas- and radiation-detection instruments, and the use of first aid and life-saving methods and equipment. Today's firefighter must also be familiar with the great number of potentially dangerous plastic and chemical products in use. Universities are beginning to offer courses in specialized fields of police work and in fire science and fire engineering.

Moreover, in both police and fire departments, the men who will become officers must have certain leadership and administrative qualifications beneficial to positions of responsibility and authority. As our cities become more complex, both police and fire protection become more scientific and specialized, and men in these leadership positions must be experts in their field.

In the area of collective bargaining, the firefighters are well organized. On February 28, 1918, Samuel Gompers presented an A.F. of L. charter to a fledgling organization formed from local firemen's benefit associations. The new union, christened the International Association of Fire Fighters, was founded because of inadequate wages, poor working conditions, and the appointment of incompetent men to the fire service as a result of their political connections.

The IAFF, which claims to be the oldest municipal employee union in the nation, has consistently taken stands to improve the occupation of firefighters and constantly encourages its membership to seek not only more general education but also more education in the field of firefighting technology. For the past seven years the International has also conducted seminars for local union officers in leadership training and collective bargaining. As a result, many locals have been able to achieve marked increases in wages and vastly improved working conditions. Through the efforts of state associations, several states have adopted statutes concerning collective bargaining for firefighters while in other states, the state IAFF organizations have cooperated with the rest of organized labor in obtaining collective bargaining laws for all public employees. Roswell L. Atwood, director of research and education for the IAFF, said this is a continuing effort which will be expanded as time goes on.

In addressing the International Association of Fire Fighters

at their fiftieth anniversary banquet in 1968, AFL–CIO President
George Meany paid tribute to the success the IAFF has achieved
in advancing the welfare of their membership and in developing
better, more efficient fire departments throughout their jurisdiction.
Granting that collective bargaining for municipal employees poses
problems, Meany went on to say:

> The question must be solved. They should have a right
> to bargain just like everyone else. No matter where a man's
> work is, he has the same living problems as everyone else.
> Perhaps some system of voluntary arbitration is the answer
> —someone who can look at the problem with a heart and
> a sense of justice for the workers.

Proceeds from this banquet were donated to the Muscular
Dystrophy Association. Support of this cause and other projects
such as repairing Christmas toys in many communities has in the
past helped to give the firefighters a closer identification with the
community than that of other public employee unions. In a recent
statement Ross Atwood said:

> The IAFF is vitally concerned with the adoption of suit-
> able collective bargaining laws in several states. At the
> present time only a quarter of the states have collective
> bargaining laws of any kind, and fewer have adequate
> laws. It is our contention that public employees deserve the
> same kind of legal protection as that afforded private em-
> ployees for the past thirty years. In particular we know that
> firefighter wages, although they have increased, are still far
> below those of other skilled workers.

Unlike the IAFF, the police have no national labor organization. Some departments have been given charters from the American Federation of State, County and Municipal Employees, the
Service Employees International Union, and the International
Brotherhood of Teamsters, but these are actually few in number.
In February 1969, the Executive Council of the AFL–CIO
authorized George Meany to grant a charter to a national police
organization if and when a significant number of police officers in
the major cities asked to become part of such an organization.
The New York Times reported in January 1969 that one of the

police groups most interested in affiliating with the labor federation is the New York City Patrolmen's Benevolent Association, which at that time was in the process of negotiating a contract with the city of New York to cover its 23,000 members. The president of the New York Association, John Cassese, and some of his associates went to Washington late in 1968 to discuss the possibility of a national police union.

There has been, however, some reluctance in the house of labor to grant a charter to the police because of the antagonism which often develops during strikes between police and pickets. There is also a movement afoot in several large cities outside of New York for policemen to form a union national in scope but independent of the AFL–CIO.

On the question of a national police union there are arguments on both sides. Advocates point out that it would give police a strong national voice when they are under fire during a period of social upheaval. Also, seminars such as those on collective bargaining and leadership conducted by the firefighters' union would prove helpful in bringing more knowledgeable police negotiators to the bargaining table.

Those opposed to a national police union feel that police officers should stand outside the labor movement entirely because of the nature of their jobs. In addition, police officers themselves are inclined to be conservative and some feel they would be uncomfortable in such an organization. Other opponents believe that exposing policemen to labor thinking will make it even more difficult to reshape police departments into the organizations that will be needed to handle the present social upheavals.

4

WHERE ONE UNION STANDS

Although younger than the Fire Fighters, the union which seems destined for first place in the public employee field is the American Federation of State, County and Municipal Employees AFL–CIO. This union grew out of the AFL federal labor union of the Wisconsin State Employees and was formed as an International AFL union in 1936 with 9000 members.

From 1936 until 1964 the union was under the leadership of Arnold S. Zander of Wisconsin. In 1964, after a close election, the leadership of the union passed to Jerry Wurf, executive director of the New York City District Council 37. Under Wurf's aggressive leadership, the AFSCME has won new respect both at the bargaining table and within labor councils on the state and central body levels of the AFL–CIO.

Today almost one out of every three members of the union's 400,000 is a white-collar worker. Close to half of this membership works for cities; the rest are employed by the states and counties. As the organization of public employees spreads, the AFSCME is facing stiffer competition from public employee departments of other big international unions such as the Service Employees International Union, the Laborers, the Teamsters, and the Hospital Division of the Retail, Wholesale and Department Store Employees.

The following articles express the beliefs of the American Federation of State, County and Municipal Employees union through a policy statement of their executive board and two addresses by their president, Jerry Wurf. These are followed by articles taken from the Public Employee Press, a tri-weekly publication of District Council 37 in New York City. In June 1968, this press was selected as the Best Labor Paper by the International Labor Press Association.

POLICY STATEMENT ON
PUBLIC EMPLOYEE UNIONS:
RIGHTS AND RESPONSIBILITIES
Adopted by International Executive Board
AFSCME, AFL–CIO—July 26, 1966

In recent years, there has been a substantial growth in the number of public employees who have joined unions. This trend seems certain to continue at an accelerated pace as public employment— already the largest single work force in the United States—expands still further and as the labor movement intensifies its efforts to organize public employees.

As this growth continues, the necessity for logical, orderly methods of settling labor-management disputes in the public sector becomes more and more evident. Progress has been made in this area. President John F. Kennedy, in his historic Executive Order 10988, established a basic approach toward collective bargaining procedures in the field of Federal employment. Several states and local governments have, through statute, ordinance, or executive order, set up collective bargaining procedures for their employees. Some of these attempts have been highly successful. Others have been at least partial failures, primarily because they represented gestures in the right direction but, in practice, amounted to form more than substance.

Public employers occasionally tried to hide behind the "sovereignty concept" of government, a concept rooted in English law dating from the period when the right of kings, i.e., of government, was considered divine. The concept has long since been abandoned in this nation—except occasionally where public employees are concerned. The attempt to invoke this outmoded doctrine in situations which cry out for democratic procedures and mutual understanding is to single out these workers as unworthy of dignity.

Government's refusal to bargain with its employees carries with it a substantial threat to the entire democratic concept which marks labor-management relations in the United States. It is absurd to believe that a governmental unit which signs contracts for buildings, for supplies, for services, for the purchase of real property, and for a thousand and one other things—virtually all of them secured under conditions regulated by the generally applicable rules of labor-management relations—would seek to deny equal treatment to its own employees. The use of public funds is the same in either case.

We believe that good labor-management relations in government, as in the private sector of the economy, must be concerned with fundamental problems and fundamental relations. The certification and collective bargaining processes used in private industry have worked well, where tried, in the public area. They can be improved and expanded in the public employment field by the continued application of sound principles. Public officials must recognize that they must deal with the problems of their employees, not sweep them under the rug and hope they will stay out of sight. If public officials and public employee unions approach the problem responsibly, sound solutions will be found. Collective bargaining does work in the public interest.

Inevitably, in any discussion of the right of public employees to bargain collectively, the question of their right to strike is also raised. Because we believe that the position of this Federation should be perfectly clear, we adopt and announce the following policy:

AFSCME insists upon the right of public employees—except for police and other law enforcement officers—to strike. To forestall this right is to handicap the free collective bargaining process. Wherever legal barriers to the exercise of this right exist, it shall be our policy to seek the removal of such barriers. Where one party at the bargaining table possesses all the power and authority, bargaining becomes no more than formalized petitioning.

The right to strike, however, is not something to be exercised casually. It should be exercised only under the most extreme provocation or as a final resort if an employer acts in an irresponsible manner. Further, let it be clearly understood: It is beyond the authority of any officer of this Federation or of the International Executive Board to call a strike. The decision to strike or to accept an agreement to end a strike can be made only by the members of a local union involved in a dispute.

We point out, further, that the prohibition on the use of the strike weapon by police and other law enforcement officers is, in this Union, absolute. For the entire existence of this Union, we have placed in the charter of every local union which includes such officers the words:

> This charter is issued with the understanding by the parties hereto that it will be revoked immediately if the members of Local —— who are employed as law enforcement, police, or penal officers call or participate in a strike or refuse in concert to perform their duties.

We have insisted that the same language be included in the constitution of such local unions. This practice is reaffirmed as a continuing policy.

It is not the policy of this Union to make mere gestures at collective bargaining and then resort to strikes to achieve our objectives. We look upon collective bargaining as the most democratic—and the most realistic—method of settling disputes over the substance of agreements between organized workers and their employers. We welcome the use of outside mediators and of genuine third-party factfinding processes as means of resolving impasses in bargaining. But efforts of this kind can be successful only if both the Union and the employer enter into bargaining in good faith. The will to reach an agreement must be present at the table.

It is for this reason, as well as because of our unwillingness to turn over to strangers the final voice in determining the wages and working conditions of our membership, that we reject the concept of compulsory arbitration to resolve bargaining disputes. Bargaining is, by its nature, a give-and-take process in which compromise and flexibility are frequently important features. If both parties know that, ultimately, an outside party will be brought in to make a binding decision on such matters as wages and hours there is not only no pressure on the parties to reach an agreement but even a fear of making any change in their original bargaining positions, lest the final arbitrator use this attempted compromise as a starting point for further compromise. Thus, positions become hardened, resistance to the other party's proposals is increased, and the whole "bargaining" process becomes a game that is played out until the whistle blows and the referee, in some mysterious fashion, determines and announces the final score.

We believe there is a place for arbitration of disputes, but that place is the voluntary use of such procedures to settle disputes over the meaning or the application of the provisions of an existing collective bargaining agreement or in the final settlement of grievances which may arise under the terms of an agreement.

AN ADDRESS TO THE MAYORS
by Jerry Wurf

> *Mr. Wurf, international president of the American Federation of State, County and Municipal Employees, AFL–CIO, delivered this address to the United States Conference of Mayors in Honolulu, Hawaii, on June 19, 1967.*

I am delighted and pleased at this opportunity to present the point of view of my international union. Since many of you will be dealing with our locals, this discussion may be especially relevant. Hopefully, it will also be useful.

I shall spare you—and myself—those tedious platitudes concerning the incalculable value of ongoing dialogue and the virtues of communication. Dialogue has frequently been used as a term to describe people talking past each other. Alleged breakdowns in communication are often not that at all, but reflect fundamental disagreements which ought to be forthrightly confronted so that resolution might follow. Resolution of conflict seems improbable if we are all thrashing about in the sticky spider web of jargon.

Further, we ought not be quite so timid—or apprehensive—about such conflict. It is not invariably verbal and it does, at least occasionally, reflect diverse interests in a gratifyingly diverse society. It was the accommodation of these diverse interests that so preoccupied James Madison in the Federalist papers as this country went about the business of adopting a constitution. And it is the accommodation of these diverse interests, rather than their repression, that is the distinctive feature of a democratic society.

Unions of employees constitute a major interest group. Like others, it is not totally without blemish. Few human institutions

Reprinted with the permission of the United States Conference of Mayors.

are. The labor movement in this country has had its share of opportunists and scoundrels, its quota of individuals who abused the power conferred by their constituents, and its proportion of shortsightedness and lack of vision. I need not remind a conference of mayors that we hold no monopoly on such limitations.

On balance, I would suggest that the pressure of labor unions for collective bargaining on the terms and conditions of employment has been both desirable and socially constructive. Despite occasional lapses, there is general consensus on this as it relates to the private sector of our economy. What seems new, and what appears threatening to some, is the relatively recent introduction of this process into public sector labor relations.

It is now almost half a century since the Boston police strike of 1919. A relatively obscure governor, Calvin Coolidge, was propelled by those events into national prominence and ultimately, the Presidency. His terse telegram is by now well known: "There is no right to strike against the public safety by anybody, anywhere, anytime."

This is neither the appropriate forum for a seminar in labor history, nor do I entertain any pretensions of expertise in this area. Several aspects of the Boston police strike, however, have painful relevance a half century later.

1. The police in that city had had their Social Club for approximately 13 years. They had lobbied, long and unsuccessfully, for wage increases. Repeated failures induced them to turn to traditional unionism. Their announcement of intention to seek affiliation with the A.F. of L. was met by the Police Commissioner arbitrarily forbidding such affiliation. It was this unilateral prohibition and his obdurate denial of all compromise and mediation proposals which precipitated the strike.

2. Although the issues were generally known, and were certainly reflected in the press, little genuine effort was made towards settlement by the responsible parties. Boston's mayor deplored police unionism, unhappily conceded that the dissatisfaction had some foundation, and was exercised at the prospect of a suspension of services. Unfortunately, he had no control, and apparently little influence, over the Police Commissioner. This gentleman devoted the weeks preceding the strike to bland reassurances that things were under control.

3. The strike, as most of you know, was broken. All participants were discharged; no one was reinstated. It was, however, a
Pyrrhic victory—and here our traditional histories are inadequate.
The new policemen were hired at precisely the pay schedules demanded by those who had struck and lost.

4. The action at Boston reflected a growing restiveness
among police and firemen throughout the country. The mass dismissal undoubtedly intimidated colleagues in other cities. But, if
subsequent pay scales are any indication, the strike that failed was
actually an impressive success. If police were intimidated, their
communities were not insensitive to what transpired in the Bay
State. Police pay improved significantly in city after city.

Candidly, now, is this not a familiar, if not a classic, pattern?

At the risk of belaboring a point, I call your attention to the
ingredients: A widening gap between compensation in the private
and public sectors. The failure of public sector pay to keep abreast
of a war-induced increase in the cost of living. Refusal to even sit
down at the negotiating table. Diffusion of authority between the
mayor and the Police Commissioner: the one reluctantly willing,
but unable; and the other able, but adamantly unwilling. And,
finally, the ruthless discharge of over a thousand men in affirma-
tion of a hollow and unjustifiable principle, followed rapidly by
exactly the settlement which could have avoided the strike in the
first place.

It was a philosopher, was it not, who wryly observed that
those who did not learn from history were destined to relive it.
Perhaps no better demonstration exists than labor relations in the
public service. Until quite recently, management and workers in
this sector appeared trapped in a grotesque minuet, the score for
which was written a half century ago. This was an imposingly
formal dance. We have been stumbling through the ritualistic steps
with the thoughtlessness of zombies.

A careful reexamination seems long overdue.

We live in a country with undreamed-of wealth, a staggering
productive capacity, and the most advanced technology known to
man. Yet we pay many public employees at levels which would
qualify them for welfare supplements. We are confronted, across
the nation, with chronic shortages of policemen, firemen, teachers,
nurses, and welfare workers. In many places recruiting is crippled

by tragically inadequate pay scales. In some places, we manage to recruit but are unable to retain employees as private industry pay and work conditions exert an understandable and irresistible magnetism. Many vital public services have been transformed by these factors into employment turnstiles, inducing simultaneously administrative inefficiency and excessive operational costs.

Yet employee efforts to improve wages and working conditions have been regarded as arrogant and unbridled self-interest and treated in a manner more appropriate to major insurrections. This disparity, ironically enough, operates largely at lower levels and in what we term social services. Executive assistants, administrative heads, and top-level staff are recruited and retained by salaries in the $15,000–$30,000 bracket. We appear to have little difficulty in rationalizing this; given market realities and the need for talent such compensation appears unavoidable. It is at the $4,000–$10,000 level that we balk and resort to pious and passionate declarations of the requirement of a sense of dedication to public service.

We have been governed since the 1930s by a public policy which specifically repudiates unilateralism in labor relations. We declared, by statute, that employees had a right to form organizations of their own and that employers were obligated to bargain in good faith. Yet this fundamental and sound public policy applied only to private industry. Government officials appeared curiously reluctant to adhere to the rules they imposed upon others.

Government representatives who regularly negotiated, directly or indirectly, with private sector unions for the construction of schools, highways, hospitals, and government office buildings found similar negotiations with their own employees to operate these facilities an unacceptable intrusion. Officials who, in pursuit of their duties, unhesitatingly executed contracts involving fiscal commitments far into the future, suddenly discovered an implacable inability to negotiate the terms and conditions of employment beyond the current legislative session or administrative term.

In some instances, journalists and others are agitated over what they deem excessive concentrations of political power. But public employees, paradoxically, in these same situations are unable to locate anyone with sufficient authority to even discuss, let alone resolve, their problems. Denied traditional unionism and collective bargaining, some public employees resorted to lobbying. The postal service is probably the outstanding example. Need I remind this group of the jungle of administrative regulations and laws which for many years prohibited even this? There is a nightmarish quality, in retrospect, to a ruling which provided disciplinary action for a letter carrier who visited Washington on his own time, at his own expense, saw his own Congressman, and discussed his own working conditions. Fortunately, this is no longer true.

But even now, a public employee union barred from or frustrated in genuine collective bargaining which turns to legislators to correct inequities is condemned as irresponsible, denounced for flexing political muscle, and regarded with the jaundice conventionally reserved for extortion. It would appear that public employee unionism was inappropriate, collective bargaining was illegal, and recourse to normal legislative processes was immoral.

Perhaps the greatest irony of all involved the evolution of the Civil Service system. No exhaustive review is necessary to suggest that this reform originated in the desire to curb the abuses of patronage and to develop a cadre of qualified and competent public servants who could perform with some degree of security, relatively immune to some of our political vagaries. It was, at the time, an admirably progressive step, and continues to be a valuable adjunct to the process of running government. The principle of merit employment is not to be discarded lightly.

But the system of Civil Service, either at the Federal, state, or local level, ought not to be regarded as sacred and immune from the same evaluation and criticism applied to other human instrumentalities. Parkinson's Law, that work expands to fill the space allotted to it, has been repeatedly validated. Similarly, another proposition, that bureaucracies will always establish justification not only for their existence, but for perpetual expansion, can be demonstrated. I venture to suggest that this applies equally to the corporate world and to government agencies. Though I might be unhappy with excessive publicity on this score, even some unions are not immune to this virus.

Nor is Civil Service. A vast, sprawling bureaucracy with self-validating characteristics has developed over the years. Not surprisingly, it is neither all good nor all bad, but its good features should not serve as a shield for its shortcomings. There is no "irrepressible conflict," to use the phrase associated with the Civil War, between collective bargaining and all aspects of Civil Service. The incompatibility is far from total, as demonstrated by years of co-existence, sometimes amicable, occasionally strained.

There are, admittedly, some tensions. The uncompromising objectivity of the system is rendered questionable when, as in one major city, the Civil Service Commissioner is simultaneously the Director of the City Department of Labor and wears both hats at the pleasure of the mayor. Scientifically constructed job classifications and career and salary plans are at best dubious in a free market economy. No one has yet defined that weary cliché, a fair day's work for a fair day's pay. What we are dealing with is nowhere near as precise as it appears, but, rather, rough approximations rationalized by an internal logic.

But the integrity of even this more modest approach is relentlessly undermined by those who accommodate the pressures of the market, but who persist in accomplishing this through under-the-counter deals, thus maintaining the fiction of the plans' validity.

Easily the most significant source of incompatibility, however, is that, even under the best circumstances, even with the most dedicated and competent personnel, even in the greatest absence of political pressures, Civil Service continues to represent unilateralism in labor-management relations in the public service. This is something we have difficulty communicating to executives and commissioners who characteristically respond as if they had been personally attacked.

There is, I submit, a legitimate—and critical—difference between my requesting something of you, but leaving the final determination in your hands and my insistence that we sit together at the negotiating table as equals.

Collective bargaining is more than simply an additional holiday, or a pay increase, or an improved pension plan, or a grievance procedure. It is, of course, all of these, and their importance can hardly be overestimated. But it is, in its most profound sense, a process. It is a process which transforms pleading to negotiation. It is a process which permits employees dignity as they participate in the formulation of their terms and conditions of employment. It is a process which embraces the democratic ideal and applies it concretely, specifically, and effectively at the place of work.

Public employees and collective bargaining have engaged in sporadic flirtations with each other for decades. It is no longer a flirtation. It is a marriage. And it will endure. Recent years have witnessed a sharp increase in government employment and a dramatic spurt in public employee unionism. Total government employment soared from 7 million in 1955 to 10.5 million in 1966. Projections suggest it will continue to climb; the latest available estimate puts it at approximately 15 million by 1975. If these statistics are accurate (and there seems no reason for skepticism) government employment will constitute 15 per cent of the total labor force by 1970.

Some people—possibly a few in this room—mutter darkly about the uncontrollable expansion of the Federal bureaucracy. But most of this recent expansion has occurred at the state and local level. Currently approximately 75 per cent of all government employment is here. The Federal level has been remarkably stable. We are, therefore, considering one of the fastest growing sectors in our society.

Most certainly we are considering the fastest growing sector in the American labor movement. More specifically I am here as a representative of what has been termed, by others, as the fastest growing union in the country. I say this with considerable pride, but without, I hope, boastfulness. On the contrary, it is offered with genuine gratitude. All that we are, we owe to you.

You represent our best organizers, our most persuasive reason for existence, our defense against membership apathy and indifference, our perpetual prod to militancy, and our assurance of continued growth.

Some observers glance at the statistics of employment, slide to union membership totals, and conclude that organized labor had crested in the major industries and was turning avariciously towards public employees, hungry for the per capita dues that would flow in upon their capture.

Whether or not this is true—I find discussions of human motivation singularly unrevealing—the important thing is that it is irrelevant. Unions would be unable to sign up a single employee if he were satisfied, if his dignity were not offended, if he were treated with justice. What is important is not the motives of union officials in organizing public employees, but the astonishing rapidity and success of their efforts. Barren ground yields poor crops, but here the ground is fertile beyond belief.

But the statistics of government employment have a far greater significance which merits fuller consideration. They suggest a major transformation in the structure and nature of our society. Fifty years ago, when Calvin Coolidge sent his telegram, the private and public sectors were discrete. They were separate entities, relatively easy to distinguish one from the other. Even if one adds the necessary qualification that every major form of transportation was heavily subsidized in one form or another, or that government-imposed tariffs provided shelters for our industry, even with all this the world of the private entrepreneur and the world of public enterprise was easily identifiable in 1920.

Governor Coolidge may have been tart or he may have been politically motivated or he may have been sincerely concerned with the public welfare. He at least had some grounds for his position. Those grounds no longer exist. A massive erosion has occurred. And if we fail to recognize this we run the risk of further irrelevant discussion.

In 1920 needy people, if they received any assistance at all, received it from private philanthropies. In 1967, public welfare is a major activity and a significant and growing budget item. Revealingly enough, government involvement has not obliterated private philanthropic efforts; the two complement each other.

Some public transportation is publicly owned, as in New York City, and some is privately owned, as in Washington, D.C.

Our public school system is staggering under the load of additional students, but private school enrollment climbs correspondingly. State universities are flourishing, but so are their private counterparts and their roles are indistinguishable. Furthermore, Federal funds underwrite major construction and research programs at leading private universities as well as at public institutions.

For several decades we have had public housing authorities whose objective was the construction of low-income accommodations. Serious consideration is currently being given the possibility of private nonprofit corporations to renovate entire areas.

The other side of the coin is the development, at breathtaking government expense, of a communications satellite, which promptly becomes the monopoly of a private consortium.

If our emulation of the Japanese high-speed trains succeeds, will the Boston-New York-Washington run be a public or a private triumph? It will be both. A private railroad will operate, presumably for profit, the special trains over special track placed on special roadbeds, all designed at public expense.

The examples could be multiplied endlessly: aerospace research conducted by private companies with government support and using civilian and military personnel almost interchangeably; government "think tanks" which compete in brilliance with our most prestigious private universities; government-generated electric power in the Tennessee Valley and private utilities elsewhere.

The clear demarcation between private and public sectors is gone. With some exceptions, it has vanished beneath a maze of overlapping functions, parallel efforts, and incredibly complex relationships. Magically, all this has occurred without violating our historic apprehension of government. Magically, it has taken place within our democratic framework and, astonishingly, it has indeed strengthened it.

If this necessarily brief and admittedly oversimplified summary is valid, then one other thing has occurred. Traditional distinctions between labor-management relations in the private and public sectors have become irrelevant. One cannot argue logically about the uniqueness of public service confronted by public bus drivers in New York City and private bus drivers in Washington performing identical services.

Reasonable men cannot really be expected to accept the thesis that all public services are equally crucial. The parks attendant is performing an important function, but social catastrophe is not imminent in his temporary absence. That decorative secretary in a government agency is really not performing differently from her sister in the private world.

This assertion has simply been repeated so frequently that it has gained unwarranted stature and credibility. I invite you to reflect on it for a moment. In our society where are the critical functions concentrated? Our farms and factories are private. The facilities which transport their products are private. We are dependent for medical research and care upon a profession which is ferociously private in orientation. In war we rely on private enterprise and stake our national survival on its successful performance.

At the same time, I have no desire to commit a similar error in reverse. Certain public services are undeniably critical, in the same way that some private services are. Our international union, consequently, constitutionally regards its police members somewhat differently than its other members. I am arguing here for reasonable and thoughtful distinctions and against the kind of wholesale and unsupportable generalizations with which we have been afflicted.

I would be remiss if I concluded without commenting on the vexing issue of public employees and the right to strike.

If there is a uniquely American style it is characterized by a pragmatic approach. We have historically tinkered and "made do," preferring the tentative experiment to complex and abstract theorizing. Discussions of public employee strikes have displayed a regrettable preoccupation with hypothetical constructs and abstract theories (and spurious ones at that). In discussing the problem of strikes, I would point out that our union constitution recognizes that law enforcement groups cannot be allowed the right to strike. However, the prohibition cannot and must not be applied across the board to all public employees.

Actually, we have a wealth of experience on which to draw. We know, for example, that public employee strikes have been and are illegal in every jurisdiction which does or does not have a law on the subject. We know, further, that in some jurisdictions the penalties for violation of the strike prohibition are relatively mild and in others they are extremely harsh. We know, in addition, that in some places elaborate labor-management machinery has been devised and in others no structure is visible.

But certainly both our knowledge and experience are richer than this. We also know that public employee strikes have occurred in jurisdictions which proscribed them. They have occurred where the penalties were mild and where the penalties were severe. They have occurred where there was special legislation and elaborate machinery and in the absence of both legislation and machinery.

Court injunctions and confiscatory fines have not been demonstrably successful in the private sector; limited experience suggests they will be no more successful in the public sector.

Earlier I spoke of collective bargaining as a process. It is a process which occurs among equals. It is a process to which the

American labor movement is committed. It is not always neat, not always orderly, not always precise. It is occasionally disruptive and it sometimes inconveniences people. To be candid, it is on occasion totally exasperating.

Nevertheless, we have knowingly, consciously, and, I think, wisely, chosen this process in preference to the authoritarianism of price and wage controls and centralized, presumably scientific, administration of our economic activities. With all of its faults, with all of its occasional lapses, with all the exasperation it sometimes induces, it has worked admirably in the private sector of our economy.

We are determined that it will have the same opportunity in the public sector. But I refer here to genuine collective bargaining, which, I remind you, occurs among equals.

Strike prohibitions are not simply ineffectual, though they are undeniably that. What is far more serious, they warp this vital process. They bring employees to the bargaining table, but as inferiors. Simultaneously they provide false reassurance to management representatives and induce less than genuine negotiations. Ironically, they create the very tensions, exacerbate the very situations, provoke the very strikes they were allegedly formulated to prevent.

It is time we learned from experience and applied its rich lessons. The democracy of our political life deserves full extension into the labor relations of our public life. Public employees will not have it otherwise.

THE USE OF FACTFINDING
IN DISPUTE SETTLEMENT
(*or, the Impasse over the Impasse*)
by Jerry Wurf

The following speech by Mr. Wurf was made at the meeting of the National Academy of Arbitrators held on January 31, 1969.

Reprinted with the permission of the American Federation of State, County and Municipal Employees, AFL–CIO.

It is evident that factfinding will be used increasingly in public sector dispute settlement and that arbitrators with private sector experience will be called upon to be factfinders and arbitrators in public employment disputes. One service I can perform is to give you a capsule view of your future employment opportunities. It seems to me that it would be fruitless to discuss public employment factfinding without a clear understanding of the broader system in which it will be expected to function. Most private industry practitioners are woefully ignorant of labor relations as malpracticed in public employment.

As a veteran with over twenty years of seniority who is still struggling in the battle of public employees to win their full collective bargaining rights, I suppose it should give me some pleasure to be able to say that the impasse concerning public sector collective bargaining has moved leftward. Today we have moved beyond the elemental issue of the right to organize into the area of dispute resolution. But we cannot intelligently discuss the resolution of disputes without first understanding the framework in which bargaining in the public sector occurs.

Only a decade ago, many people questioned the right of public employees to join unions and sit at a bargaining table. Public employees were excluded from coverage of the National Labor Relations Act. And, state legislatures, with their heads in the sand, refused to believe that any problem existed. Contrast this with a very recent Gallup Poll which indicated that over 60 per cent of U.S. citizens now believe that teachers, police, and firemen should have the right to join unions. This figure would probably be even higher for less essential occupations.

Unfortunately, state and local legislative bodies apparently have not yet caught up with public opinion. Today, seven years after Executive Order 10988 was issued by President Kennedy, giving Federal employees the right to organize and to engage in collective bargaining on certain matters, only 17 states provide machinery to establish majority representation—and only 10 of these states require anything resembling true collective bargaining. But all public laws contain the broadest management rights clauses, and often attempt to limit bargaining to matters not covered by the civil service system, which I shall consider later.

What about public sector collective bargaining in the absence of legislation? At the risk of bewilderment—mine as well as yours—over the contradictions, anomalies, and ironies currently existing in the majority of states without collective bargaining legislation, let's briefly examine the "state of the art."

In some states public sector collective bargaining has been introduced without enabling legislation. Bargaining relationships and legal framework to deal with *de facto* bargaining have been established in many government jurisdictions, especially municipalities. *De facto* bargaining may be viewed in two extremes: As a result of the combination of the union's muscle and the city's enlightened political leadership, bargaining developed in Philadelphia on an increasingly sophisticated basis for more than twenty years. And in Memphis bargaining was accomplished despite the opposition of an antediluvian mayor—but only after a bitter struggle over the fundamental right of recognition—a struggle culminating in the assassination of Dr. Martin Luther King, Jr.

Certainly Memphis is an extreme example, but it is a vivid demonstration.

In other cities, after a hard-fought collective bargaining agreement is achieved, the boss may thumb his nose at the agreement knowing that the union will have some difficulty getting the agreement enforced. And as you know, the most typical method for a boss to thumb his nose at the union is to refuse to arbitrate, a matter which should be of no small concern to this body. For example, a few weeks ago newly elected county commissioners in Indiana, where there is no law requiring collective bargaining, decided they would like to hand out a few jobs in the public roads department to their supporters. When the collective bargaining agreement, which contained a typical provision requiring that discharge be for cause, got in the way, the commissioners conveniently arranged for a few job applicants to file a lawsuit, as a result of which the county was restrained from enforcing the agreement. The restraining order was issued without notice to the union.

We might add, parenthetically, that although the lawyers representing the county were present, they stood silent when the county's contract with our union was attacked. Significantly, although the court's order merely made the contract unenforceable, the commissioners interpreted the order as requiring the discharge of all of the employees who had supported the union. We expect to appeal and hope to establish that in Indiana, where there is no legislation requiring collective bargaining in the public sector, that a collective bargaining.agreement is enforceable.

When faced with the task of how to give employees the right to join unions and bargain collectively in the absence of legislation, union leaders and their lawyers have developed some ingenious approaches. For example, in Arkansas and other states, the infamous right-to-work laws have been used to accomplish the reinstatement of employees who had been discharged for having joined a union.

And in recent months we have learned that public employees don't have to rely on right-to-work laws in order to keep political leaders from discharging employees when they seek the elemental right to organize. Two Federal Courts of Appeals—in Chicago and St. Louis—have now held that "Union membership is protected by the right of association under the First and Fourteenth Amendments" to the U.S. Constitution, and that damages and injunctive relief may be awarded to the dischargees. While these court decisions may provide a remedy for the right of public employees to join a union, they do not reach the broader issues of collective bargaining. Moreover, it is evident that the court route for correcting each case of discrimination is far too cumbersome, and that some administrative machinery must be established to protect the rights of public employees to join unions and engage in collective bargaining.

These examples merely illustrate the nineteenth-century attitude held by the typical public official. A study recently published by the International City Managers' Association reveals labor relations policies in council-manager cities of at least 10,000 population:

67% have no policy with respect to permitting employees to join nationally affiliated organizations.

2% do not permit employees to join such organizations.

29% permit employees to join such organizations.

66% have no policy with respect to authorizing management to punish employees for organizational activity.

29% do not permit such punishment.

3% admit to permitting such punishment.

66% have no policy with respect to permitting recognition of a majority unit.

21% do not permit such recognition.

11% do permit such recognition.

72% have no policy with respect to authorizing signed negotiated agreements.

15% do not permit signed negotiated authorization.

10% do permit signed negotiated agreements.

68% have no policy with respect to authorizing arbitration of disputes.

24% do not authorize arbitration.

4% do authorize arbitration.

In the face of this lack of preparation and understanding, is there any question why public-sector employment relations are in such turmoil?

Even where state legislatures have been sufficiently enlightened to enact mandatory collective bargaining legislation, there is generally a wide gulf between such legislation and the rights necessary to enable public employees to sit down at the bargaining table as equal participants.

One major issue of contention is the scope of bargaining. Key issues such as wages, pension plans, vacations, and the like are generally not negotiable.

All too frequently civil service regulations preempt large areas of what manifestly is bargainable in the private sector, such as seniority, discipline, grievance arbitration, and occupational classifications. Contrary to the myth that civil service is impartial, it is in fact nothing more nor less than the personnel arm of the public employer, and it exercises what amounts to the broadest management rights clause imaginable. They enjoy this not by dint of negotiating prowess, but rather by virtue of laws which unfortunately state that nothing in the bargaining agreement may conflict with civil service regulations or other legislation.

Another devilish relationship is that between bargaining and government fiscal procedures. Where we do bargain over wages and other economic matters, we can't be sure that the bargain reached at the table won't become undone when it must be approved by the legislature, which has relatively little understanding of the collective bargaining process.

And we've learned that government officials, no less than private employers, must be restrained from engaging in unfair labor practices. A recent experience occurred in New York State, where the public law does not provide for unfair labor practices. There the state continued to bargain for a new contract with an independent association while our union's petition for representation was pending before New York's Public Employee Relations Board. The NLRB as well as the New York Board for the private sector has long held that bargaining with one union while a valid claim for recognition was pending by another union constitutes an unfair labor practice. Our membership believed it was given a Hobson's choice: Sit back and watch the state violate the spirit of these laws and thereby destroy our union in New York State, or strike and risk violating the New York State law. The alternative was costly: two of the leaders were sent to jail for violating the restraining order; many workers were suspended and the union is threatened with the loss of all checked-off dues for a period up to 18 months.

The hottest fight is, of course, over the matter of impasse resolution, including the right to strike. This is where the issue is joined. Permit me to quote, in part, from a statement concerning the importance of the right to strike which expresses my feelings on this issue:

> Considering the numerous cases in which disputes are not settled until after there has been resort to a strike, it may seem odd that confidence in the value of collective bargaining nevertheless persists. This is so for three reasons. The first is that *we know that the strike or the threat of a strike is an essential part of negotiations; without it there could hardly be an approach to equality in bargaining power of the kind which our law seeks.* The second is that *the denial of the right to strike would be incompatible with tradition and would strip the element of voluntarism from the labor agreement which is, after all, the objective of the process of collective bargaining as we understand it. . . .* The third is that we have not been able to devise a method of establishing the wage rates and other conditions of em-

ployment which is more efficient and at the same time consistent with our basic political thinking. The totalitarian kind of imposition and prohibition is abhorrent to us, and no authoritative voices have been raised to advocate such a course.

An anti-strike law should at best be addressed only to a case of genuine emergency, one in which we see as a fact that very acute harm is being done to the community; in other words, a situation, unlike any we have ever had, which approaches the proportions of disaster. . . .

This is excerpted from *Report to Governor Robert B. Meyner by the Governor's Committee on Legislation Relating to Public Utility Labor Disputes,* September 1954, David L. Cole, Chairman.

And George Taylor waxed enthusiastically over the need to maintain the strike when he said:

Each substantial narrowing of latitude and every restriction upon the right to strike weakens the structure of collective bargaining. . . . No one should have any doubt about the unlikelihood that collective bargaining can be maintained in the absence of the rights to strike and to lockout. . . . [The strike] serves as a motive power to induce peaceful settlements.

What eloquent statements! But times have changed. You may know that Mr. Taylor and Mr. Cole, and other distinguished arbitrators who wrote the report leading to the passage of New York State's Taylor Act, which bans strikes in public employment, are all vigorous defenders of the right to strike—in private industry. They are all equally vigorous opponents of the right to strike— in public employment.

Do they attempt to differentiate in terms of public interest between the acceptability of a strike in a publicly operated and a privately operated local transit system, or a publicly operated and a privately operated trash removal, or a publicly operated and a privately operated swimming pool? They explain that there is no right to strike against the government, by anybody, anywhere, at any time. Shades of Calvin Coolidge. I must respectfully disagree that the right of public employees to strike can be dismissed in such a cavalier fashion.

Let me then suggest conditions under which factfinding might play a useful role in the public sector. The union must be permitted the opportunity to stand as an equal in the bargaining relationship. In short we want rights—and responsibilities—equal to our sister unions in private industry. This would necessitate the passage of public sector collective bargaining legislation that would give public employees the rights long held by employees in the private sector—to organize and bargain collectively.

This may require that the legislature cede some of its authority to the employer-bargaining agent. It would also require that we develop a mechanism for assuring that the administrators of the law would not be beholden to the chief executive—the employer—who appointed them. As you know, New York City has resolved this problem by establishing an impartial tripartite board, with the impartial members being selected by the employer and union representatives.

Current public sector collective bargaining laws provide for factfinding or some other form of impasse resolution, but there is no driving force for agreement since strikes are outlawed. Under these conditions, however, the union is not an equal party to the factfinding proceedings. If the union disagrees with the factfinder's report, what alternatives does it have? Does the union veto the report and attempt to return to negotiations when the employer knows it has no leverage—the right to strike—or does the union attempt to bypass the bargaining table and run to the legislature out of sheer frustration? Or, does the union conduct an illegal strike?

On the other hand, the employer may reject the recommendations of the factfinder with virtual impunity in the face of a strike ban, and simply stand on its last offer.

Although a few states seem bent on competing to escalate the price of martyrdom for labor leaders, strikes for essential rights in public employment will continue—legal or illegal—as long as public employees are deprived of their dignity. Attention must be focused on resolving these disputes prior to a work stoppage, rather than on devising penalties that eventually prove difficult, if not impossible, to apply.

While I believe that public employee unions are entitled to the right to strike, I do not, however, favor strikes except as a last and desperate resort. Like private employers, public employers must also, on occasion, have the threat of a strike hanging over their heads to engage in good faith bargaining.

But what are the alternatives? Virtually no one wants compulsory binding arbitration over contract terms. It would serve little purpose to recite the pros and cons of compulsory arbitration. Suffice it to say that it may enervate collective bargaining and encourage parties to maintain rigid positions. And, most importantly, it does not stop strikes. It also tends to result in awards which do not permit, for example, low-paid hospital workers to catch up with auto and steel workers. Experience in Australia, New Zealand, and Great Britain as well as rather limited exposure in this country all indicates that compulsory arbitration has not eliminated strikes.

In any case, very few legislatures are likely to delegate this kind of authority to an outside "neutral" third party. They would view it as an intrusion on their sovereignty.

The recently released draft, "Report of the President's Review Committee on Employee-Management Relations in the Federal Service," suggests the form that compulsory arbitration could take in public employment. It emphasizes voluntarism in dealing with the impasse, with factfinding and voluntary arbitration only as a last resort. But what happens in a really "up tight" impasse that defies solution? The boss is still the final arbiter. Here is the way it would work.

The chairman of the Civil Service Commission would serve as chairman of the proposed Federal Labor Relations Panel. This is somewhat akin to appointing the personnel vice president of a company to chair a "neutral panel." Other members of the panel would be the Secretary of Labor and the chairman of the National Labor Relations Board. Only the latter designee could be described as relatively free of control by the executive branch of government. Although the panel may hear the case itself, or submit the matter to experts from within or without Federal service for recommendations, it holds the authority to issue a final and binding decision.

At the risk of offending the very distinguished members of the academy who served on the advisory panel to the review committee, my reaction is "a boss is a boss is a boss is a boss." Make no mistake about it. The chairman of the Civil Service Commission is "top hand." He is the protector of the personnel establishment. This certainly implies no disrespect to past, present, or future Civil Service Commission chairmen. Experience, particularly at the state and local levels, shows, however, that this individual—whoever he happens to be—cannot act as a neutral in Federal service labor-management matters.

Although it is saddled with several of the disadvantages of compulsory arbitration, factfinding—coupled with recommendations—does, however, present a maximum amount of flexibility and permits the parties to make the final decision. It appears to offer the best hope compatible with the concept of collective bargaining for the parties to reconcile their differences. Factfinding in public employment disputes will work best where there is a legal framework around collective bargaining. This framework must treat the union as a party of equal standing, not as a supplicant. But if the strike threat and the strike are prohibited, factfinding will have limited value.

Factfinding must take place within specified time limits. Any cooling-off period, either built into the factfinding process or added on following a possible breakdown in factfinding, must also conclude within a specific, reasonable time limit. Lengthy, unwarranted delays exceeding sixty days or thereabouts would substantially weaken the process. During this period the status quo would, of course, prevail. Thus far, then, we have not prohibited the strike, we have merely delayed it.

Factfinding should be available at the request of both parties or upon determination by the Public Employment Labor Board that factfinding should be explored, or that it is warranted, after which the factfinder should be selected jointly by the parties.

Let us understand that the term factfinding is somewhat misleading. Most frequently the parties know and understand the facts. The problem is that these facts are interpreted from positions of self-interest and therefore lead rational people to conflicting conclusions.

Maximum flexibility for the factfinder is essential. For example, he should have the right to determine that conditions are not yet ripe for factfinding—and thus send the dispute back to the parties for some serious bargaining. Or, if deemed appropriate, he may conclude that the parties are in need of quick guidelines for further negotiations and engage in mediation which may include general preliminary recommendations. Such a procedure would clearly put the parties on notice as to the factfinder's thinking and his ultimate recommendations. Thus, he is slowly making the transition from mediator to factfinder—but always preferring to mediate.

Preferably formal, written recommendations would not be made until rather late in the process, again in an effort at voluntary settlement and in order to keep positions unfrozen. As a last resort only would he make the recommendations public.

I tend to believe that public disclosure of recommendations may be more important in public sector factfinding than in the private sector. Two aspects of public employee collective bargaining lead me to this conclusion. One is the visibility of the parties. Public sector bargaining is often conducted in a fish bowl. This is especially true when critical occupations are involved or when an impasse develops. Secondly, the kind of real pressure applied by both parties is political rather than economic. The headlines read "City Workers Raid Public Till," or "City Is Sweatshop Boss." Both parties must strive to maintain creditability in the public eye.

The factfinder could even recommend that the sharply defined few remaining issues be submitted to voluntary, binding arbitration. The factfinder would strive for voluntary agreement until the expiration of his assignment.

While I have urged the greater use of factfinding machinery, with the factfinder being given the widest possible latitude to mediate, to make private or public recommendations, and to refer the case back to the parties, we are not unaware of what it takes away from truly free collective bargaining. Indeed, it may present an excuse to the parties to engage in little or no bargaining and to depend upon the factfinder. And then, of course, there are those who believe that the recommendations of the factfinder may be based upon the acceptability rather than upon the merits of the conflicting claims.

In the event that agreement is not forthcoming and the impasse remains after factfinding, we must accept the possibility of a strike. I place an extremely high priority on the right to strike and its efficacy as a means to resolve conflict. I do not claim, however, that this right to strike must take precedence over all other competing rights. AFSCME's constitution, for example, prohibits law enforcement personnel from striking.

In any event, we should be aware of the door which the Federal courts may have opened to strike against a public employer's refusal to recognize the right of employees to join unions, i.e., the Chicago and St. Louis Courts of Appeals cases I mentioned earlier, which held that a state may not deny employees the freedom to associate, i.e., to join a union.

This poses an interesting question. The Supreme Court has ruled that a strike against an employer's unfair labor practices is protected under certain circumstances, and in civil rights cases the Supreme Court has upheld an individual's right to violate a state law which conflicts with the Constitution. Is a strike in protest of a public employer's illegal discharge of an employee, in violation of the First and Fourteenth Amendments to the Constitution, now protected?

Most people believe that a community cannot tolerate strikes that present a clear and present danger to the health and safety of the people. But such strikes, I submit, are very, very rare. Hopefully they will become more rare as public employment collective bargaining techniques improve. However, if and when they do occur, they should be treated in a manner somewhat similar to the emergency dispute-settling machinery in the Taft-Hartley Act. An injunction could be issued for a limited period of time, say 60 or 90 days. This period would afford another attempt to settle the dispute.

In the unlikely event that a dispute continues after the expiration of an injunction, a rare experience under Taft-Hartley, the legislature could take action in determining the best method to resolve the impasse.

Since you are a captive audience of "opinion makers," I frankly want to take one further advantage of you before concluding. I want to get something off my chest about civil disobedience. Government, in the form of the public employer, can't close off all of our options and then scream because we shut down the operation. If the public employer sits on his sovereign rump and majestically violates the Constitution by refusing to recognize our right to belong to a union, or that we are a majority union, or, if he refuses to engage in good faith bargaining—then we are going to strike.

Similarly, if the government, in the form of bigoted politicians playing to the lowest common denominator, violates the Constitution by trampling on the civil rights of our black citizens—then there will be civil disobedience.

To expect less is to characterize us as less than men. And I might add that the most predominant picket sign throughout the nine-week strike in Memphis was the one that proclaimed: "I Am a Man."

And now an admission. I am quickly approaching my fiftieth year. This is much too late in life to be a violent revolutionist. I, like most of my black brothers, want a peaceful revolution.

While the members of the National Academy of Arbitrators cannot be expected to "mediate" all of this nation's problems, you do possess a unique expertise in your understanding of union-management relations. In this respect, it seems to me that you have a duty to turn your attention to new problem areas—what the academicians refer to as the "emerging sectors" of collective bargaining—to come forward and contribute new ideas and fresh concepts. I beseech you to do so.

STATE HOSPITAL STRIKE A WINNER!
by Collin Gonze

> *Mr. Gonze is a staff writer for the* Public Employee Press.

Tens of thousands of New York State employees won themselves an unforgettable Thanksgiving Day this year: a union victory climaxing a 10-day strike.

The strike, called at four state mental institutions, was aimed at forcing Governor Rockefeller to keep his long-delayed promise to hold elections for bargaining agents among 124,000 state workers. The labor-shy Governor was trying to wrap up this enormous state work force with a long-range secret contract with the company union of his own personal choice, the Civil Service Employees Association (CSEA), an insurance company representative. Rockefeller had selected the CSEA without an election. Neither he nor the CSEA dared to go before the employees in a secret ballot vote.

The average weekly take-home pay of a state mental hospital attendant is $77.50. Compared to city workers covered by our DC 37 contract, they have totally inadequate pensions, no career ladder to speak of, no shift differentials, and an ancient and creaky grievance mechanism.

The Governor was going to give them an across-the-board 4 per cent increase (that's around $5 a week for most employees).

Led by our own Lillian Roberts, the Council 50 locals at Creedmoor, Manhattan, Bronx, and Buffalo State hospitals struck one by one, starting on November 18.

Ten other locals were preparing to strike in their turn. But the Governor, utilizing the Public Employment Relations Board (PERB) as a facesaver, surrendered after 10 days. He agreed to stop negotiating with the CSEA and to go along with the PERB-ordered elections for bargaining agents. The election will probably be held in February or March.

The amazing success of the strikes, the first of their kind in state service, was partly due to the emergency assistance freely given by DC 37 members and staff. Many sacrificed their own time to join the picket lines in fair and foul weather. Several Blue Collar organizers, well known for the generous capacity of their voices, were reduced to hoarse whispers after a couple of rainy days on the line.

Our AFSCME International Union also played an important role in winning the strike. International President Jerry Wurf worked ceaselessly both behind the scenes and at meetings of the strikers. The breakthrough came when PERB hurriedly issued a long-awaited decision on how state employees should be divided for bargaining purposes, and then ordered the Governor to cease negotiating with his hand-picked CSEA.

The state workers' struggle to win real union representation for themselves is by no means over. The Governor, apparently deeply humiliated by his defeat, is actually threatening to have all strikers fired. This action, right out of the Middle Ages, is apparently meant to intimidate the formerly docile state workers into voting for the company union.

The jailing of Lillian Roberts for 30 days—the harshest sentence ever handed out under the Taylor Law—is a saddening example of his tactics.

But the plain fact is that state workers have seen what a real union can accomplish in the city . . . and they want some of that freedom too. Just like city workers, they are demanding a $6,000 minimum starting salary. This kind of militancy is unheard of in state service. And it is sure to lead to a victory for Council 50 at the polls.

LILLIAN ROBERTS' CAUSE
by Bayard Rustin

Mr. Rustin is executive director of the A. Philip Randolph Institute. This article first appeared in Rustin's column in the Amsterdam News *and was later reprinted in thirty other newspapers, including the* Public Employee Press.

There have been a lot of strikes in New York during the past few years. Many of these have been public employee strikes. And each time such a strike has been called (whether by transport, sanitation, hospital, or welfare workers and teachers) a representative of the state or city government has denounced that strike as being against poor people. The reasoning goes as follows: poor people need public transportation; they need their garbage collected by the city, etc., and any work stoppage—even if it ultimately improves those services—is against the poor people who rely on them. This is divisive and dangerous reasoning.

Let us examine the latest strike "against the poor." Its leader was Mrs. Lillian Roberts of the American Federation of State, County and Municipal Employees, AFL–CIO. She is a black woman who has worked in behalf of the poor all of her life. She was sentenced to a 30-day sentence for leading a strike of mental hospital attendants. (Incidentally, this was the harshest sentence given a labor leader under the Taylor Law.)

Mrs. Roberts represents a group of Negro and white workers who are among the working poor. A hospital attendant in New York State earns $90 a week to begin with, and after fifteen years service earns $120. The ten-day strike at several mental hospitals was not for higher wages, however. It was for the elementary right of workers to elect a union to bargain in their behalf. For years Governor Rockefeller and state officials have negotiated with the timid Civil Service Employees Association. And for years working conditions at our hospitals have deteriorated. Turnover among workers has been high as the most fortunate of them moved on to better-paying jobs. The less fortunate attendants have had to take on one or two extra jobs or have been forced to live just above the poverty line if they had a family.

District 50 struck for 10 days, and finally the Public Employment Relations Board ruled that an election should take place. Despite this, Mrs. Roberts was sentenced to spend Christmas in jail—away from the three children in her care. She was subsequently released on Christmas Eve.

Was the ten-day strike at mental hospitals a strike against the poor? I think not. It is unfortunate that mental patients and their families had to suffer during the strike. But attendants provide vital services for these patients; they should be well trained, well paid and happy in their jobs.

Thus, we should be applauding Mrs. Roberts in her efforts to win union recognition and improved working conditions for hospital workers. She served a jail sentence in behalf of black and white workers and in behalf of the poor mental patients. She represents the fight for economic equality, dignity, and the right to organize that has been waged for more than one hundred years by the labor and civil rights movement in this country.

Beyond this, she joins that noble group of black women who have stood in the forefront of our progress—Sojourner Truth, Harriet Tubman, Mary McCloud Bethune, and Rosa Parks. Her great sacrifice is as much a part of our history as of theirs. All black people should salute Lillian Roberts.

5

THE BATTLE FOR THE TEACHER

The National Education Association and the American Federation of Teachers AFL–CIO are currently attempting by different approaches to obtain collective bargaining in school systems. Both organizations are also lobbying for legislation to control this bargaining.

Some educators regard this contest as offering modern education a challenge equal to those problems stemming from the curriculum, the building of schools, or the nature of professional courses for teachers.

Since 1960 the nation has seen the public school teacher change from a docile educator into an angry professional employee. Why and how this has happened is discussed in the following selections which give a brief history of the two organizations and the views of people leading or working for them.

THE TOUGH NEW TEACHER
by J. Douglas Muir

This article appeared in the November 1968 edition of the American School Board Journal. *Professor Muir is an assistant professor on the Faculty of Business Administration at the University of Alberta in Edmonton, Alberta, Canada. The article was written while he was attending Cornell University's School of Labor Economics and Industrial Relations where he was completing requirements for his doctoral degree.*

Reprinted, with permission, from *The American School Board Journal*, November 1968. The National School Boards Association. All rights reserved. Permission also granted by the author.

Just because you're a member of a school board, don't allow yourself to become too comfortable with the idea that the real power decisions about the schools are likely to remain the exclusive property of you and your fellow boardmen.

Teachers have a different idea. Backed by one of two powerful organizations—the National Education Association or the American Federation of Teachers—they are organized, financed, trained, determined, and in a fighting mood to win higher (much higher) salaries, improved working conditions, and a strong say in what you might think is your responsibility, policymaking.

AFT was the first of the two groups to get tough about higher salaries and better working conditions for teachers. It took NEA a few years to get the idea, but it, too, caught on—to the tune of calling this year for a teacher salary range of $10,500 to $21,000 and for a hand in the establishment of all school board policies on recruitment, evaluation, and personnel.

If you think it all happened fast, it's because it did. Only a couple of years ago, it was possible to distinguish clearly between the actions of the "teacher union" (AFT) and the "professional association" (NEA). That distinction is no longer easy to make. In just eight years, there's been something like a 350-degree turn in NEA's position concerning collective action. The remaining ten degrees needed to complete the about-face probably will be turned next year when NEA members vote on whether to establish a million-dollar "defense fund" to tide teachers over a walkout.

This report will attempt to describe how it all happened and what school boards might expect from teachers in the near future now that not one but two forces of teacher militancy have been unleashed on public education in the United States.

If you want to grasp what's happened to the National Education Association and the more than 50 per cent of American teachers it represents, watch the dowdy spinster on the beer commercial, who drops her inhibitions along with her cello and comes alive at a swinging party. NEA has shed its image of an aging sisterhood of spinster teachers and has come alive to the will of its members, 80 per cent of whom are teachers, a group that is getting younger and bigger all the time.

Nowhere is the big change more visible than in NEA's development since 1960 of "affirmative action" (my phrase) policies on collective bargaining, strikes, and sanctions. They represent a complete turnabout from the days before 1961 when NEA opposed *any* procedure that might interrupt school operations.

What caused the about-face? Two of many factors stand out: (1) demands by NEA's teachers that the association assume responsibility for improving their occupational needs, and (2) the ominous example provided by NEA's rival for teacher members, the American Federation of Teachers, which has been demonstrating what can be obtained from school boards by use of the big stick.

How was the change accomplished? Carefully and completely through a series of aggressive policy maneuvers—sparked mainly by NEA's teacher members—that has seen NEA change gradually from an association unwilling to concede that the word "strike" was part of the language to an action organization that backs its striking locals with money and muscle.

Professional Negotiations

In 1960 NEA's assembly turned down, strongly, a resolution suggesting that "representative negotiations" are "compatible with the ethics and dignity of the teaching profession."

So a new resolution, which avoided the term "negotiations," was introduced and passed in 1961. That was NEA's first policy on negotiations; it stated simply that NEA believed that professional education associations should "be accorded the right . . . to participate [with school boards] in the determination of policies of common concern," including salaries.

The resolution ruled out "arbitrary exercise of unilateral authority" by boards of education or strikes by teachers. In case of an impasse, a board of review of professional and lay educators —something calculated to preclude the use of state labor mediation or arbitration boards—should be called in.

It was the year 1962 that unquestionably marked the turning point in NEA's attitude toward collective bargaining. By 1962 NEA was "insisting" on the right of teachers to negotiate with school boards—even though the word "negotiation" had not yet crept into official wording of the policy.

Strikes were still anathema, as were labor mediation boards: "Under no circumstances," declared the 1962 resolution, "should the resolution of differences between professional associations and boards of education be sought through channels set up for handling industrial disputes." The rationale: "Industrial-dispute machinery, which assumes a conflict of interest and a diversity of purpose between persons and groups, is not appropriate to professional negotiations in public education."

This resolution passed in spite of objections from the floor of the delegate assembly that it focused too much attention upon the professional-union controversy, that it could be interpreted as being directed against the union movement in general and the American Federation of Teachers in particular, and that it handicapped affiliates that were required to support local mediation efforts.

The 1962 resolution didn't spell out how boards and teachers were to reach agreement in impasses, except to recommend that "procedures," including "provisions for appeal through designated educational channels," should be established.

The delegates, in 1963, decided these still-undefined procedures "must" be established, and this was the only change made in the negotiations resolution. The urgency of setting up workable negotiations machinery may have been somewhat in reaction to a speech by the president of the National School Boards Association, who pointed out that NSBA policy urged all boards "to refrain from compromise agreements based on negotiations or collective bargaining," and to avoid mediation or arbitration.

The 1964 assembly cleared the way for NEA affiliates to resolve disputes with school boards through mediation and arbitration boards originally designed for resolving industrial disputes. The entire section outlawing such action was deleted from the previous year's negotiations resolution. Affiliates were called upon to make a greater effort to develop negotiations procedures and adopt written agreements.

One small but significant change was made in 1965. The word "strike" was deleted from that section of the resolution which previously banned the use of strikes along with "arbitrary exercise of unilateral authority" by school boards. The revision read: "The

seeking of consensus and mutual agreement on a professional basis
should preclude the arbitrary exercise of unilateral action by boards
of education, administrators, or teachers."

A strong plea was made by the 1965 delegates for an amendment to the resolution in order to allow local associations of classroom teachers to negotiate with school boards separately from
administrators, but it was defeated. Had it passed, it would have
established a bargaining group of classroom teachers within NEA
parallel to that of the AFT membership. This could have opened
the door for an AFT–NEA merger, or it simply may have helped
AFT raid NEA affiliates.

In 1966, William G. Carr, then NEA's executive secretary,
reported that the association's push for development of legislation
governing teacher-board negotiations had been successful—11
states had passed statutes covering them. From the floor of the
1966 delegate assembly came a motion to write some sort of
grievance procedure into the negotiations resolution. "To have one
without the other is going half way"; NEA must protect teachers
through the right of appeal of grievances, argued the delegate.

A majority agreed. The title of the resolution was changed
from professional negotiations to professional negotiations and
grievance procedure, and this paragraph was added:

> The National Education Association insists on the
> right of individual teachers, through officially adopted pro-
> fessional grievance procedures and with the right to profes-
> sional association representation, to appeal the application
> or interpretation of board of education policies affecting
> them through educational channels which include third
> party appeal if necessary, without fear of intimidation, co-
> ercion, discrimination, or other forms of reprisal.

Everything NEA either had condemned or avoided saying
about negotiations in the early 1960s was included in the completely revised resolution presented to the 1968 assembly in Dallas.
Negotiations agreements, says the latest resolution, "must" be established between teachers and school boards. These agreements
"shall provide" for negotiations, mediation, factfinding and appeal
of impasses, and for grievance procedures that include binding
arbitration.

The resolution also calls on NEA members and affiliates to push for state bargaining laws.

Sanctions

Just as 1962 ushered in a marked change in NEA negotiation policy, so, too, did that same year see the NEA delegate assembly adopt the first resolution supporting sanctions (blacklisting of school districts) "as a means for preventing unethical or arbitrary policies or practices that have a deleterious effect on the welfare of the schools." The resolution called on NEA affiliates to help develop guidelines for invoking "professional sanctions."

A few points about this revolutionary resolution bear mentioning. It came from the floor, not from the NEA executive, suggesting perhaps that the NEA hadn't intended taking the big step then. It came directly on the heels of heated debate over a negotiations resolution that may have influenced the delegates' thinking. And it came at the end of a long morning after two motions for adjournment, a fact probably influencing its quick, uneventful passage.

At their 1963 convention, NEA delegates decided that complete authority for imposing and removing nationwide sanctions should rest with the executive committee. The guidelines established that the executive committee would impose sanctions only after a request by a state affiliate was received and after the NEA Commission on Professional Rights and Responsibilities had made an investigation.

Nationwide sanctions against all the school districts in Utah were invoked by NEA in May 1964 on grounds that the Governor had refused to increase the education budget. No major change was made in the sanctions resolution that year, but the NEA board of directors provided a little more insight into the use of sanctions: They should be applied only "when the total conditions in a district are such that the professional people there cannot perform the services in the interests of the children for which they have been trained."

In 1965 the sanction against Utah was lifted after 300 days. But sanctions were imposed that year against Idaho (only briefly) and Oklahoma. The tactics, initiated in the Oklahoma case, were clear: *censure*—wide publicity on education conditions in the state; *notification*—informing placement services throughout the country of the sanction and conditions in Oklahoma; *warning*—to active and student NEA members that accepting employment in Oklahoma might be considered unethical conduct; *assistance*—helping teachers in Oklahoma leave the state.

Speaking to delegates at the 1965 assembly, NEA executive secretary Carr laid down some specific sanctions ground rules:

> Before sanctions are invoked [he warned] the educational deficiencies should be established by an impartial study. These documented deficiencies must be serious enough and general enough in scope to warrant so drastic a measure. The profession itself must be substantially united and resolute. The group against whom the sanctions were directed must be legally and financially capable of removing the deficiencies which led to the sanctions. Sanctions should be applied only after due warning, and with a complete absence of threats or vindictiveness. They must be preceded and accompanied by a persistent campaign of public information.

A 1965 addition to the sanction resolution gave the association, for the first time, some effective control over members who ignore sanctions: ". . . violation of sanctions by a member of the profession is a violation of the Code of Ethics of the Education Profession. Therefore, the offering or accepting of employment in areas where sanctions are in effect should be evaluated in terms of the code. . . ." The NEA delegates also changed the association's bylaws to give the "Committee on Professional Ethics power, after notice and hearing, to censure, suspend, or expel" violators.

The 1966 NEA convention brought no change in wording of the sanctions resolution from 1965. Recommending use of sanctions over strikes, Carr assured delegates that sanctions do not violate contracts or encounter court injunctions. They are directed at legislatures and other public bodies, not against students. "They [sanctions] constitute," he said, "a procedure which is more powerful, more respected, and more successful than any other."

Worried about that section of the resolution making it unethical for a superintendent whose school district is under sanction to offer a position to a teacher, delegates to the 1967 convention revised part of the resolution to read: "the offering, without informing the prospective employe of sanctions, or the acceptance of employment in areas where sanctions are in effect should be evaluated in terms of the code. . . ."

Somewhat surprisingly, this entire section on violation of sanctions was deleted from the resolution presented to the 1968 assembly in Dallas. It is possible that this represents a change in the association's policy concerning the internal disciplining of its members who fail to adhere to an NEA-imposed sanction.

Otherwise, the 1968 sanctions resolution remained as revised through the years, affirmatively stating when sanctions should be invoked, how they should be imposed and lifted, and calling upon affiliates to apply the guidelines.

Strikes

By far the greatest change in NEA collective bargaining policies has come on the issue of teacher strikes, sometimes euphemistically called "withdrawal of services" or "professional holidays" by NEA.

Only eight years ago the teachers recognized an "obligation to maintain the uninterrupted operation of the public schools." Between 1961 and 1964, NEA policy followed this general line, emphasizing that seeking of agreement between teachers and school boards "should preclude . . . the use of strikes. . . ."

All reference to the word "strike" was deleted in the 1965 collective bargaining resolution. Whether this change was designed to pave the way for strikes in the future or because of an aversion on the part of many teachers to the word "strike" isn't known.

Although they hadn't condoned teacher strikes, there's no question that NEA leaders recognized the importance of the developing teacher militancy to strengthening the association. Carr said so publicly before the 1966 delegates, warning that such new-found power must be exercised with responsibility, within the framework of the Code of Ethics, and with due regard for public interest. He emphasized that strikes or threats of strikes shouldn't be a requirement for successful professional negotiations. Legislation on bargaining rights and impasse settlements, he added, would lessen the need to resort to strikes—a step some affiliates already had taken on their own.

In 1967 NEA's board of directors took a new position toward striking affiliates. While continuing to recommend that strikes be avoided, the directors decided that, in the future, NEA would "offer all of the services at its command to the affiliate concerned to help resolve the impasse."

The directors' position on the support of affiliates' strikes was upheld by the 1968 assembly. This support was possibly influenced by an NEA research division survey showing teachers who believe in striking rose from 53.3 per cent in 1965 to 68.2 per cent this year. Although the 1968 resolution still recommends that impasses be resolved with procedures other than strikes, it actually calls a strike a strike, admits they will occur, and pledges association support to the striking affiliate.

In part, the resolution reads:

> . . . under conditions of severe stress, causing deterioration of the educational program, and when good faith attempts at resolution have been rejected, strikes have occurred and may occur in the future. In such instances, the association will offer all of the services at its command to the affiliate concerned to help resolve the impasse.

The resolution also clarified NEA's attitude toward use of strike breakers: The association "denounces the practice of staffing schools with any other personnel, when, in an effort to provide high quality education, educators withdraw their services."

To leave no doubt that teachers intend to use the strike weapon in the future, the resolution also urged NEA affiliates to work toward the repeal of state laws that prohibit strikes.

The last hurdle probably will be jumped next year when delegates vote on a proposal, tabled this year, for a $10 per year increase in membership dues for a "defense fund" to "prevent reprisals and unjust actions against teachers" and to meet "other" needs.

Throughout the 1960s—the period when these dramatic changes took place in NEA collective action policies—the specter of NEA's rival, the American Federation of Teachers, rose high over the association. Indeed, it's fair to conclude the AFT indirectly but significantly influenced the changes in NEA.

In a historical discussion of teacher-labor movement relations before delegates to the 1962 assembly, Carr expressed worry that the AFL–CIO "after decades of cooperation with the NEA suddenly moved in on the teaching profession" by supporting the AFT. Concern may have been nurtured when James A. Cary, president of the United Electrical Workers, told delegates the NEA had failed, and would continue to fail, to win wage increases for teachers unless it took on more of a "trade union" relationship with school boards. Unless the basic position of the NEA was changed, he theorized, janitors would get more money and job security through their union than teachers would through NEA.

After hours of heated discussion about the place for trade union activities in NEA, delegates resolved:

> Certain actions of this convention have been misinterpreted as action designed to sever the long-standing friendly and cooperative relations of the National Education Association with the American labor movement. Such misinterpretation could seriously damage the effectiveness of American public education. The National Education Association therefore declares its intention to continue its friendly and cooperative relations with the American labor movement, as it shall with all other segments of American society, in an atmosphere of mutual respect while retaining its identity as an independent professional organization.

But by 1964 NEA had become jittery over the activities of AFT and the support AFT was receiving from the AFL–CIO. A warning came from Carr: Through "substantial financial resources" and "considerable political influence," challenges in local representative elections, and opposition of labor councils to increases in school taxes, organized labor—namely the AFL–CIO and the AFT—was making jetlike headway in its move to overtake the teaching profession. NEA affiliates, he reported, won 12 out of 15 representative elections in 1963–64, but the AFT won the big ones—Detroit and Cleveland.

Definite steps would have to be taken, Carr warned, to counteract the AFT or else the "AFL–CIO program, as defined by its leadership, would, if successful, destroy the National Education Association and its state and local affiliates." Some of those steps were to take the form of cemented collective action policies.

Why this fear of the AFT? Statistics on membership, representative elections, and strikes hold the answer.

Membership. Although NEA members outnumber AFT members almost seven to one, comparative growth of the AFT has been greater. Since 1963, NEA membership has increased only at the same rate as the U.S. teaching force; for the past five years, NEA has represented 52 per cent of teachers. Membership of the AFT, while representing only 8 per cent of U.S. teachers, has jumped an average of 18 per cent yearly since 1959—and most of that growth is in cities. Result: NEA started a membership drive and has "unified" local, state, and national membership.

Another reason for AFT influence on NEA policy is that many NEA members—especially the more militant-minded classroom teachers*—find AFT occupational objectives most attractive. And NEA cannot afford to snub its Association of Classroom Teachers, which accounts for 80 per cent of its membership.

Representative elections. Between 1961 and 1965, there were 35. NEA won 17; AFT, 18. NEA added 14,600 represented members through these elections; AFT, 76,000. AFT also came away with the bigger victories—New York, Milwaukee, Detroit, Cleveland, and Philadelphia. Since 28 of the elections took place in 1964 and 1965, it's understandable that NEA delegates were especially concerned about AFT activities during those years.

Teacher strikes. Strikes by teachers, especially under NEA auspices, were virtually unheard of before 1966. The 33 strikes held in 1966 alone—followed by another 11 in the first quarter of 1967—nearly doubled the total number of strikes from 1960 to 1965. NEA affiliates initiated 11 of the 33; AFT, 20; independent organizations, 2. These strikes averaged 1.8 classroom days compared to 14.1 employee days for all strikes during 1966. Reasons for the teacher strikes, according to the Bureau of Labor

---

* Obvious differences in policy objectives between NEA's teacher and administrator members have produced serious problems within the association. At the 1968 convention in Dallas, a walkout by school administrators was only narrowly averted.

Statistics: salaries or hours, 16; attempts to organize, 9; school conditions and policies, 8. It would appear that NEA's move toward strikes stems, in part, from AFT's successful use of the tactic in the past (substantial salary boosts resulted from 14 of the 16 strikes over salaries in 1966).

What does the development of these stronger collective action policies mean for the future of NEA?

Most importantly, the new policies and their development show clearly that classroom teachers hold the upper hand in NEA. Had it not been for their insistence that the NEA become concerned with occupational objectives, they probably would have defected to the AFT, causing NEA membership to decline drastically rather than merely level off. Acceptance of classroom teachers as the association's strong arm hasn't come easy to administrators and supervisors.

More stress will be produced within the NEA membership as the association struggles to function as an occupational as well as an educational organization. Experience in industry and other professions has shown that there's an inherent difference between the occupational views of those who manage and those who are managed. That being so, NEA can expect even more conflicts— not easily resolved—between administrators and supervisors on the one hand, and classroom teachers on the other.

To deal effectively with these differences, it's going to be essential that NEA establish an organizational structure that goes beyond the internal reshaping the association approved in Dallas in July.

Somehow NEA is going to have to devise an umbrella structure that will allow classroom teachers to bargain separately from administrators and still maintain an educational tie with them. It will have to be a structure that will satisfy not only NEA's educational interests but also its divergent occupational interests. How else will the same organization be able to serve the needs of groups who find themselves on opposite sides of the bargaining table?

The change in basic NEA policies, started in 1962, is not yet complete. The next couple of years are critical for NEA and for teachers. The decisions NEA makes in the immediate future will not only determine the association's ability to enforce its occupational demands on school boards, but also will establish the organizational structure of NEA, which in turn will affect the future strength and unity of teachers.

THE TEACHERS' ADVOCATE
by Robert S. Kowalczyk

This article appeared in the January 1969 edition of the National Education Association's publication, Today's Education, *under the title of "The Teachers' Advocate." Mr. Kowalczyk is the executive secretary of the Warren (Michigan) Education Association, a professional organization of 1300 members. A former high school teacher, he has served on the bargaining team and the grievance committee of the association.*

We sincerely—and most firmly—believe that our efforts to become first-class citizens, under the law, will provide a better school system in Warren, for Warren school district children. Somehow, sometime, someone must call out the shortcomings of this school system and its operations and make it the kind of leading educational system that Warren citizens have long indicated they prefer. If not now, when? If not teachers, who?—Warren Education Association.

These are teachers. They walk picket lines. Among them are veterans of World War II or Korea, gray-haired women, and miniskirted beginners. They have a common bond and interest. Aware of the service they provide, they have pooled their intelligence and power. Experts in their field, they question their exclusion from the development of educational policy. They view themselves as the best qualified persons to make decisions in matters dealing with the classroom. They realize that they have a right to say what salaries and what conditions are satisfactory.

Teachers have not changed; their attitude has. This new attitude affects teacher associations. Teachers are organizing associations in order to achieve results. They are demanding more of

Reprinted with the permission of the publisher and author.

their organizations and are revamping or abandoning ineffective patterns of organization. Having an annual tea party is no longer sufficient.

If associations are to be successful, the leaders must adhere to a basic concept—simple yet vital: The overruling influence in an association must be the will of its membership. A prime example of this overruling influence takes place in professional negotiation.

In professional negotiation, associations represent their teacher-members in across-the-table bargaining with boards of education or their duly authorized representatives. The negotiation culminates in a written agreement, a contract which sets forth who teaches, how he teaches, and under what conditions.

Traditionally, boards have assumed prestige, authority, and autonomy. Reluctant to change, they have operated as if the teacher taught in a vacuum isolated from the decision-making process. Because teachers do not go along with these hypotheses, a militant mood pervades the arena of professional negotiation.

The negotiating posture of the Warren Education Association serves as an example. The association's negotiating team, mandated by teacher opinionnaire, seeks smaller classes, more planning time, duty-free lunch periods, more clerical and technical assistance for teachers, a clearly defined grievance procedure with binding arbitration, clearly described seniority rights, an improved transfer policy, and more realistic teaching loads.

The WEA bargaining proposals also include revised and updated instructional policies. The association seeks better provisions for disturbed or maladjusted children, more adequate counseling for students, teacher relief from minor administrative and clerical chores, curriculum provisions for potential dropouts, a more direct role for teachers in curriculum change, cultural enrichment programs for students, a larger school role in the development of values and morality, greater diversity of materials in each classroom, more teaching aids, a greater say in instructional budgets, and provisions for usable curriculum guides.

Bargaining proposals such as these lead to a relationship between board and association in which the association is challenging the board's assumed autonomy—its exclusive right to determine all instructional policies. This is an adversary relationship.

The result of this relationship is not chaos, for adversary relationships can be productive and wholesome. A division remains, however. The board's negotiating team reflects the board's views. The association, through its negotiating team, represents the views of teachers.

Negotiation subjects both sides to extreme pressure. Neither side can ignore the other's position and arguments. The proposals lay bare problems: Who is affected? How many are affected? What has been done in the past? Is it proper? Is a change necessary? Is the proposal workable? What is the cost? The adversary relationship forces both groups to point out problems, understand them, agree on basic principles, and work out the details in contract language. Proposals produce counterproposals which, in turn, produce more discussion and counterproposals until agreement is reached.

Maintaining that the status quo is sufficient, the board's team can refuse every proposal. If the association acquiesces to the refusals, it shuns its obligation. Once aspirations of the members are known, the association must muster its force and reserves to achieve them.

If the adversary relationship is to be productive in fulfilling teacher aspirations, it demands a partisan advocacy of the teacher's point of view. The association must stand behind, support, and argue for each of its teacher demands. If, in the negotiating process, an association considers itself as a mediator—an objective third party reconciling teacher desires—that group loses its thrust and it will lose the serious game of negotiation.

Professional negotiation demands that the association know its members' desires and that it be able to predict its opponent's responses and moves. (*Opponent* is not used lightly here. The better prepared team has an edge. Often, the more determined wins out.)

The board is, as it were, a shopper looking for values. The teachers own the product. Their association sets the price as directed by the collective decision of the teachers. Just as no corporation dares undersell the desires of its stockholders, no association should dare sell the teachers' product for less than it is worth.

The partisan advocacy in behalf of a point of view can best be illustrated in grievance processing, an area directly related to negotiation. If a teacher is discharged and considers his dismissal unfair, he appeals to the association for help. The association considers the facts of the immediate case. Has the board demonstrated that it has just cause for its action? If, for example, it fired the teacher because it expected a performance not properly expected of him, it has no just cause for action, and the association, the teacher's advocate, defends him.

Similarly, the association defends the teacher in cases of too severe or unfair penalties, or when the board has failed to follow proper procedures. Even in debatable cases, as long as a shred of evidence supports the teacher's position, the association is his advocate.

In professional negotiation, teachers select an agent to speak for them. This agent and its spokesmen take on the role of teachers' advocate, just as the association assumes that role when pursuing the right of one teacher. The dynamics of negotiation require that the spokesmen be well charged, that they know what they will set out to attain. Opinionnaires, committee work, personal contacts are vital for planning and fulfilling the expectations of members. The contact with the membership and the intense preparation for negotiation help the negotiating team determine what form its prejudiced advocacy should take. The team then plans its tactics with this in mind.

There are alternatives to a prejudiced advocacy in regard to a point of view. Warren tried it all ways. We used to be a teachers' club. Once a year we were guests of the board at a roasted-corn picnic. The superintendent worked with our salary committee. At that time he was the only person allowed to speak to the board. He did his job well. He presented a prejudiced advocacy in behalf of a view—his own and the board's. The teachers received little. Finally, we bade him adieu and tried formal requests, which were tantamount to begging.

At last we gathered together our thousands of hours of training, experience, and education; organized; and selected a group to speak for us. We made certain that this spokesman group was our advocate. We reasoned that if advocacy worked in litigation and international diplomacy, it should work in dealing with our employer. The Warren Education Association became our advocate.

Teachers in Warren have changed their attitudes. They do

not consider themselves public servants; they consider themselves individual practitioners, like lawyers and doctors, who have banded together to promote their own cause.

Obviously, as the attitudes of individual teachers change, the attitudes of associations change. Effective associations are now purging themselves of patterns that do not reflect attitudes of the general membership. They will move forward when the will of their membership has become the overruling influence in all their undertakings.

NEEDED: MORE TEACHER STRIKES
by David Selden

This editorial originally appeared in the May 15, 1965, edition of the Saturday Review. *Mr. Selden is the president of the American Federation of Teachers, AFL–CIO. Prior to assuming that post, he was the director of organization of AFT Local 2 in New York City.*

What American schools need most is more teacher strikes. Instead of putting work stoppages by teachers in the same category as matricide and spitting on the flag, school board members and superintendents should be delighted when they have a group of educators who care enough about the schools and their own professional status to lay their jobs on the line in order to bring about improvements.

By every standard of measurement—drop-out rate, reading retardation, overcrowding, teacher academic training—our schools have failed to keep pace with the demands placed upon them. Yet year after year, most of our school systems go along on a business-as-usual basis.

And teachers, who have had first-hand knowledge of the neglect of our educational enterprise, have gone along, too, protesting weakly, grumbling to each other in teacher rest rooms—and all the while "making do" with what they have been given to work with.

What is so terrible about a strike by teachers? The traditional answer is, "Think of the children!" Yet it is often more harmful to the children for teachers *not* to strike than it would be to close down the schools for a while. When New York City teachers were criticized for striking in April 1962, Charles Cogen, then the union president, declared, "It is better for a child to lose a few days or weeks of schooling now than go through life handicapped by years of inferior education."

As a result of the one-day shutdown, $13,000,000 was added to the school budget. Most of the new money was used to expand direct services to children.

During the course of a year schools are closed for a dozen holidays of varying significance, and they are shut down for two weeks at Christmas time, a week at Easter, and two to three months in the summer. No one thinks of these "work stoppages" as harming the children. But let teachers close the schools for even one day, for the purpose of making the schools better, and the pillars of society tremble.

Perhaps some of this public opposition to strikes by teachers comes from the public's proprietary interest in the schools. No employer likes a strike. But this doesn't tell the whole story. Strikes by bus drivers, for instance, are not regarded as affronts to the dignity and status of the government. Bus drivers are expected to take drastic action when negotiations break down, but the pedagogues are expected to keep right on working.

Should our children be taught by spineless economic illiterates lacking enough professional commitment to insist on decent school buildings, classes of teachable size, proper instructional materials, and salary schedules that can enable school systems to recruit teachers from the top of the graduating class instead of the bottom?

Where the right—and the willingness—to strike exists, most disputes will be settled without an actual walkout. Both sides then have an incentive to negotiate in good faith.

There are four alternatives to the strike, and all are much worse than a possible work stoppage. Disputes can be "settled" by: 1) continuing the status quo, 2) carrying on a cold war

between teachers and school authorities, 3) political action, or
4) arbitration. The first of these alternatives, the "don't complain"
philosophy, is unthinkable if we really want good education. The
second, the long-festering contest of little meannesses between
teachers and school authorities, erodes morale and seldom results
in any real solution to the problems confronting the schools. The
other two alternatives require more detailed discussion.

Teachers certainly have a *right* to appeal a school board's
action to the voters. But political action is often far different in
practice than in theory. Frequently the choice of opposing candidates offers little hope for improvement. Furthermore, politics is a
two-way street; it is often hard to discover who has more control,
the politician who depends on teachers for votes, or the teachers
who depend on the politician for favorable action.

When teachers have the right to strike, very real political
decisions must be made by the authorities. Issues are dramatized,
and the way the board resolves them becomes a factor in the next
election.

The final alternative, a pet panacea of the no-strike supporters, is a devastating influence on negotiations. Neither side
will bargain if it knows that the dispute is going to wind up in the
hands of an arbitrator. It is not good tactics to yield any points in
advance. The arbitrator functions within the limits set by the two
parties to the dispute, and he is apt to issue Solomon-like judgments that are mere compromises. Arbitration turns negotiations
into a debating contest, and the outcome is seldom the kind of
meeting of the minds that results when each side has something to
gain from good-faith negotiations, and something to lose from unreasonable stubbornness.

B. Frank Brown, one of the nation's leading school administrators, told a recent meeting of the North Central Association of Colleges and Secondary Schools, "Administrators are
demurrers who are afraid to expose themselves to dangerous and
heady ideas." Not only administrators but teachers, too, suffer this
disability.

It is time teachers were released from their conformist
bondage. Anyone who really worries about education ought to
kick, prod, cajole, wheedle, and exhort teachers to far greater
militancy. When teachers are willing to stop work rather than

continue under substandard conditions, they will have gone a long way toward attaining the professional status to which they have given lip service for so many years.

THE PUBLIC SCHOOL TEACHER AS ORGANIZATION MAN
by Robert G. Doherty and Walter E. Oberer

> *The following selection is a chapter from the authors'* Teachers, School Boards, and Collective Bargaining: A Changing of the Guard.
>
> *Mr. Doherty is professor of industrial and labor relations at Cornell University. He has also taught in public schools in Oregon and New York State, at Teachers College, Columbia University, and at the State University College at Oneonta, New York. He also conducts conferences and seminars on teacher-school board relations for teachers and public school officials.*
>
> *Mr. Oberer is professor of law and industrial and labor relations at Cornell University. An active arbitrator in teacher representation and bargaining disputes, he serves as co-chairman of the Committee on the Law of Government Employee Relations, Labor Law Section, American Bar Association. From 1957 to 1959 he was executive director of the Public Review Board of the United Auto Workers.*

It is rare that two organizations markedly dissimilar in origin, structure, and style should come to pursue identical objectives in similar fashion. Yet as one looks at recent activities of affiliates of the National Education Association and the American Federation of Teachers, organizations which over the years have held widely differing views on the proper role of teacher associations, one is impressed more by similarities than by differences. The catalyst has been the movement to formalize the employment relationship in

Reprinted with the permission of the New York State School of Industrial Relations, Cornell University, Ithaca, N.Y., 1967.

public schools, and the organization that has done most of the reacting has been the NEA. The circumstances created by collective bargaining have forced a great many NEA affiliates to adopt functions and even an outlook more typical of trade unions than of professional organizations. The AFT has veered less from its appointed course. One sees in the AFT's current interest in problems of education distinct from the employment relationship, however, a somewhat determined effort to achieve professional respectability.

But while it is true that the two teacher organizations are beginning to show a strong resemblance to one another, many differences remain. And one can probably get a better understanding of the current movement among teachers to formalize the employment relationship by briefly exploring these differences.

One of the most obvious differences is in longevity. The NEA was founded in 1857, as the National Teachers Association, when representatives of ten state teacher associations gathered to form a national organization they hoped would "elevate the character and advance the interests of the profession of teaching, and . . . promote the cause of popular education in the United States."[1] Reflecting the masculine domination of the profession of that era, the new association limited its membership to "gentlemen."

The first sixty years of the NEA did not prove to be very promising. Although membership rose to over 9,000 in 1887, it fell to little more than a thousand in the late 1890s and did not achieve 10,000 until 1918, when it enrolled about 5 per cent of American public school teachers.[2] Only five departments—school administration, vocational education, science education, business education, and kindergarten education—were created in the nineteenth century, and it was not until 1914 that the Classroom Teachers Association, today the largest of the NEA departments, was organized.[3]

By 1966, however, membership totaled about 900,000, with an additional 600,000 teachers and administrators affiliated with state associations. The number of departments, divisions, and commissions had risen to seventy-four, providing services to such diverse groups as social science and mathematics teachers, elementary teachers, school administrators, curriculum specialists, teacher-training institutions, and parent-teacher associations.

The AFT was organized in Chicago in 1916 when the Chicago Teachers Federation, which had been in existence since 1897, joined with the Chicago Federation of Women Teachers, the Chicago Federation of Men Teachers, and a teachers' local in Gary, Indiana, to secure a charter as an affiliate of the American Federation of Labor.[4] From the beginning, the AFT seems to have concentrated on conditions of employment. The two primary objectives stated in its constitution were to "obtain for [teachers] all the rights to which they are entitled," and "to raise the standards of the teaching profession by securing the conditions essential to the best professional service."[5] The way to "elevate the character of the profession of teaching," evidently, was to put the stress on teachers' freedom and economic well-being. And there was a lesson to be learned from unionized craft workers of that era who, because they bargained collectively with their employers, seemed to enjoy more on-the-job freedom and economic well-being than did teachers. Although collective bargaining did not become an immediate objective of AFT affiliates, it eventually became the most distinguishing feature separating the union from the NEA.

Like the NEA, the AFT had difficulty getting off the ground. Twenty years after it was founded, it had only 13,000 members. But it doubled its membership during the depression (while the NEA was losing members) and took another spurt between 1962 and 1966 when membership rose from 60,000 to over 120,000,[6] making it one of the fastest growing trade unions of modern times.

The AFT is still very largely an employee organization. True, it has recently expanded its research efforts and in 1966 launched a new "professional" journal, *Changing Education,* and a series of pamphlets in its Grassroots Research Project dealing with problems in education. It has also developed an interest in teacher training and recruitment, and in its More Effective Schools program has been instrumental in bringing about some imaginative innovations in staffing and educational practices in slum schools in a handful of cities. But for the most part AFT activities have been self-serving with some activities being carried out, it would appear, only in an attempt to "one-up" the NEA.

Since the NEA is essentially a professional association and the AFT primarily an employee organization, there are, as one might expect, significant structural differences. Membership in the

NEA, for example, is direct, teachers usually having the option of joining the national, state, or local organizations (or all three) on an individual basis. State and local affiliates are only loosely tied in with the national association.

The AFT is organized along more typical trade union lines. Teachers join an AFT local, which usually claims jurisdiction over an entire school district or system, and the local in turn pays a per capita tax to the national organization. In those states where there is a state federation, it too derives its funds from a per capita tax on the locals.

The real strength of the NEA is in its state affiliates. More than half again as many teachers are members of the state associations as of the national. In New York State, for example, NEA membership is about one-third that of the New York State Teachers Association.[7] The reason for this, beyond the fact that state associations existed long before the NEA was organized, is that public education, in the final analysis, is a function of the states. It is the state legislature, NEA spokesmen point out, that establishes teacher tenure laws, retirement and welfare plans, and minimum (which often turn out to be maximum) salaries. State governments also provide a large per cent of school revenue, over 40 per cent on the average, to local school districts. Thus, it is argued, if one truly wishes to represent the interests of teachers one must organize to deal with those who make the most significant decisions affecting teacher welfare—the state legislature and education department.

The AFT, on the other hand, while certainly not ignoring developments in state capitals, has put most of its eggs in the local school district basket. The state legislature might have an important hand in determining the size of total educational appropriations, but it is usually the local school board, union members point out, that determines how this money shall be spent. Furthermore, if AFT affiliates are to bargain over conditions of employment, they must strike the bargain with local authorities who, as distinct from state officials, have sufficient discretion to make adjustments in the employment arrangement in the here and now. The strike, or threat thereof, has become the most potent union weapon for gaining concessions.

State and local associations have, until recently, relied almost exclusively on sanctions for the same purpose. Teachers are warned that employment conditions in a given state or locality are unsatisfactory, and those employed in the areas under sanctions are assisted in finding employment elsewhere. The publicity accompanying a vote of sanctions, moreover, can have a chilling effect on governors, legislatures, and local school boards and administrators. The NEA's use of sanctions is partly due to its aversion to the strike but, equally important, because it is a measure that is consistent with its unique structure. If one wants to apply pressure on a state governor or legislature, as state associations have done in Utah, Kentucky, and Oklahoma in recent years, then the pressure must be statewide. If the problem is at the local district level and the local association is weak, as most of them are, then only the state and the national association can muster the necessary leverage, via sanctions, to win concessions from the school board.

Another significant difference between the two organizations is in the composition of the local affiliates. NEA groups, in keeping with the national organization's principle of community of interest between teachers and administrators, typically seek to recruit all certificated school personnel as members. Thus in 1966 school superintendents were eligible for membership in almost 75 per cent of local teachers' associations. Only 12.4 per cent of local associations confined membership to classroom teachers.[8]

AFT affiliates are more inclined, as are most trade unions, to restrict membership to nonsupervisory personnel. Only 17.6 per cent allow principals as members, according to a 1966 survey of 262 locals comprising about 70 per cent of AFT membership, and 19.5 per cent admit assistant principals. Department heads in junior and senior high schools are eligible for membership in 58 per cent of AFT locals, however.[9]

The significance of the composition of the two rival organizations lies in the influence this composition has on determining the bargaining unit when teachers begin to press for formalization of the employment relationship in a local district. Ideology aside, the group that has the largest number of members voting in a representation election has a better chance of being selected as the exclusive bargaining agent. Thus one finds NEA affiliates very often demanding all-inclusive units, since they have considerable membership among administrative personnel, and AFT groups plugging for units consisting of classroom teachers only where *their* strength is concentrated.

The AFT's position on limiting the bargaining unit to non-supervisory personnel has had an unexpected advantage, however. The NEA is associated in teachers' eyes with the educational establishment, and teachers who feel aggrieved by the conditions of their employment often blame the establishment for their predicament, or at the very least accuse it of not doing enough to improve their circumstances. The NEA and its state and local affiliates have long been *the* organizations in public education, and to many teachers they just have not delivered the goods. To support the association in a representation election then would be tantamount to giving one's approval of doing the same old business at the same old stand. Thus, in Philadelphia, the local AFT affiliate went into a representation election in 1965 with slightly more than 2,000 members against the association's 5,200, yet won the election handily.[10]

Another advantage enjoyed by the AFT is that the NEA has long had a reputation of using subtle, and sometimes not so subtle, administrative pressure to get teachers to join the organization. Probably there has been a marked decline over the last several years in the number of school districts where association membership is, for all practical purposes, compulsory. But teacher resentment lingers, and the privacy afforded by the secret ballot in a representation election provides an excellent opportunity to show it.

If the AFT has accomplished anything, it has exposed the efforts of school administrators to force association membership on reluctant teachers. Yet compulsion does remain in some quarters. As recently as 1965, the California Senate Fact-finding Committee on Governmental Administration reported that "the right of certificated public school employees to 'join' . . . or 're-fuse to join' . . . employee organizations of their own choosing," a right guaranteed under California law, "is being interfered with, abridged, and violated on a widespread basis. . . ."[11] The report continued that legal remedies available to provide redress did not provide practical relief, that ratings, promotions, and recommendations for tenure were very often dependent on membership in the California Teachers Association, that subtle oral pressure was as influential as official written policy, and that such pressure is bound to continue so long as administrators, who do the rating and make the recommendations, are also members of the association.[12] California might be an extreme case, but it is not easy to understand how the Teachers Association of the State of Washington could boast of a 100 per cent membership in 1966[13] without assuming overzealousness on the part of local school administrators anxious to fill their membership quotas.

Of course, the NEA aspires to be a professional association, the function of which is to enhance the status of education, rather than to serve merely as an employee organization. And it should be pointed out that the high percentage of teachers and administrators in state associations, about 84 per cent on a national average, is about on a par with the degree of professional affiliation of the two most respected professions, medicine and law.

An interesting sidelight on the NEA's competition with the AFT is that one of its most important professional tenets—the obligation to police its own ranks—seems to be eroding away. As a professional organization, the NEA has felt over the years that it should be as much concerned about the professional conduct and teaching competence of its members as about their economic welfare. One gets the impression, in reading the literature of the Committee on Professional Ethics and the Commission on Professional Rights and Responsibilities over the past years, that the NEA and its affiliates were to be judges as well as advocates, that responsibilities of teachers were to be given at least as much importance as their rights. By 1966, however, with the pressure to win representation elections and the duty to represent teachers, a duty that collective bargaining imposes in a rather special way, there seems to have been a sloughing off of the obligation to judge, and teachers' rights appear to be stressed more vigorously than their obligations. The lesson, evidently, is that if one competes with a union, one ends up playing by the union's rules.

Superficially viewed, there are no significant differences between the rank-and-file members of the two organizations, except that, as William Lowe has pointed out, the AFT has a much higher percentage of males than does the NEA and the profession generally.[14] The AFT also has a higher percentage of junior and senior high school teachers, but that is where the men are. Also, as Professor Lowe has indicated, AFT members are more inclined to be members of professional bodies such as the National Council for the Teaching of Social Studies or the National Science Teachers Association, both organizations, incidentally, organs of the NEA. But, here again, these are associations that cater to subject-matter specialists who are almost always on the junior and senior high school level, a high percentage of whom—over half—are men. As to other characteristics, dissatisfaction with teaching as a career, the degree to which they feel intimidated by administrators, professional competence, interest in the welfare of school children—there seem to be no significant differences.[15]

There is a rather striking difference in the matter of style, however. While the NEA has a record of solid accomplishments in the professional area, it is also, paradoxically, plagued by a reputation for complacency in the face of real educational problems. There is little sense of urgency in its manner, not much tough-minded intellectualism in its posture. The 1965 NEA Convention in New York City, wrote Fred Hechinger, was "a mixture of conventioneering corn and prissy schoolmarmism . . . an embarrassing kind of image building, in conflict with the aims of action-minded and intellectually oriented delegates. . . . Embarrassingly little discussion of educational substance, philosophy, issues of research came from within the public school ranks."[16]

But if the NEA often seems prissy and complacent, the AFT sometimes gives the impression of stridency—its criticisms of school boards, administrators, the "establishment" being characterized more by their shrillness than by their telling accuracy. The AFT has opted for, and appears to relish the role of the abused underdog, clashing valiantly with school boards and the competing association. One finds in its literature, the monthly *American Teacher*, in its occasional publications, even in its new professional quarterly, *Changing Education* (the front cover of the first issue carried an Osborn cartoon showing a supervisor sitting on top of the head of a bound and gagged teacher), a sense of victimization that almost borders on the paranoiac. Brave and dedicated federation members, evidently, are daily being exploited by cruel and reactionary administrations.

Two recent actions by the AFT, both prompted by its affiliation with the AFL–CIO, and the subsequent reaction of the NEA, serve as excellent examples of stylistic differences between the two organizations. One had to do with the AFT's support of a strike by five unions against the Kingsport Press in Kingsport, Tennessee, one of the nation's largest manufacturers of school textbooks. The background of the dispute, briefly, is that the unions struck against Kingsport in 1963 for higher wages and other benefits, but the company kept operating with the help of supervisors, workers who had abandoned the strike, and "permanent" replacements. By the spring of 1966, over 1,000 of the original 1,600 strikers were still out.[17]

At its 1965 Convention, the AFT adopted a resolution supporting the strikers and urging member locals "to call on their local boards of education to refrain from purchasing books printed by the Kingsport Press."[18] By 1966, two big city school boards, New York City and Cleveland, had been persuaded by the AFT and other unions, mostly in the printing trades, to boycott Kingsport Press books if, in the judgment of building principles, other books of "equal value" were available. The unions argued that taxpayers' money should not be used to support firms paying substandard wages.

"The AFT demonstrated, beyond a shadow of a doubt, where its first loyalties lay," the NEA *Urban Reporter* charged in the fall of 1965.

> Given a choice between the principles of academic freedom for teachers and youth's right to learn vs. paying off its debts to other labor unions on whose financial and manpower support it is so completely dependent, the AFT chose the latter.[19] . . . Clearly, the price of unionism is costly for teachers. They are, in effect, being asked to forfeit professional judgment and responsibility and leave educational decisions to nonprofessionals who are motivated by responsibilities and interests which are, and must remain, extraneous to the teaching-learning process.[20]

The NEA position was that professionally trained teachers should be intimately involved in the selection of textbooks and other teaching materials. And while the association held no brief for the uncompromising stand of the employer in the Kingsport dispute, it maintained that the dispute itself should not be allowed to intrude into the schools. The consequence of a school board boycott would be to make teachers "voiceless bystanders, indifferent to questions of educational excellence,"[21] a circumstance that is in rather sharp contrast to the role both the AFT and the NEA would like teachers to play.

The other issue on which the two organizations are divided is support of the sales tax as a source of school revenue. Because of their affiliation with state and local AFL–CIO bodies, which oppose this form of taxation, AFT locals have fought against passage of sales-tax laws or increases in several states, counties, and municipalities.[22] The argument against the sales tax, of course, is that such taxes are regressive. They place the burden on low-income families which spend a higher *proportion* of their income on consumer goods than the well-to-do and therefore have to pay a disproportionate percentage of the tax.

The counterargument, originally advanced by John Kenneth Galbraith, but picked up by the NEA and its state and local affiliates, is that unlike other forms of taxation—property, income, excise—the yield of the sales tax responds immediately to increases in the production of consumer goods. And as wants increase for consumer goods more revenue is created for public use. As Galbraith has put it, ". . . by making private goods more expensive, public goods are made more abundant. Motion pictures, electronic entertainment, and cigarettes are made more costly so that schools can be more handsomely supported."[23]

The sales-tax issue has put many AFT locals in a difficult position. They are allied, or at least closely identified, with organizations that oppose the tax, even though much, sometimes all, of the revenue is earmarked for support of public education. AFT locals in Oklahoma and Louisiana evidently lost a great deal of momentum in their organizing drives when the state labor bodies came out against sales-tax increases.[24]

Like the textbook boycott, the AFT's position on the sales-tax issue will probably prove to be a source of embarrassment to its members. Certainly it will not help the union in its organizing drives. Nor is the AFT's stand on the textbook ban calculated to endear it to the intellectual community.

II

In the previous chapter we pointed out some of the reasons many teachers are demanding some type of formalized employment arrangement with local school boards. The dramatic increase in the number of men teachers, low salaries, unsatisfactory working conditions, the mounting frustrations of public school teaching headed the list.

But there is another reason—the growing competition between the two major teacher organizations—that might be as important a cause of organizational activity as all the other reasons combined. This competition has its roots in the changing character of the work force and the frustrations it presents to the labor movement. "Feeling the effects of declining employment and membership in manufacturing and other traditional areas of union strength," Ronald Donovan has observed, ". . . and generally concerned about a decline in strength and influence, the labor movement sees the governmental sector as a promising field."[25]

Public employment is indeed a beckoning frontier for a stagnated labor movement. Employment in state and local government rose by 74 per cent between 1951 and 1964, when it reached a total of 7.16 million[26] with only about 1.5 million represented by trade unions.[27] At the same time, there has been a significant increase in white-collar employment, 27.7 per cent from 1950 to 1960; yet as of 1964 only about 11 per cent of white-collar workers were organized.[28] This area too, in Professor Donovan's expression, is a promising field for organized labor to harvest.

Teachers, being both public employees and white-collar workers, posed a fat target for unionization. Salaries were low; there were numerous complaints about working conditions; the major teacher organization appeared to be indifferent to the employment arrangement, or at least unable to make improvements in it; and there was already a union of teachers, albeit small and ineffective, which had been affiliated with the American labor movement for a good many years. It was also thought that, if teachers could become organized and receive substantial benefits thereby, this might serve as an inducement to other government and white-collar workers to join up.

Thus, when the United Federation of Teachers in New York

City, an AFT affiliate, led a successful strike in 1962 that culminated in the first comprehensive collective agreement covering teachers, the labor movement was encouraged that this might be just the "breakthrough" it was waiting for. So it was viewed at least by the AFL–CIO's Industrial Union Department, a collection of former CIO and other industrial unions which for some time had been spearheading the drive to organize white-collar and government employees. Money was poured into AFT organizing drives and representation elections, $362,000 between 1963 and 1965,[29] highly skilled manpower was donated to assist AFT locals in election contests, and in 1965 prestige was added to money and manpower when AFT president Charles Cogen was made an IUD vice president. With IUD help, the AFT went on to win representation elections in Detroit, Cleveland, Philadelphia, Boston, Yonkers, and dozens of smaller school systems.

To the NEA, what had been merely an irritant had now become a major threat. It could either play the union's game, the two chief rules of which were exclusive recognition and collective bargaining, or face the possibility of being eased out as a viable organization in urban and suburban communities. It chose to play, sometimes by demanding representation elections before the union could muster sufficient strength, as in Rochester, New York, but in other cases responding successfully to union-initiated requests, as in Newark, New Jersey. Once elected as the exclusive bargaining agent, the association had no choice but to negotiate comprehensive, very "union-like" agreements. This was particularly the case in those instances where the union was in the wings, waiting for the association to fall on its face—Newark, New Haven, New Rochelle.

In the process, several local associations became transformed. Salary requests came to be called salary demands, consultation was changed to negotiation, professional associations began to look and sound like employee organizations. Teachers who had never dreamed of bilateral determination of employment conditions now talked in the jargon of trade unionism, and school administrators and school boards who had once been thought of as captains of the team were now in a few instances being regarded as exploiters. To be sure, competition between the two organizations had its origin in unsatisfactory employment arrangements, but by

1966 this competition seemed to be its own *raison d'être*. Issues were raised as much for the way in which they served the institutional interests of competitors as for their merit. Collective bargaining which emerged as a consequence of teacher unrest was, because of the intensity of the AFT–NEA rivalry, proving in some cases to be its cause.

The emergence of a viable AFT has also been responsible for a rather significant transformation of the NEA at the national level. The attitude of the NEA toward bilateral determination of working conditions, at least as reflected by its Delegate Assembly, has since 1960 undergone a rather profound change. Thus in 1960 when a rather innocuous resolution on the "representative Conference," a term used by the NEA at that time as a euphemism for professional negotiations, was brought to the convention for adoption it was considered a bit too rich for the blood of most delegates and was sent to the NEA Board of Directors for further consideration.[30] The following year a similar resolution, saying that professional associations *"should* be accorded the right . . . to participate in the determination of policies of common concern including salary and other conditions for professional service"[31] passed the convention by an overwhelming majority.

Not until 1962, however, did the Delegate Assembly really get down to the business of spelling out what this new process, now called professional negotiations, actually meant. The fact that the UFT had negotiated a comprehensive agreement that spring, and that the AFT had picked up almost 10,000 members between 1960 and 1962 undoubtedly caused some consternation among NEA leaders. The 1962 resolution, which is regarded by the association as a new departure in its thinking on how school boards should be dealt with, is reproduced below in full.

> The teaching profession has the ultimate aim of providing the best possible education for all the people. It is a professional calling and a public trust. Boards of education have the same aims and share this trust.
>
> *The National Education Association calls upon boards of education in all school districts to recognize their identity of interest with the teaching profession.*
>
> The National Education Association *insists* on the

right of professional associations, through democratically selected representatives using professional channels, to participate with boards of education in the determination of policies of common concern, including salary and other conditions of professional service.

Recognizing both the legal authority of boards of education and the educational competencies of the teaching profession, the two groups should view the consideration of matters of mutual concern as a joint responsibility.

The seeking of consensus and mutual agreement on a professional basis should preclude the arbitrary exercise of unilateral authority of boards of education and *the use of the strike by teachers.*

The Association believes that procedures should be established which provide an orderly method for professional education associations and boards of education to reach mutually satisfactory agreements. These procedures should include provisions for appeal through designated educational channels when agreement cannot be reached.

Under no circumstances should the resolution of differences between professional associations and boards of education be sought through channels set up for handling industrial disputes. The teacher's situation is completely unlike that of an industrial employee. A board of education is not a private employer, and a teacher is not a private employee. Both are committed to serve the common indivisible interest of all persons and groups in the community in the best possible education for their children. Teachers and boards of education can perform their indispensable functions only if they act in terms of their identity of purpose in carrying out this commitment. Industrial disputes conciliation machinery, which assumes a conflict of interest and a diversity of purpose between persons and groups, is not appropriate to professional negotiations in public education.

The National Education Association calls upon its members and upon boards of education to seek state legislation and local board action which clearly and firmly establishes these rights for the teaching profession.[32]

The resolution adopted in 1963 was essentially the same as the 1962 resolution. But in 1964 the delegates voted to drop the caveat about local associations using "channels set up for handling industrial disputes" and added a section commending school boards, superintendents, and associations that had already "initiated and entered into written negotiation agreements."[33] The following year the phrase condemning "the use of the strike by teachers" was omitted, and while the 1965 resolution did not go so far as to say that there was an inherent conflict between teachers and school boards, it did for the first time "recognize[s] that the school board, the superintendent or administration, and the teaching staff have significantly different contributions to make in the development of educational policies and procedures."[34] Truly, a lot had happened since 1960.

It was probably in connection with this new mood that the delegates acted during the 1965 convention to drain much of the substance from the charge that the NEA was administrator-dominated and, therefore, little more than a "company union." If local affiliates were to compete successfully with the AFT, the NEA would have to persuade classroom teachers that the parent organization was not only for them but of them as well. "At present our opponents' contention is that the NEA is moving too slowly to give vital assistance to classroom teachers in this country,"[35] one delegate complained. And if there was a ring of truth in this contention it might have been, as Thelma Davis, president of the Classroom Teachers Department, pointed out, because: "Since the year 1947 up to 1964 we have had no representation on the Board of Trustees . . . [and] since 1950 no members who were classroom teachers have been elected by the Board of Directors to serve on the Executive Committee."[36]

The teacher delegates voted overwhelmingly to rectify the matter. The NEA bylaws were changed so that at least one of the two members elected by the Board of Directors to the Executive Committee would be a classroom teacher, as would at least two of the four members elected by the convention. The change also provided that at least two members of the Board of Trustees elected by the Board of Directors should be classroom teachers. The amendments passed by votes of 4,669 to 1,298 and 4,472 to 1,366, respectively.[37]

Other developments within the association also pointed to a changing attitude toward the manner in which teachers should participate in the formulation of school policies affecting the employment arrangement. The Office of Urban Services, in effect the NEA's collective bargaining arm, although not established until 1962, had by 1965 a budget that accounted for 13 per cent of all NEA expenditures.[38] It is also instructive to look at the changes that have taken place in the various revisions of the NEA booklet, *Professional Negotiations: Selected Statements of School Board, Administrator, Teacher Relationships.* First published in 1963, the booklet was designed as a guide for local associations contemplating a more formalized relationship with their school boards. In both the 1963 edition and the 1964 revision, the majority of examples of professional agreements cited were of the Level I and Level II variety, providing only for "recognition" and "recognition plus outline of negotiation procedure," respectively. In the 1965 revision, however, there was but one example each of the Level I and II categories. The remaining space was devoted to excerpts from Level III agreements, which are very much like the comprehensive labor-management contracts used in private employment. We shall have more to say about the nature of these agreements later; it need only be said here that by 1965 the NEA had evidently come around to accepting the same type of elaborate document the AFT had long been advocating.

If NEA affiliates are less inclined to strike than union locals, there nonetheless appears to be declining aversion to work stoppages among NEA members. The local association in Newark did go out in the spring of 1966 when it reached an impasse with the board over salaries, and in the same year in Michigan four NEA affiliates were out on strike at the same time. Elsewhere there have been strike threats and threats of mass resignation when local boards were slow in granting minimum concessions. The deletion of the stricture on strikes from the NEA resolution on professional negotiations in 1965 might have been in anticipation of this kind of militancy. The delegates might also have been anticipating the results of an NEA survey under way at that time. For when the association asked a national teacher sample in late 1965 and early 1966 if teachers should ever strike, it found that, while only 3.3 per cent thought teachers should have the same strike rights as any other group of employees, 50 per cent believed strikes were permissible under extreme circumstances. Sixty-one per cent of this group thought low salaries an extreme circumstance. Not surprisingly, male teachers and teachers in large school districts opposed strikes to a markedly lesser degree than women or those from small districts.[39]

And when the NEA Convention dropped its opposition to using "industrial channels" for establishing election procedures and dispute-settlement machinery, the reason might have been that, in those states where laws covering employee relations in public service forced affiliates to operate under the industrial model (Wisconsin and Michigan), local associations were doing very well indeed. As of the spring of 1966, Michigan NEA affiliates had won 48 of the 68 representation elections conducted under the public employee bargaining statute, and represented 51,900 teachers, as against the union's 15,770, including 10,500 in Detroit. The association's record was even better in Wisconsin, where it had won 18 of 23 elections and had been designated as exclusive representative through stipulations in 100 more.[40] And while they might have found it upsetting, it probably came as no surprise to members of the Wisconsin School Boards Association when the Wisconsin Education Association passed a resolution at its annual meeting late in 1965 stating: "The Wisconsin Education Association *opposes* action which seeks to nullify or amend Statute 11.70 [providing for collective bargaining for municipal and county employees] in such ways as to exclude teachers from enjoying the benefits, rights and prerogatives listed therein."[41]

III

The quintessence of the formalized employment arrangement is the collective agreement, or contract, which sets forth in detail those employment conditions that have been bilaterally determined. There is no better way to compare the ultimate objectives of AFT and NEA affiliates, at least as far as employer-employee relations are concerned, than to examine the contents of the agreements that have been negotiated by both organizations.[42]

While the overwhelming majority of the agreements negotiated by the NEA have been in the Level I and II category, the recent tendency has been for association affiliates in large school districts, Newark, New Haven, Rochester, for example, to press for comprehensive and elaborate documents. In all likelihood, many of those affiliates which settled originally for rather simple and uncomplicated agreements will during the next go-around negotiate with their boards over a greater number of employment conditions. So too, of course, will those AFT affiliates which for one reason or another were unable to secure agreements that provided for anything more than a statement of recognition, a salary schedule, and a grievance procedure, if that much.

In the meantime, if one concentrates on those agreements that have been negotiated by both organizations in the large school systems, one finds that there is little difference in the scope or subject matter of the bargain. The subject matter of agreements in Rochester, New Haven, and Newark, where associations are the bargaining agents, is in the main no less comprehensive than it is in the contracts negotiated by the federation in New York City, Boston, and Philadelphia. This conclusion may be verified by a perusal of representative provisions of the New Haven and Boston agreements.*

Similarly, the Newark and New York City agreements have almost identical provisions, which would seem to indicate that the association in Newark was more sensitive to what had recently happened across the Hudson than whatever recommendations might have been emanating from NEA headquarters in Washington. Both agreements cover salaries, leaves, sabbaticals, relief from nonteaching duties, utilization of teacher aides, assignments, transfers, seniority, class size and number of classes taught, hours of work, the school year, number and duration of faculty meetings, teacher facilities, and a grievance machinery. The New York agreement does provide for binding arbitration (when not prohibited by law or board bylaws), while Newark's is advisory only. This latter difference is less a matter of differing philosophies than it is of differing bargaining environments in local districts. The New Haven contract, for example, negotiated by the association

* See the Appendix to *Teachers, School Boards, and Collective Bargaining: A Changing of the Guard,* by Robert G. Doherty and Walter E. Oberer (Ithaca, N.Y.: New York State School of Industrial Relations, 1967).

contains the same kind of binding arbitration provisions as that of the federation agreement in New York, while in Pawtucket, Rhode Island, the federation accepted a grievance procedure in its 1966 contract that leaves the school board as the final arbiter.

Of course, from a teacher's point of view the subject matter is less important than the language itself. If the agreement is merely a rewrite of the board's policy manual into contract language, little is gained by collective bargaining. Our impression, after studying several agreements negotiated by both organizations, is that the federation more often has been able to place a somewhat greater number of restrictions on board prerogatives than has the association. But this has not always been the case. Thus when the AFT newspaper, *The American Teacher,* chided the association affiliate in Grosse Pointe, Michigan, for accepting in its contract the clause, "Attendance at and participation in PTA meetings is a normal professional responsibility,"[43] it forgot for the moment that in a contract the federation had agreed to in Highland Park, Michigan, at about the same time, the PTA obligation read: "It is understood that attendance at a PTA 'Open House' function is *required* [italics added] unless the teacher is excused by the principal."

Since each school district has its own special character, comparing agreements to see which of the two teacher organizations writes the better contracts is a somewhat inexact science. Some boards are tougher and some school districts are poorer than others. On the surface it would appear that the employment conditions negotiated by an NEA affiliate in Rochester are superior, from a teacher viewpoint, to those negotiated by an AFT local in Pawtucket. But this probably says less about the relative strength or viewpoints of the two teacher organizations than it does about the two communities and their school administrations.

We do have one school system, however, New Rochelle, New York, where both teacher organizations have tried their hands at negotiating a collective agreement. The New Rochelle Teachers Association represented the system's teachers from 1964 to 1966; the New Rochelle Federation of Teachers, after winning a representation election in the spring of 1966, negotiated an agreement the following summer.

There are some rather striking differences between the two

agreements. In the AFT settlement, salaries were increased substantially: $350 per year for holders of bachelor degrees on step one to a $750 increase for those holding doctorates at step 16. The new agreement established an "Educational Policies Committee" for joint teacher-administration planning on educational policies, curriculum, and other academic matters. The grievance procedure was also changed to conform more closely to the multistep procedure common in private industry. The association had bargained for the grievance procedure then being promoted by the NEA which utilized an *ad hoc* screening committee (a committee of peers to judge the merit of each grievance) and specified that, in cases of impasse, a "disinterested person of recognized competence in the field of public education" would render an advisory decision. The final step in the AFT agreement also provides for advisory arbitration, but the arbitrator is to be selected from an American Arbitration Association panel, definitely not an educational channel.

There are other, though less significant, "improvements"—a somewhat more liberal sick-leave policy and a provision for granting in-service credit for teachers who supervise student teachers. There is also at least one setback. Class size, which had been spelled out in the NEA agreement, was now merely to be a subject for "continuing study."

On balance, then, the union seems to have come up with an agreement that better serves the employment interests of New Rochelle teachers. The difficulty with this kind of judgment, however, is that we will never know what kind of agreement the association might have negotiated had *it* been elected bargaining agent in 1966. As we pointed out earlier, a great many things had happened within the NEA in the intervening two years and, had the New Rochelle Teachers Association been the victor in 1966; it would have been influenced by a different set of precedents from those prevailing in 1964.

Our conclusion, then, guided solely by the scope of the collective agreements negotiated by both teacher organizations, is that there is very little difference between the two when it comes down to the manner in which teachers are to be represented at the local level. In a great many cases, NEA affiliates are beginning to act very much like trade unions. Indeed, when an NEA affiliate participates in a representation election, wins the election and assumes the role of exclusive bargaining agent, enters into negotiations with the employer over a comprehensive agreement, goes out on strike when its terms are not met, wins the strike and administers the agreement with vigor and determination—when an affiliate does all this, it does not seem right to speak of it as anything but a union. Yet increasingly this appears to be the kind of role NEA affiliates are opting to play. The struggle then seems to have become not a contest between rival ideologies, between "professionalism" and "trade unionism," but between rival unions, reminiscent of jurisdictional fights in private employment before the AFL–CIO no-raiding pact.

IV

If the contest between the AFT and NEA, particularly as it manifests itself at the school district level, has indeed become essentially institutional rather than ideological, what purpose is served by perpetuating two teacher organizations? Would not the public school teacher be in a much stronger bargaining position, be able to have greater influence over the educational enterprise, if there were a single teacher organization?

Certainly there are several "public" arguments favoring merger or assimilation, not the least of which is that the competition between the two teacher organizations in some cases has had a divisive effect on the school program. Representation elections, like political elections, require issues and personalities to feed on. And if the issues are bland and the personalities colorless, they are sometimes made to appear controversial and sinister. Campaigns are frequently heated. Teacher organizations hurl charges at one another and on occasion both accuse the board and administration of callousness, if not downright perfidy. Sometimes the organizations feel they must adopt a pose as the most militant of militants. It is of the utmost importance, evidently, particularly in those school systems where the employment relationship has been something less than amicable, that the opposing organization not be allowed to get to one's left. And the best assurance against this eventuality, apparently, is to make charges, demands, and promises that are as extravagant as the opponent's.

The dust of battle settles, but wounds are very often slow to heal. Teachers who fought bitterly in the election campaign are now expected to cooperate on educational and professional concerns. Administrators who were the *bêtes noires* during the campaign are now expected to provide educational leadership to their faculties.

It may have been partly because he was shaken by problems such as these that retiring NEA President Richard Batchelder urged during his presidential address at the 1966 NEA Convention that the two organizations join forces in a single, united teacher organization: "I . . . invite our colleagues in the AFT to sever ties with labor and unite with the National Education Association so that we can present one common front for the improvement of the teaching profession and can assure that all teachers can serve the needs of all children."[44]

The AFT response was quick but not sympathetic. "We have read with interest your recent public statement that the American Federation of Teachers and the National Education Association form one common front for the improvement of the teaching profession," replied AFT President Cogen. "The AFT stands for a united teacher organization free from administrator domination and dedicated to the improvement of American society. Our AFL–CIO affiliation has been a great benefit in pursuing this objective. We therefore have no intention of forsaking our affiliation with organized labor."[45] A month later, at its annual national convention, the AFT again responded to the NEA invitation to join forces by inviting the Association's Classroom Teachers Department to join the union.[46]

So the issue stood as of the fall of 1966. The NEA, although willing to act very much like a trade union at the local level, was adamant that teachers should retain their independence from other social and economic groups. The Kingsport Press issue and the union position on the sales tax were persuasive arguments that affiliation with the labor movement could at times force teachers to take positions that were at odds with high quality education. And, while the NEA seemed to be ridding itself of administration domination or control at both the national and local level, and local affiliates were on occasion striking against these very administrations, a rather heavy emphasis was still put on the community of interest existing among all segments of the profession.

The AFT, on the other hand, profits by its affiliation with organized labor, sees no inconsistency between its AFL–CIO alliance and its professional stance, and is more ideologically attuned to the idea of conflict of interest between teachers and their employers.

There is, moreover, the matter of institutional interests, completely apart from ideological differences, that are served by separation and competition. It has been argued that we have passed the point where this competition serves any real social purpose. But history is replete with examples of institutions that lingered on long after their usefulness had been outgrown. Merger would mean a considerable shuffling of personnel, a loss of status for several of the hierarchy in both organizations, a loss of strongly held institutional identification for thousands of teachers. And, given the intensity of the struggle and the degree of animosity that has been generated by both sides over the last several years, one wonders if either organization is prepared to eat the amount of crow that merger would demand.

Finally, there seems no question that teachers have benefited from this competition. Certainly fewer teachers would be protected by the coverage of a collective agreement had not the AFT challenged the NEA's role as sole guardian of teachers' rights. Competition has moved the NEA to act more militantly, to reassess its obligations to teachers in their employment capacity, and to press harder at the state and local level for greater teacher benefits. Take away this competition by merging the competitors and a substantial part of the motivation for vigorously serving teachers will have been dissipated.

The public may grow increasingly exasperated at the divisive effect this competition has upon the educational enterprise, just as it may continue to worry about the consequences illegal teacher strikes might have on children's understanding of the importance of law and order. It is likely to be some time, however, before the two organizations will see fit to accommodate their differences. Too much is to be gained by separation.

REFERENCES

1. Edgar B. Wesley, *The NEA: The First Hundred Years* (New York: Harper & Brothers, 1957), pp. 23–24. The organization changed its name to National Education Association in 1870.
2. *Ibid.,* p. 397.
3. *Ibid.,* pp. 278–281.
4. The Commission on Educational Reconstruction, *Organizing the Teaching Profession* (Glencoe, Ill.: The Free Press, 1955), pp. 27–28.
5. *Ibid.,* p. 28.
6. American Federation of Teachers, *Representing Today's Teachers* (Chicago: AFT, 1964), p. 69; *American Teacher,* May 1966, p. 1, col. 1.
7. *NEA Reporter,* June 17, 1966, p. 2, col. 1. NEA membership seems to be concentrated in the West. As of 1966 only California and Colorado of all the Rocky Mountain and Pacific Coast states had less than 75 per cent of all school employees enrolled in the NEA. By contrast, Louisiana had 11 per cent and Rhode Island 12 per cent. Of the large cities, New York, where the United Federation of Teachers—an affiliate of the AFT—has represented all teachers since 1962, has the lowest percentage: 3 per cent. AFT strength, as of 1965, was concentrated in Rhode Island, where 26.9 per cent of all teachers were members; New York, 22.8 per cent; Illinois, 20.0 per cent; Minnesota, 16.3 per cent; Michigan, 14.5 per cent.
8. Information in a letter to the authors from Glen Robinson, director, Research Division, NEA, August 23, 1966.
9. Pete Schnaufer, *Report on Supervisory Membership in the AFT and in Other International Unions,* A Report Prepared for the Executive Council of the American Federation of Teachers, 1966, p. 1.
10. *White Collar Report,* no. 413, February 4, 1965, p. A–4.
11. *Final Report on Compulsory Membership in Professional Organizations Among Credentialed California School Employees.* Senate of the State of California, 1965, p. 16.
12. *Ibid.*
13. *NEA Reporter,* June 17, 1966, p. 2, col. 1.
14. William T. Lowe, "Who Joins Which Teachers Group?" *Teachers College Record,* vol. 66, no. 7 (April 1965), pp. 615–616.
15. *Ibid.,* pp. 617–618; Lesley Hughes Browder, Jr., "Teacher Unionism in America: A Descriptive Analysis," Ph.D. dissertation, School of Education, Cornell University, 1965, pp. 194–226.
16. Fred Hechinger, "NEA Convention Rich in Hoopla," *New York Times,* July 4, 1965, sec. 4, p. 5, col. 2.
17. *New York Times,* February 13, 1966, p. 65, col. 2.
18. American Federation of Teachers, AFL–CIO, *Proceedings of the Forty-ninth Annual Convention, Los Angeles, California, August 23–27, 1965,* p. 115.

19. "AFT's 'Ban-the-Books' Caper Imperils Academic Freedom," *Urban Reporter,* vol. 4, no. 3 (November 1965), p. 1.

20. *Ibid.,* p. 6.

21. "New York City Board Votes to Ban-the-Books," *Urban Reporter,* vol. 4, no. 6 (April–May 1966), p. 1.

22. "New Jersey School Support Battle Pits the NJEA Against the AFL–CIO," *Urban Reporter,* vol. 4, no. 6 (March–April 1966), p. 8; "AFL–CIO Opposition Fails to Defeat Baton Rouge Sales Tax for Schools," *Urban Reporter,* vol. 4, no. 5 (January–February 1966), Barbara Cater, "The Teachers Give Oklahoma a Lesson," *The Reporter,* vol. 33, no. 4 (September 9, 1965), p. 35.

23. John Kenneth Galbraith, *The Affluent Society* (Boston: Houghton Mifflin Company, 1958), p. 315.

24. Cater, p. 35; "AFL–CIO Opposition Fails to Defeat Baton Rouge Sales Tax for Schools," p. 6.

25. Ronald Donovan, "Labor Relations in the Public Service," *Industrial and Labor Relations Report Card,* vol. 14, no. 3 (March 1966), p. 3.

26. *Ibid.,* p. 1.

27. *Ibid.,* p. 3.

28. Everett M. Kassalow, "White-Collar Unionism in the United States," *White-Collar Trade Unions: Contemporary Developments in Industrialized Societies,* Adolf Sturmthal, ed. (Urbana: University of Illinois Press, 1966), pp. 307, 338.

29. *Government Employees Relations Reporter,* no. 115, November 22, 1965, p. B–1.

30. National Education Association, *Addresses and Proceedings of the Ninety-eighth Annual Meeting, Los Angeles, California, June 26–July 1, 1960,* p. 160.

31. National Education Association, *Addresses and Proceedings of the Ninety-ninth Annual Meeting, Atlantic City, N.J., June 25–30, 1961,* pp. 216–217 (italics added).

32. National Education Association, *Addresses and Proceedings of the One-Hundredth Annual Meeting, Denver, Colorado, July 1–July 6, 1962,* p. 397 (italics added).

33. National Education Association, *Addresses and Proceedings of the One-Hundred-and-Second Annual Meeting, Seattle, Washington, June 28–July 3, 1964,* p. 446.

34. National Education Association, *Addresses and Proceedings of the One-Hundredth Annual Meeting, Denver, Colorado, July 1–July 6, 1962,* p. 397 (italics added).

35. *Ibid.,* p. 120.

36. *Ibid.,* p. 122.

37. *Ibid.,* p. 223.

38. *Ibid.,* p. 379.

39. "Teacher Opinion Poll: Should Teachers Strike?" *NEA Journal,* vol. 55, no. 5 (May 1966), p. 54.

40. *Government Employee Relations Reporter,* no. 140, May 16, 1966, p. B–5. The Masachusetts statute covering bargaining rights for public employees did not go into effect until February of 1966, too short a time before this was written to permit an assessment of how well the association was doing.
41. Quoted in an address by George E. Watson to the Joint School Board-Administrator Convention, Milwaukee, January 21, 1966 (italics added).
42. The agreements alluded to here and throughout this section are: *Agreement between the Board of Education of the City of Detroit and the Detroit Federation of Teachers, Local 231, AFT,* June 29, 1965–July 1, 1966; *Agreement between the Grosse Pointe Board of Education and the Grosse Pointe Education Association,* July 1, 1966–June 30, 1970; *Agreement between the Highland Park Board of Education and the Highland Park Federation of Teachers,* July 1, 1966–July 1, 1967; *Agreement between the New Haven Board of Education and the New Haven Teachers' League* (affiliated with the NEA), January 17, 1966–January 16, 1969; *Agreement between the New Rochelle Teachers Association and the Board of Education of the City School District of New Rochelle,* July 1, 1964–June 30, 1965; *Agreement between the Board of Education of the City School District of New Rochelle and the New Rochelle Federation of Teachers, Local 280, AFT,* July 1, 1966–June 30, 1967; *Agreement between the Board of Education of the City of New York and the United Federation of Teachers, Local 2, AFT,* July 1, 1965–June 30, 1967; *Agreement between the Newark Board of Education and the Newark Teachers' Association,* July 28, 1965–July 27, 1966; *Contract between the School Committee of the City of Pawtucket and the Pawtucket Teachers' Alliance, Local 930, AFT,* September 1, 1966–August 31, 1969; *Agreement between the Board of Public Education of the School District of Philadelphia and the Philadelphia Federation of Teachers, Local 3, AFT,* September 1, 1965–August 31, 1966; *The Contractual Agreement between the Board of Education of the City School District of Rochester, New York and the Rochester Teachers Association,* July 1, 1965–June 30, 1966.
43. *The American Teacher,* May 1966, p. 7, col. 3.
44. Richard D. Batchelder, "Free to Teach," Speech at 104th Annual NEA Convention, Miami Beach, Florida, June 26–July 1, 1966, p. 6.
45. American Federation of Teachers News Release, June 30, 1966.
46. *AFL–CIO News,* September 3, 1966, p. 2, col. 1.

COLLECTIVE NEGOTIATIONS
IN PUBLIC EDUCATION
by Charles Cogen

Charles Cogen was first elected president of the American Federation of Teachers AFL–CIO in 1964 and was reelected in 1966, serving until his retirement in August 1968. He was a classroom teacher in the New York City school system for many years and is also an attorney. This article is taken from the text of a speech which was delivered at an educational conference in Rhode Island in 1965.

In April 1965, as president of the American Federation of Teachers, I addressed a telegram to the president of the Department of Classroom Teachers of the National Education Association. I proposed that the DCT and the AFT engage in a dialogue for the purpose of establishing a nationwide "Code of Observance" for the conduct of teacher representation elections. What we in the AFT were seeking was a united front of teachers in establishing uniform rules for choosing local exclusive negotiating representative organizations, regardless of whether the organization chosen by the teachers was an AFT local or an association affiliated with NEA or its state branches.

Increasingly, educational commentators have proposed that the AFT and the NEA merge into one organization. We would not rule out such a possibility. The AFT favors "teacher unity," but there are fundamental points at issue between the two organizations and many of these revolve around the question of the proper relationship between teachers and their employing boards of education. We reasoned that if teacher unity in an organizational sense is not possible, at least we ought to be able to agree on the rights which teachers should have, and stand united in our insistence that these rights be recognized by boards of education.

Within this framework the two organizations could then compete for teacher support.

Our efforts to establish a common framework of teachers' rights as employees were rebuffed by the Department of Classroom Teachers. Instead, the DCT supports legislation defining the negotiating relationship on a state-by-state basis. We consider this action irresponsible and harmful to teachers. It seems motivated more by the desire of the associations to maintain the organizational status quo than by any consideration for improving the position of teaching as a profession. At best the state-by-state approach can result only in a patchwork of unsatisfactory compromises, achieved after decades of effort, and it is likely to lead to a prolonged guerilla war in which teachers become embroiled in unproductive attacks against each other while the great issues confronting the schools are neglected.

If there were to be a nationwide negotiating code, what would it look like?

WHAT A NATIONAL CODE FOR TEACHER NEGOTIATIONS
WOULD INCLUDE

In general, the AFT favors the same sort of relationship between teachers and their boards of education as that which has been established for employees in the private sector through the National Labor Management Relations Act.

We favor the principle of exclusive recognition of a single bargaining agent. We are opposed to "members only" bargaining, in which two or more organizations have separate but equal rights to negotiate with the board. We are opposed to "joint committees," whether they are chosen on an organization basis or by direct election of individual committee members.

Where there are two or more organizations vying for recognition, we favor recognition of the organization which achieves a majority of those voting in a secret-ballot election. We are opposed to recognition on the basis of membership lists except where only one organization is seeking exclusive recognition. Even here, due notice should be given so that any other organization could force an election upon making a sufficient showing of interest.

We favor "continuing recognition" until such time as a significant proportion of the members of the negotiating unit petition for a new election. We are opposed to required annual or biannual elections of negotiating agents.

We favor negotiating units composed of nonsupervisory educational employees only. We are opposed to units composed of "all certificated employees" which include principals and other administrators and supervisors.

We would place no limit on the scope of negotiations, the items which are subject to the bargaining process. Anything on which the two parties can agree should become a part of the agreement; anything on which they cannot agree will, of course, not appear.

We favor written agreements between boards of education and negotiating agents. These agreements should be legally binding.

We favor development of a code of unfair labor practices and definitions of what constitutes good faith negotiations.

We favor according teachers the right to strike; we are opposed to antistrike laws, and we are opposed to the use of injunctions in teacher-board disputes.

We favor the use of skilled mediators to resolve impasses. We are opposed to compulsory arbitration of negotiable items.

We favor individual grievance procedures under the contract, with outside arbitration as the final step. We oppose grievance procedures which place the board or the superintendent in the position of final arbiter.

Any nationwide teacher-board relations code would include the items I have noted. Many variations in detail are possible and these we are perfectly willing to discuss and even compromise on, but it is obvious that even the compromises least advantageous to teachers and most favorable to those who are in the management end of the school enterprise would constitute a tremendous advance in teachers' rights. Neither the AFT nor the DCT–NEA could bind its local units to any such code, of course, nor would agreement between the two teacher organizations mean that all boards of education would accept the code. Most local teacher organizations, however, want guidance, and many boards of education are willing to help establish some order in what is now a chaotic situation. At the very least we have an obligation to set standards of right and wrong in this field.

APPROPRIATENESS OF LABOR-MANAGEMENT CONCEPTS
TO EDUCATION

Some educational commentators decry the trend toward collective negotiations on the grounds that bargaining between teachers and their employers is not appropriate to education. Teaching, they say, is a profession, and education is not a business. Now, some might deny that teaching is, at present, a profession, and everyone can agree that education is not a business in the usual sense, but semantic arguments of this sort advance us very little.

Teachers certainly are *employees* of the board of education regardless of their professional status or the lack of it. If one were to place a schematic drawing of the staff structure of almost any school system alongside a schematic drawing of the staff structure of a typical private business corporation of comparable size, the little boxes and circles would be about the same for each. The same stresses, strains, and conflicts which exist in such structures in private enterprise are also to be found in enterprises owned by the public, whether they be school systems, fire departments, or bus lines.

The "nonprofit" argument, too, is fallacious. Schools are just as much in the marketplace for their share of consumer dollars as any manufacturer of automobiles or safety pins. People pay taxes because they want schools, just as they put up $3000 for a new automobile or 10¢ for a packet of pins because they want these items. Boards of education and superintendents are elected and employed to produce education, and their obligation is even set forth by law. Their success, like that of private managers, is measured by an equation in which public approval is balanced against costs.

Many superintendents, principals, and other supervisors and administrators resent efforts to classify them as "management," as though there were something disgraceful about the term, and most of the opposition to applying established labor-management concepts to education comes from this quarter. Their attitude is reflected by the nonunion associations, and a large "literature" of circumlocutions, rationalizations, and antilabor propaganda has emerged from the effort to avoid labor-management terms and concepts. Yet, ironically, one of the most widely read educational

magazines among administrators and school board members is—
School Management.

SUPERVISORS AND ADMINISTRATORS SHOULD NOT BE IN TEACHER UNITS

A basic labor relations tenet is that management employees should not be in the same bargaining units as nonsupervisory employees. There can be no question about the predominantly managerial status of a school superintendent. Even legislation sponsored by the various nonunion state associations excludes superintendents from the bargaining unit. As for principals and others in middle management, the determining questions are "How much discretionary power do they have?" and "With whom do they identify?" Two categories are debatable. Teaching department heads, for instance, who have little discretionary power and who in the main are treated as teachers, probably should be included in the bargaining unit. Assistant principals, who usually exercise the authority of the principal, and who are usually paid or given other benefits based upon those given the principal, probably should be excluded.

Only in a few of our largest cities is there anything approaching a civil service merit system for the selection of administrative personnel, and even where such a system operates, the superintendent retains a great deal of power in determining who gets promoted. The standard practice in private enterprise—of allowing the chief executive a free hand in the selection of his subordinates —has been applied to the educational enterprise. The increasing tendency to require specialized certificates changes the status and power factors very little. Getting a certificate is a matter of getting the credits. In some cases, acting appointments are made and then confirmed after the person chosen has acquired his certificate.

Basing the salaries of administrative personnel on percentages of the teacher salary, or "indices," does not materially change the concept we have been discussing, either. True, under an index, every time the teachers get a raise the administrators get one too, which ought to produce friendly feelings toward teacher salary campaigns. But when hard negotiations begin, or a strike occurs, and the order comes down from the superintendent to tighten the rules or cross the picket line, it is a rare administrator who will uphold the teachers' cause.

The supervisors' salary index idea is bitterly resented by many teachers because the very people who try to curb teacher action end up by benefiting the most from teacher success. Also, the index freezes in a status relationship which many teachers do not acknowledge. The relationship existing now between supervisory personnel and teachers is mainly superordinate-subordinate, not primarily collegial.

In normal employee-employer relations, those who have authority to hire and fire, settle grievances, or make specific job assignments are excluded from the employee bargaining unit. Placing these positions firmly on the management side acts to check possible abuses of power, and allows nonsupervisory employees to make group decisions without being subjected to undue influence and undemocratic pressures from supervisors. We would see no objection to middle management administrators and supervisors forming bargaining units of their own, but these should be separate from those for nonsupervisory personnel.

We in the AFT think it unwise—even downright silly—to ignore the experience which has been amassed in labor-management relations over the years. The principles and concepts which have evolved apply to industries of widest possible diversity, and there is no reason to segregate educational employees and attempt to establish a new body of rules for them. In fact, teachers can only lose from such a development.

ORGANIZATION, NEGOTIATION, AND PROFESSIONALISM;
THE SCOPE OF BARGAINING

Effective organization, negotiating rights, and greater professionalism are all parts of the same problem with which teachers are now confronted. It is worse than useless to have the *right* to negotiate where teachers have no *power* to negotiate, and the development of rights and power by teachers must be accompanied by a much higher degree of involvement in matters of professional concern.

Most administrators would agree with this last statement, at least in principle; where they would disagree is on the question of priority. The administrators would say, as some Southern governors say about civil rights: "They aren't ready for it. First they have to show that they know how to handle these rights and privileges."

Many of us in the AFT might, in turn, agree that teachers must be much more willing to accept responsibility for matters which they all too often abjure, but progress in this direction will come as a concomitant to the increased power and rights of teachers rather than as a prerequisite. As teachers achieve improved status, more able and aggressive individuals will be attracted to enter—and to remain in—the profession. As teachers become more "professional," they will achieve greater power and more rights. I do not want to add to the torrent of definitions of professionalism which has come forth from lecturers, panelists, writers, and after-dinner speakers over the decades. When I use the term I am referring to our commitment as teachers to accept responsibility, to welcome innovation, and to be firm in our insistence on proper standards so that the quality and quantity of education is constantly improved and enlarged. This sort of professionalism can develop only in a society of equals, in which all have an equal responsibility to the common enterprise.

Collective negotiation is the logical, practical, and meaningful way to develop greater professionalism among teachers. In the past, when teachers depended primarily upon public relations, research, lobbying, and paternalism, their progress toward professionalism was tortuously slow. As they assume the new rights and responsibilities which go with collective bargaining—or collective negotiation—their progress is speeded up.

Those who seek to place limits on the scope of teacher bargaining are basically antiprofessional. A professional insists on professional standards, conditions of work which permit him to use his professional skills to the greatest advantage. In New York City, the Board of Education representatives take the position that the proper size of a class is not a proper subject for negotiations, while the union asserts the right of its members to exercise their collective professional judgment on this question. Would a doctor allow a hospital superintendent to determine the time he can spend with each patient, or the number of patients on whom he must operate in an hour?

What should be the "professional" role of the superintendent of schools in the negotiating process? The NEA, in its rapidly expanding literature on "professional negotiations," talks of the "dual role" of the superintendent. The superintendent does have a "dual role," but not quite the same sort of duality as that meant by the NEA. Rather than have one role as adviser of the board and another as adviser of the teachers, the two roles of the superintendent are both management in function. On the one hand he is an administrator, responsible for the efficient operation of the educational enterprise. On the other he is an educational adviser, responsible for making policy recommendations to the board of education. The superintendent has as great an obligation to negotiate on professional matters as on business affairs.

In a clothing factory the workers negotiate about wages, fringe benefits, and conditions of work, but garment workers are not expected to set clothing styles. Teachers, however, as professionals, have an obligation to exercise their professional judgment, to share the educational policy-making function.

I look for a great expansion in the effective scope of negotiations between teachers and school management. Obviously class size, number of classes taught, curriculum, hiring standards, textbooks and supplies, extra-curricular activities—in fact, anything having to do with the operation of the school—is a matter for professional concern and should thus be subject to collective bargaining. At least, the method of determining these matters, such as curriculum, should be negotiable. The fact that these items also involve budgetary arrangements is an added reason for including them in the scope of bargaining.

Through local and eventually statewide and possibly national negotiation, teachers can even use their collective power to control standards of entry into the profession.

SOME LEGAL PROBLEMS

In many states during the past few years we have run into legal obstacles to establishing the right of teachers to negotiate. Sometimes these obstacles have been created by boards of education; sometimes they have been created by the nonunion associations.

In Taylor Township, Michigan, a teacher, using the same law firm retained by the Michigan Education Association, obtained a restraining order prohibiting recognition of any exclusive bargaining representative which might be chosen as a result of a forthcoming election. The election was held, after a two-month delay, but on an advisory basis only. The board of education has thus far refused to enter into an agreement with the Taylor Federation of Teachers, which received a majority of the votes.

In Detroit, legal obstacles to exclusive recognition delayed a representation election in 1964 and nearly precipitated a strike. The election was held and the union won, but one of the stipulations under which the election was authorized by the Detroit Board of Education was that a new election would be held in a year. On the eve of the second election, the Detroit Education Association sought a court order to grant administrative and supervisory personnel the right to vote in the election. When the judge refused to rule immediately, the DEA withdrew from the ballot, and a committee representing the union was then recognized as the exclusive bargaining agent for the teachers. While the legality of any agreement in Michigan was at first in doubt, peculiarly enough, in April 1965, in Hamtramck, Michigan, the board ratified a written agreement reached between its negotiating committee and that of the union.

In New York, the status of the exclusive recognition of the United Federation of Teachers has been upheld by the State Commissioner of Education, but the contract between the board and the union has not yet been tested in court (as of 1965). A question has been raised due to the fact that the contract contains a compulsory arbitration feature on grievances as a final step, which tends to make it self-enforcing, and also due to the no-strike clause which is the union's quid pro quo in making the contract. If the board breached the contract, the union could consider itself free of its agreement not to strike during the duration of the contract.

Many boards of education fall back on the doctrine of "sovereignty" to deny teachers bargaining rights. They say that signing a contract would restrict their freedom to act during the duration of the contract. Not infrequently, as in St. Louis, associations have reinforced the board's view that exclusive recognition is illegal.

There are really very few recent court decisions concerning the legality of exclusive recognition. Unfortunately, state attorneys general tend to repeat court doctrine and opinions of their predecessors in office which were handed down prior to the growth of unionism among government employees during the past decade. The fact remains that in spite of adverse legal opinions, the number of written and unwritten collective bargaining agreements based on exclusive recognition is increasing at a very rapid rate.

THE IMPASSE PROBLEM

I wish to conclude my remarks by stating our view toward the problem of resolution of impasses in negotiations. We believe that work stoppages by teachers should be a last resort in attempting to resolve such impasses. Every possible effort to reach an agreement should be made before a work stoppage occurs. However, we also believe—as does the NEA, as evidenced by its sanctions policy—that work stoppages by teachers are morally justifiable under certain circumstances.

AFT locals are urged to follow the normal procedure of collective bargaining. When an impasse occurs, they usually resort to some sort of public appeal: a demonstration, informational picketing, leaflets, newspaper, radio, and television advertisements, and marshaling of support from the labor movement and parent and civic organizations. If these efforts fail to move the board from its position, the members sometimes set a strike date.

We strongly advocate the use of skilled mediators in attempting to resolve negotiating impasses. In addition to his experience and skill, the impartiality of the mediator must be above question. We do not think that most state superintendents of public instruction qualify for the mediation role on either count. Few have had mediation training or experience, and even the "fairest" state superintendent is apt to have a pro-management bias. Perhaps standing educational mediation panels could be approved by state teacher organizations and the state school boards association. Mediators for any particular situation could then be chosen from this panel.

In most cases when a strike date is set, a settlement is reached before the deadline. However, there are occasional impasses which are settled only after the walkout occurs. Few of these work stoppages have lasted more than a day or so. Teachers have shown great reluctance to use the strike to resolve an impasse, and one reason for this hesitancy is that in most states a strike by public employees is enjoinable, either under a specific antistrike statute or under common law. The lurking fear of court action, added to the distaste of many teachers for such drastic action, has limited the willingness of teachers to strike. Teacher strikes tend to be more in the nature of demonstrations to call public attention to the points at issue.

Legally, no one can be forced to work. A group of public employees who are determined enough can withstand court fines and jailings of their leaders and threatened loss of vested rights, just as the social workers in the New York City Welfare Department did in January of 1965; and when they do, they usually win. However, teacher groups are only now approaching such solidarity. In the meantime, methods of avoiding the legal entanglements of antistrike laws and injunctions should be explored. (Penalties have become more burdensome since this speech was prepared.)

The most desirable step toward giving teachers bargaining power in negotiations would be to outlaw the use of the injunction in teacher-board disputes, just as the Norris-LaGuardia Act outlaws injunctions in labor disputes in the private sector. The Michigan Board of Education recently declared in favor of granting teachers the right to strike, but widespread acceptance of this right to strike is not an immediate likelihood.

Perhaps the best avenue to explore is the "no contract-no work" concept. When teachers understand that they are to work only under the terms and conditions of a collective bargaining contract, no formal action would be required to set a deadline for a work stoppage. Lack of a contract or the acceptance of a contract is a self-evident fact, and teachers would simply act accordingly. Certain types of picketing, advertising, and communications are usually subject to court restraint, but no court can force a union to sign an agreement. So long as teachers remain true to the "no contract-no work" principle, a legally permissible work stoppage can be carried on.

In some respects the "no contract-no work" policy is similar to the code of ethics approach of Myron Lieberman and others, and it also bears strong resemblance to the sanctions approach of the NEA, at least as projected in the Utah and Oklahoma situations.

If teachers have a code of ethics involving standard of salaries, class size, teaching program load, and other vital matters, and agree that they will teach only under these ethical conditions, a work stoppage is implicit when conditions fail to meet these standards. The difficulty with this approach lies in its rigidity. There is such a variation in the ability of local school districts to provide adequate professional conditions that either exceptions would have to be made or the code itself would be so substandard as to be meaningless in many situations. However, the code of ethics could have meaning if considered in conjunction with local collective negotiations and the "no contract-no work" principle.

The sanctions approach of the NEA has possibilities for development into an effective professional weapon, but in its present formulation it has many pitfalls and drawbacks. The basic idea underlying sanctions—that teachers should not work in districts which do not maintain adequate professional standards—is sound. It is the same principle underlying the no contract-no work idea. However, if a district is not a fit place in which to teach, all teachers—those presently employed as well as applicants for teaching positions—should refuse to teach there. We see no moral or logical defense for condoning teaching by those who are already there while new applicants are urged to go elsewhere. Furthermore, this strangulation approach is unduly attenuated, and a great deal of harm can be done to the children and to public education in general while the process runs its course over a long period of time.

Another problem with the sanctions idea is that of "who invokes and who revokes." An impasse in local negotiations or in a state educational program occurs. The local or state association declares in favor of sanctions. Then an investigating team comes in, ostensibly to make an evaluation of the professional conditions which prevail. In actuality the "evaluation" is a sort of under-the-table negotiation in which local teachers as a collective force are removed from the process. Let us assume, however, that following the evaluation, sanctions are applied in their most extreme form and teachers are encouraged to pick up their goods and chattels and teach elsewhere (a vengeance harder on the avenger than on the avengee). Who decides the point at which conditions have become acceptable? And then does everybody move back into town?

Compared with a strike, or a no contract-no work policy as a way of resolving an impasse, sanctions are slow, uncertain, potentially harmful to children and the schools, difficult to enforce, a hindrance to teacher involvement in the problems which concern them, and lacking in democratic controls. If sanctions procedures could be modified to correct these defects, what would emerge would be essentially a no contract-no work policy.

In all the foregoing I have avoided mention of arbitration as a method of settling negotiating impasses. While we favor arbitration to enforce an agreement once it is negotiated as a final step of a grievance procedure, we are opposed to its use in negotiations for a variety of reasons which are too lengthy to go into here. (These are outlined in a brief policy paper available from the American Federation of Teachers, 1012 14th Street, N.W., Washington, D.C. 20005.)

CONCLUSION

I now come back to my original thesis: the principles involved in establishing collective negotiation are too important to be settled on the basis of organizational advantage. Rather, the two organizations—NEA and AFT—ought to make every effort to agree on these principles and mutually uphold them.

We must never lose sight of the fact that it is the *teachers* whom we represent and serve. Any temporary organizational advantage which might seem possible by pursuing some expediential course which is contrary to sound principles of teacher-board relationships will be swept aside as teachers march toward their goal of greater dignity and professional status.

6

PUBLIC EMPLOYEES AND THE LAW

BACKGROUND
by Robert E. Walsh

Thomas Jefferson wrote in the Declaration of Independence, "Governments are instituted among Men, deriving their just powers from the consent of the governed." The preamble to the Constitution starts with the words, "We the people of the United States. . . ." Thus, the supreme power in our government belongs to the people, and the word used to describe this concept is sovereignty. It is this concept which traditionally gives the state its immunity from lawsuits. The people holding this power in turn delegate it to representatives to run their government.

It is evident that the only way one can bargain with a sovereign is by the sovereign agreeing to give up some of his inherent power; this is exactly what happens when a state legislature votes to bargain with its state employees or allows municipalities to bargain with employees on a local level.

The Massachusetts Legislative Research Bureau in a 1968 study found that thirty-eight states granted the right, at least to some of their employees at the state or local level, to organize and bargain collectively. Ten states did this by constitutional amendment, twenty-six by statute and the remaining two by executive order. Three states, North Carolina, Georgia, and Virginia prohibit public employee unions as of 1968.

State laws vary widely in their dealings with public employees. Some states allow their employees to organize and deal collectively with the state while forbidding employees of local jurisdictions the same rights. Other states allow local employees the right to organize and bargain but forbid the same rights to state employees. Also, in some states only certain groups of public employees such as teachers, or firefighters, or employees of a state university are granted this right. No two states treat the subject exactly the same way and even the procedures for handling the recognition of the bargaining agent or disputes differ. With one exception all states agree on one point: they prohibit *strikes* by public employees. The one exception is California which has remained silent on the question.

These laws prohibiting strikes, however, have not prevented them. Legislators and labor relations experts are currently seeking to improve existing laws in this field. Thus people in many states watched with interest New York State's attempt to hammer out a new law dealing with the public employee.

New York City, under an executive order signed by Mayor Robert Wagner in the late fifties, set up one of the first codes of labor relations for public employees. It established procedures for recognizing unions and dealing with disputes.

New York State generally lagged behind the city, and the state law governing public employee strikes was considered an ineffective punitive statute. The transit strike of 1966 was one of the factors contributing to a pressure for a change. On January 15 of that year, Governor Nelson Rockefeller appointed a committee of men knowledgeable in collective bargaining to "make legislative proposals for protecting the public against the disruption of vital public services by illegal strikes, while at the same time protecting the rights of public employees."

George W. Taylor, Harnwell Professor of Industry at the Wharton School of Finance and Commerce of the University of Pennsylvania, was named chairman of this committee. Those named to serve with him were: E. Wight Bakke, Sterling Professor of Economics at Yale University; David L. Cole, labor lawyer and choice of the AFL–CIO to umpire their internal disputes; John T. Dunlop, widely known professor of economics and chairman of the Department of Economics at Harvard University; and Frederick H. Harbison, professor of economics and director of the Industrial Relations Section of Princeton University.

The legislation enacted proved to be a modified version of the original committee report, and the law passed was called the Public Employees' Fair Employment Act; it is more commonly referred to as the Taylor Act.

In line with the provisions of this act, Governor Rockefeller appointed a three-man Public Employment Relations Board with Dr. Robert D. Helsby as Chairman.

One of the purposes of this new act was to bring more flexibility to public employee relations. The act and the rules set up by the Public Employment Relations Board basically do five things. They

1. Give public employees the right to join or refrain from joining any employee organization;

2. Give public employees the right to be represented by employee organizations of their own choosing and to negotiate collectively with their public employers;

3. Require public employers to negotiate with their employees and to enter into written agreements with them;

4. Establish impasse procedures for the resolution of labor disputes in the public sector; and they

5. Prohibit strikes by public employees.

DISPUTES IN THE PUBLIC SECTOR— NEW YORK'S EXPERIENCE
by Robert D. Helsby

This selection is a speech given on October 15, 1968, at the Governor's Conference on Public Employment Relations in New York City. Prior to his appointment to the New York State Public Employment Relations Board, Dr. Helsby was Dean for Continuing Education at the State University of New York. He received his doctoral degree from the New York School of Industrial and Labor Relations at Cornell University.

The two most common questions in our affluent society are supposedly "How do I lose weight?" and "Where do I park my car?" In keeping with this affluence, perhaps the most common question being asked by government today is "How do I handle my increasingly militant public employees?"

Provided by the Public Employment Relations Board.

Perhaps I should, at the outset, be as self-serving as Gilbert and Sullivan's Lord Chancellor who, you remember, declared that "The law is the true embodiment of everything that is excellent. In it you will find no fault or flaw, and I, my friends, embody the law." I may not be as immodest as all that, but the Public Employment Relations Board, of which I presently serve as chairman and which is known by the acronym PERB, does really embody the Taylor Law. We are charged with the statewide responsibility of overall administration of the law in an impartial manner to all parties concerned.

Whatever one wants to say about New York State, we can all agree that it is big, diverse, and complex. Whatever problems are likely to be found are undoubtedly going to exist in all variants and complexities—so it is with labor relations in the public sector.

DIMENSIONS OF THE PROBLEM

Before reviewing our dispute settlement experience in New York in the initial year of the Taylor Law, let me briefly describe the dimensions of the problems we face.

1. Currently, there are about 950,000 state and local employees in New York State involving more than 2500 separate public employers, ranging in size from very few employees to several hundred thousand.

2. While most other states have chosen to go into public employment relations on a piecemeal basis, New York State in "one fell swoop" brought *all* state and local public employees under the jurisdiction of the Taylor Law—teachers, university professors and state, county, city, village, and authority employees.

3. Over 750,000 public employees are now in negotiating units represented by employee organizations—60 per cent of these employees being represented for the first time.

4. Presently more than 850 public employers, whose employees are divided into some 1900 negotiating units, have either negotiated contracts or are in the process of doing so. Of these, more than 650 employers are school districts.

5. The law makes it possible for local governments to pass their own laws and establish their own public employment relations boards, if they choose to do so. These laws must be substantially equivalent to the Taylor Law and their boards must have basically

the same responsibilities as our state board. To date, some 29 local PERBs have been established, including the Office of Collective Bargaining in New York City. These boards have a potential jurisdiction of roughly one-quarter of the public employees in the state.

IMPASSE PROCEDURES

It is obvious that impasse procedures must be flexible to be workable. Negotiating experience of the parties ranges from school boards and teachers facing each other across the table for the first time to the Transit Authority and Transit Workers Union with a well-developed negotiating history.

The law faces this problem by creating two different routes: 1. They can develop their own local impasse procedures; or 2. The statutory impasse procedures may be utilized.

If the parties choose to develop their own impasse procedures, they are free to utilize any approach. There are no procedural strings attached to this route. PERB cannot intervene until such agreed-upon procedures fail or unless requested to do so.

If the parties do not establish their own procedures, PERB may, on request of the parties or on its own motion, provide conciliation services. If mediation does not resolve the dispute, PERB may appoint a factfinding board which is empowered to make recommendations if it cannot otherwise resolve the dispute.

If either or both parties reject the factfinder's recommendations, the chief executive officer of the jurisdiction involved *must,* and the employee organization *may,* submit recommendations for resolving the dispute to the appropriate legislative body which has the ultimate authority for decision.

A technical impasse exists 60 days before the budget submission date and a factfinding board is required to act 15 days before the budget date. One difficulty is that the law presumes definite budget dates, which may not, in fact, exist.

This brief outline of the impasse procedures of the law indicates that, although there are certain problems, there is sufficient flexibility. In fact, since there are no limitations on the local impasse procedure route, there are some who think there is too much flexibility. Before tracing our experience under these impasse procedures, two additional points need to be made. The first is that if the parties utilize their own procedures, they pay the bill for any third-party assistance. If PERB provides third-party assistance, the state pays the bill.

The second and more important point is the concept of compulsory third-party assistance. Thus, PERB is mandated to do all that it can do to resolve disputes regardless of whether or not the parties are operating under their own or under statutory procedures.

THE FIRST YEAR'S EXPERIENCE

Statistics are often boring at best, but a brief, factual impasse record of our first year is necessary. In the first year, PERB has rendered assistance in some 360 disputes, of which 296 have been settled. Most of these settlements involved schools—80 per cent, in fact. About half were settled through mediation. The other half involved factfinding, which either produced a settlement or served as a basis for settlement.

Forty-five per cent of the factfinding reports were accepted. Another 22 per cent were settled during the factfinding process, but without the issuance of a factfinding report. Factfinding reports were not fully accepted in the remaining 33 per cent of the cases.

In about 40 per cent of those cases in which the factfinding report was not accepted in full, it was modified by the public employer and apparently then accepted by the employee organization. Third-party intervention was required in two-thirds of the instances where substantial additional negotiations took place.

Of particular interest is what this record shows with regard to mediation and factfinding. To summarize our experience in the first year involving some 124 factfinding boards, I would draw the following conclusions.

1. There was *not* an over-reliance on the factfinding process since nearly half of the impasses reaching our board were settled through mediation. 2. Factfinding reports produced the actual settlement or provided the basis for a negotiated settlement. 3. Factfinding did *not* result—as many had anticipated—in an undue polarization of the positions of the parties. 4. The system utilized by our board of hiring per diem mediators and factfinders from a panel established by the board seems to be an effective one. 5. In all but eight of the 125 boards, we have utilized one-member factfinding boards. In the eight, we utilized three-member boards. Our

general conclusion is that except for the most complex cases one-member boards operate more efficiently, expeditiously, and economically.

To complete the picture, it should be pointed out that PERB intervention was required in only from 15 to 20 per cent of the negotiations. In other words, at least 80 per cent of negotiations in the first year were resolved without third-party assistance.

So much for the impasse record of the first year. If we had been told that we could have gotten through the year with so little difficulty, I am not sure that I would have believed it.

INGREDIENTS OF SUCCESS

The ingredients responsible for the comparative success of the past year include the following. 1. *Procedures.* The impasse procedures of the law proved to be both flexible and, indeed, workable. 2. *Timing and Costs.* It proved possible to get third-party assistance efforts underway within twenty-four hours after receipt of such a request. 3. *Attitudes of the Parties.* The parties, although handicapped in many instances by lack of experience, negotiated in good faith.

1. *The Procedures.* There were many who felt that Taylor Law impasse procedures were too rigid to be workable. Many of these contentions centered around criticism of factfinding, particularly the provision for making recommendations available to the parties and to the public simultaneously. These critics overlooked the option which permits the parties to develop their own procedures. This option basically makes the law equally applicable to those situations in which the parties have a long negotiating history and to those in which there is little, if any, such experience.

This is not to say that the present impasse procedures represent perfection. For example, the law does not clearly resolve the question of finality. It was the clear intention of the Taylor Report that the appropriate legislative body would resolve the dispute if all other steps failed. It was presumed that negotiations would be between an executive—city manager, chief school officer, etc.—and the employee organization, and that the monetary aspects of the agreement would be effectuated through budget recommendations to the legislative body.

However, in many types of local government in New York

State there is no executive. In other instances, members of the legislative body have actually done the negotiating. For these reasons, it is not clear what happens when a factfinding report is rejected. Additional negotiations are the inevitable result, but the process has to end somewhere.

So far, this has not proved to be an insurmountable problem. Employee organizations are obviously not enamored by the lack of finality. On the other hand, there are obvious constitutional and legal problems in the imposition of third-party determinations upon legislatures, whether state or local.

2. *Timing and Costs.* The second, ingredient is found in the fact. that we were able to respond to requests for assistance promptly—normally within twenty-four hours. To accomplish this, PERB maintains a small staff of mediators and maintains a panel of nearly 200 per diem mediators and factfinders. Factfinding is done exclusively by panel members. We do not believe that it is sound public policy for our staff to act as factfinders.

In short, we were able to have a neutral into the dispute involving the full panoply of PERB while pressures were high. From what has already been said, it should be clear that we paid the bill. Also, it should be clear that we could not have moved as expeditiously as we did if we had consulted the parties as to who the mediator or the factfinder should be. We did so consult in a few instances, but in most we did not—we simply could not afford the luxury of time-consuming administrative procedures. Most of the requests for assistance came relatively near budget deadlines so that time was of the essence. This is particularly true where negotiations were conducted under local impasse procedures and we were not called upon to put out the fire until the emergency was acute—perhaps as little as twenty-four to forty-eight hours before the budget deadline.

I would recommend to other states contemplating public employment legislation that they take every step possible to insure that mediation and factfinding efforts are financed adequately. Only then can expeditious service be rendered. Our mediation and factfinding efforts have cost the state of New York approximately $150,000 in the first six months of this fiscal year. Our per diem factfinders are paid at the rate of $100 per day. Mediation efforts have averaged $375; single-member factfinding boards,

$650; and the eight three-member factfinding boards have averaged $3,050. One three-man factfinding board in the case of the New York State Triborough Bridge and Tunnel Authority cost the state about $7,000. These costs are nominal compared to the costs and disruptions of even short-duration work stoppages.

One of the more important lessons to be learned from our experience is that passage of the Taylor Law, in and of itself, would not have solved many problems. Nor would the maintenance of a panel and routine referral of names to the parties have accomplished much. The availability of an active, aggressive referee is a necessary ingredient.

3. *Attitudes of the Parties.* Even more important, however, is the willingness of the parties to stay off a collision course. I have already indicated that, although the large number of impasses in which we rendered assistance severely strained our resources, we were only involved in from 15 per cent to 20 per cent of the actual number of negotiations. Given the inexperience of the parties, the necessity to develop contracts for the first time, and the natural and understandable built-in resistance to change, it is surprising that 80 per cent or more did not require assistance.

SOME OF THE PROBLEMS

Now, I would like to cite a few of the problems which have been encountered in the first year. The parties were, of course, inexperienced. This contributed to both procedural and tactical errors. The following are some of the more common problems which we encountered.

In some situations, the parties placed undue emphasis or spent an undue amount of time quibbling over *negotiating procedures:* such items as when and where to meet, who should chair meetings, and similar matters. In other situations, one or both parties attempted to dictate who could represent the other. The introduction of these peripheral issues did not expedite the negotiating process and delayed getting to substantive issues.

Tactical errors. were common. The parties often forgot or never knew the definition of "negotiation." Employee demands were often couched in "take it or leave it" terms. Employers or their representatives sometimes placed an offer on the table which left no room for maneuvering. In some situations, neither party was initially prepared to accept the "give and take" essential to the negotiating process.

Another problem was simply lack of preparation on the part of one or both parties. It was not uncommon for the parties to have proceeded for days and weeks without really defining the issues or costing out their economic proposals. Sometimes this was not done until a mediator or a factfinder arrived on the scene. Lack of preparation and the failure to develop defined positions were basic difficulties in many situations in which PERB intervention was required.

In some situations there was such a long delay in drawing up contractual terms that the parties literally forgot what they agreed to. It is reasonable to expect that time will be required to reduce agreed-upon terms to contractual language, but to require several months for this is, to say the least, totally unreasonable. In school situations particularly, the composition of the school board, the administration, or the employee organization may change.

One of the basic problems encountered in school negotiations was the direct involvement of school boards in negotiations. I think the boards which did so made a fundamental mistake.

Under the Taylor Law, a school board is the legislative body, and the school superintendent, by whatever title, is the chief administrative officer. From an employee organization's point of view, it should not make any difference who negotiates for a public employer as long as the representative has *authority* to negotiate. Thus, an employer should indicate to its negotiator what franchise he has, and the franchise should be broad enough so that he does not have to check in every few minutes.

There is another basic reason why school board members should not involve themselves in the negotiating process. As the legislative body, a school board has the final authority on whether to accept or reject a proposal for settlement. In one situation, *three members of a school board* negotiated a settlement. Then these three joined the other four members of the board to reject the agreement. Needless to say, a strike was narrowly averted in this situation.

The Taylor Law establishes the various responsibilities of

the chief administrative officer and the legislative body. There must be adherence to these responsibilities to avoid short-circuiting the law's impasse procedures.

These are only a few of the more obvious problems.

WHAT ABOUT THE STRIKES?

We have had nine strikes during the first year from September 1, 1967 to August 31, 1968. Two—the New York City teachers' strike of last year and the sanitation strike in February—were well advertised. However, the impasse procedures of PERB were not utilized in either of these situations. This is not to say that our board would have done any better, but simply that we were not involved.

Outside of New York City there were seven stoppages. Three of these involved teachers. In the four others—a town public works department, a county water district, a town police department, and a small group of state mental hygiene employees—there were work stoppages for a day or less with a total of 1,450 employees involved. PERB's impasse procedures had been used in the three teachers' strikes, but not in the others.

Some people have come to the conclusion that if there are any strikes by public employees the Taylor Law is a failure. Others contend that a statute requiring compulsory arbitration would be a panacea. Compulsory arbitration has not necessarily prevented strikes when tried in other countries, such as New Zealand. I am convinced that no law, in and of itself, is an absolute guarantee against strikes. When the blood between parties becomes so bad that employees are willing to engage in civil disobedience—even willing to be fined or to go to jail—strikes may occur. Indeed, many knowledgeable observers predicted that the encouragement of organization under the Taylor Law would increase strikes regardless of the effectiveness of the dispute settlement procedures and no-strike provisions of the statute.

This has happened in some other states. Even without the stimulation of statutes encouraging organizational and representational rights, strikes by public employees are on the rise throughout the country. In this first year of New York's law, approximately 2,000 agreements of various types have been negotiated in the public sector and only nine strikes have occurred.

The Taylor Committee did not believe that penalties in themselves are a guarantee against strikes. The basic premise of the law is to provide public employees with fair and impartial treatment of the determination of their working conditions, and that fair treatment, coupled with reasonable deterrents on all parties, will minimize the number of illegal work stoppages.

THE CONCEPT OF PERB

The concept of one overall board responsible for the administration of a total labor relations program in the public sector is unique. In addition to its responsibilities on the impasse side, the board is responsible for the statewide administration of the law, for establishing policy, for deciding representation questions, for making certain penalty determinations if there is a strike, and for providing data and undertaking research.

Our experience to date indicates that these diverse functions, normally assigned to different agencies, can be effectively administered by one agency.

In summary, two principal conclusions can be drawn from our impasse experience. The first is that undue emphasis can be placed upon the development of procedures. While a sound law and appropriate impasse procedures are important, in themselves they will not solve many problems. The second is that there must be good faith and constructive relationships between the parties, and an ability and willingness for neutrals to intervene with all possible speed when impasses develop. Such a program, of course, costs money, but these costs are relatively minor when compared to the alternatives.

We do not contend that the Taylor Law is without its shortcomings. No legislation devised by man has reached perfection. Indeed, I submit that it will never be so. Even after more than thirty years of National Labor Relations Board experience in the private sector, no one contends that perfection has been achieved. I do believe, however, that the Taylor Law concepts, and particularly the impasse procedures, are viable, and that they offer a positive, constructive, and new opportunity to one of the most critical segments of our work force—our public employees.

THE FEDERAL INVOLVEMENT
by Robert E. Walsh

Collective bargaining for state and city employees is regulated either by state law or city ordinance, and as of early 1969, no Federal law obtains in this area. However, there are signs of increased Federal involvement with public employees of the state and city as a result of action taken by Congress in 1966.

In 1938, Congress passed the Fair Labor Standards Act, which established minimum wages, maximum hours, and overtime pay for specified employees as well as child labor standards. Through the years the number of people covered by this act has been enlarged and in amendments passed in 1966 Congress extended coverage of the law to an additional eight million workers, mostly in schools and hospitals. Under this law the Federal government was able to set minimum wages and maximum hours for a substantial number of employees of cities and states.

Maryland, along with twenty-seven other states and one school district, were parties to a suit brought against the U.S. Secretary of Labor (*Maryland* v. *Wirtz*) which challenged the constitutionality of this Federal involvement with state and city employees. In an opinion written by Justice John M. Harlan, the Supreme Court held that the 1966 amendments were constitutional and that public schools and hospitals are sufficiently involved in interstate commerce to warrant Federal regulation.

In his opinion Justice Harlan said,

> It is clear that labor conditions in schools and hospitals can affect commerce. The facts stipulated in this case indicate that such institutions are major users of goods imported from other states. For example:
>
> > In the current fiscal year an estimated $38.3 billion will be spent by State and local public educational institutions in the United States. In the fiscal year 1965, these same authorities spent $3.9 billion operating public hospitals.
> >
> > For Maryland, which was stipulated to be typical of the plaintiff States, 87% of the $8 million spent for sup-

plies and equipment by its public school system during the fiscal year 1965 represented direct interstate purchases. Over 55% of the $576,000 spent for drugs, X-ray supplies and equipment and hospital beds by the University of Maryland Hospital and seven other State hospitals were out-of-state purchases!

Similar figures were supplied for other states. Strikes and work stoppages involving employees of schools and hospitals, events which unfortunately are not infrequent, obviously interrupt and burden this flow of goods across state lines. It is therefore clear that a "rational basis" exists for congressional action prescribing minimum labor standards for schools and hospitals, as for other importing enterprises.

In another section of his opinion Justice Harlan said, "It is clear that the federal government, when acting within a delegated power (the power to regulate commerce) may override countervailing state interests whether these be described as 'governmental' or 'proprietary' in character."

Justices William O. Douglas and Potter Stewart dissented from the opinion. In his dissent Justice Douglas said,

> The Court's opinion skillfully brings employees of state-owned enterprises within the reach of the Commerce Clause; and as an exercise in semantics it is unexceptionable if congressional federalism is the standard. But what is done here is nonetheless such a serious invasion of state sovereignty protected by the Tenth Amendment that it is in my view not consistent with our constitutional federalism.

Federal regulation of public employees under the Fair Labor Standards Act next raises the question of whether or not there is a possibility that the next move may not be to extend coverage of the National Labor Relations Act to public employees and bring them under the umbrella of the National Labor Relations Board.

OTHER DECISIONS

In March 1969, the *Labor Law Journal* reported two recent decisions of U.S. courts that also carry the next effect of extending considerable Federal protection to public employees, state laws notwithstanding. Two U.S. Courts of Appeals recently ruled that public employees have a constitutional right to join a union; it also held that if they are dismissed from their employment because they join a union they can bring action for damages, in a Federal district court, against the public official responsible for their discharge.

The *Labor Law Journal* article said,

> The First Amendment to the United States Constitution protects the right of the people to assemble peacefully. The Fourteenth Amendment makes the First Amendment applicable to the states. And the Civil Rights Act of 1871 states that every person who, under color of any statute, ordinance or regulation of any state causes any citizen to be deprived of any rights, privileges or immunities secured by the Constitution shall be liable to the party injured.
>
> Putting all of these together, the U.S. Courts of Appeals in St. Louis and Chicago say that employees have a constitutional right to join a labor union and that, if public employees lose their jobs because they have joined a union, they can sue under the 1871 law.
>
> The importance of these rulings is magnified by the fact that not all of the states have statutes protecting the right of all public employees to join labor groups. . . .
>
> In the St. Louis Circuit Court case two city employees were fired because of their union membership. They sought $5000 in damages and an injunction barring the city Commissioner from further discrimination because of such activity.
>
> The Appeals Court ruled their union membership was protected by the right of association under the First Amendment, basing its conclusion on the rationale employed in a 1945 U.S. Supreme Court decision which held that the right to discuss unionism, pro or con, is a part of free assembly as well as free speech.
>
> Similarly, the Chicago Appeals Court upheld the right of two school teachers to bring suit under the 1871 law for alleged denials of employment because of union

membership. The court's conclusion was that the 1871 law gave teachers a remedy if, as they alleged, they had been denied employment because they exercised their constitutional rights by joining a union.

The journal pointed out that the decisions are important because they mean public employees can obtain remedies for anti-union discrimination by going to Federal courts and bypassing state courts.

However, the decisions do not hold that strikes by public employees are constitutionally protected activity. Also, both decisions say only that public employees' suits can get into court. Whether they will prevail in a trial on the merits is another question. To do that they will have to prove they had in fact been discriminated against because of their union membership.

As a result of these court decisions, increased activity by labor unions to bring about greater Federal involvement in the public employee field can be anticipated. The following news release from the National Education Association indicates this teacher organization is also moving in the same direction.

NEA–SPONSORED BILL AIMS AT REDUCING STRIKES BY REQUIRING TEACHER-SCHOOL BOARD NEGOTIATION

The National Education Association sent the following news release to press, radio, and television on April 7, 1969. It outlines an NEA–sponsored bill submitted to Congress that hopes to reduce strikes by requiring negotiations between teachers and school boards.

WASHINGTON, D.C., April 7—A Federal bill requiring negotiation between school boards and organizations representing public school teachers will be introduced in Congress soon, the National Education Association announced today.

Although the bill would legalize teacher strikes under certain circumstances, it is designed to reduce the incidence of such strikes by providing alternative means of resolving teacher-school board disputes.

If enacted, the legislation would represent the first full-scale effort by the Federal Government to regulate employment relationships between state and local governments and their employees.

The bill would directly affect nearly two million teachers and other professional staff and more than one hundred thousand school board members. It would have potential impact on schools enrolling about fifty million students.

Federal regulation of this type is desperately needed, according to Sam M. Lambert, NEA executive secretary.

"Although some states have provided fairly adequate procedures for regulating teacher-school board relations, many have refused to grant teachers even the basic rights that most other employees in the country have had for years," Dr. Lambert declared. The result, he added, is an "almost chaotic diversity among various parts of the country."

The statute, structurally similar to the National Labor Relations Act, would open a wide scope of matters to teacher-school board negotiation. These could include not only teacher salaries and working conditions but also "virtually everything of importance to teachers," Dr. Lambert said. An increasing number of state and local negotiation agreements now cover such areas as class size, teacher load, teacher assignment, recruiting, selection of textbooks, and use of teacher aides.

The bill would legalize teacher strikes only under restricted circumstances. Courts could issue restraining orders or injunctions if the striking teacher organization had jumped the gun and failed to use the law's entire impasse procedure, if the strike posed a "clear and present danger to the public health or safety," or if the striking group was not the official teachers' representative in the particular school system.

Robert H. Chanin, NEA's chief counsel for school board-professional staff relations, asserted that the legislation is designed to reduce—not increase—the incidence of teacher strikes.

"In our experience," Mr. Chanin said,

teachers are not strike-happy. An examination of the relatively few teacher strikes that have occurred, compared to the substantial number of negotiations that have been concluded peacefully throughout the nation, reveals that the strikes usually resulted from refusal of the school boards to consider reasonable solutions to the disputes.

When an obstinate school board knows that its position will be sustained by an injunction, there is little motivation for it to try to negotiate a compromise settlement. By giving that small minority of school boards a feeling of uncertainty as to whether an injunction would be issued, the proposed bill would encourage peaceful settlement of disagreements.

The bill provides that the organization representing the majority of the professional employees in a school system be designated as exclusive representative of all such employees in negotiating with the school board.

One important advantage of a Federal statute, Mr. Chanin pointed out, is that it would make possible the establishment of national legal precedents in the negotiation field. Presently, there is costly and time-consuming case-by-case testing of the same basic issues in various states throughout the country.

Administration of the law would be by a five-member Professional Employee Relations Commission in the U.S. Department of Health, Education, and Welfare. The members, appointed by the President with Senate approval, would be paid $27,000 a year for the full-time positions, with the chairman receiving an additional $1,500. Headquarters would be in Washington, D.C., but regional offices would also be established to administer the act on a day-to-day basis.

States having negotiation statutes essentially like the Federal one could operate under their own law, while states with laws that did not meet Federal standards could either strengthen them or come directly under the Federal act. More than 15 states have some type of negotiation law—although some are very weak—and nearly as many others are developing bills or have ones pending.

The starting point in implementing the Federal legislation on the local level would be a teacher organization's request for official school board recognition as exclusive representative for negotiation. However, a competing organization could intervene by presenting a verified membership list containing at least 30 per cent of the professional employees in the negotiating unit. In cases of doubt as to the teachers' organizational preference, a secret ballot election would be held to determine the representative.

In general, the law would cover public school professional staff at the elementary, secondary, and higher education levels, but would specifically exclude superintendents and assistant superintendents—representatives of management in the day-to-day operation of the schools. Whether such persons as guidance counselors, librarians, psychologists, and social workers, as well as principals, vice principals, and other first-line supervisors, would be included with classroom teachers for negotiation purposes would be determined locally.

It would be unlawful for a school board to impose reprisals or discriminate against teachers for exercising the rights guaranteed by the statute; to refuse to negotiate in good faith with the recognized teacher organization; or to deny that organization a place to meet, access to work areas, the use of bulletin boards and mail boxes, or the right to membership dues deduction.

The teacher organization, on its side, must not attempt to nudge the board into any of these violations and it must negotiate in good faith.

The law provides a two-step process of third-party intervention to resolve negotiation impasse. The first step is mediation. If within 15 days the mediator has failed to work out a mutually acceptable agreement, the parties—or the commission, if the parties cannot agree—can select an arbitrator with power to subpoena testimony and documentary evidence and make recommendations for settlement. The recommendations, which would not be binding upon either party, can be made public 10 days after presentation to the parties if agreement has not been reached.

It would be at this point that a legal teachers' strike could occur. However, a strike would be relatively rare, Mr. Chanin predicted, because in the vast majority of cases the parties would have come to an agreement before reaching this critical stage.

7

SPECIALISTS AT THE BARGAINING TABLE

The management of public personnel and the administration of municipal finance are today highly specialized fields. As men representing unions or independent employee organizations move to the bargaining table, they will usually find themselves facing lawyers representing a municipality, a school board, a publicly owned hospital, or an institution of higher learning. The lawyers will be well versed in labor law and the ways of bargaining, but for the answers to questions raised in bargaining, the lawyers will have to turn to the personnel and financial experts.

In the following five articles, men recognized as leaders in these fields discuss various aspects of personnel management, financial administration, and school board leadership as they apply to collective bargaining for public employees.

AN ADDRESS TO MUNICIPAL
FINANCE OFFICERS
by Louis G. Basso

This article was originally Mr. Basso's "Presidential Address," delivered before the Municipal Finance Officers Association in 1968. Mr. Basso has been the director of budget and finance of Wayne County, Michigan, since 1957. He also holds a law degree in addition to his professional work as an accountant.

COLLECTIVE BARGAINING IN THE PUBLIC SECTOR
At all levels of government from the town hall to the halls of

Reprinted with the permission of the publisher from the August 1968 issue of *Municipal Finance Magazine*.

Congress, public employees are demanding and getting the right to organize freely—to form or to join an association, union, or other labor organization. They are also demanding that the organization of their choice be recognized as the spokesman for all employees in the bargaining unit. Public employees are demanding that their governmental unit, through its designated representatives, engage with them in meaningful negotiations on wages, working conditions, fringe benefits, certain policy areas, and a variety of other topics.

Militant labor leaders also demand that collective bargaining be based openly on the right to strike rather than on a system of arbitration or conciliation for the settlement of disputed provisions and also the right to exclusive representation and the union shop. In recent years, the militancy of employee groups and unions has induced many state legislatures to enact labor relations laws which authorized the bargaining process in all areas and all levels of government.

Employment and employee organizing activity in local and state governments are growing rapidly. Figures from the U.S. Department of Labor show that as of October 1966, there were 11.5 million civilian government employees in Federal, state, and local governments as against 7.5 million in 1956, or an increase of fifty-three per cent. State and local government is expanding the most rapidly, having doubled since 1950. State and municipal employees, in October 1966, numbered 8.6 million and are expected to exceed 14.5 million by 1969. Union membership in government is likewise expanding, having increased by 540,000 to 1.4 million since 1956. Walter Reuther told delegates to the convention of AFL–CIO's Industrial Union Department, "We can organize three million teachers and government workers in the next three years."

The American Federation of State, County and Municipal Employees represents the largest number of organized workers directly employed in state and local government. In view of this tremendous growth, it is predicted that an organization of government workers in time will be one of the biggest unions, if not the biggest, in the nation.

The requirement, by law, of highly structured competitive bargaining has created a new and very difficult dimension in the administration of public affairs by public officials. Our system of representative government is built on the doctrine of separation of powers between the legislative, executive, and judicial branches. Each of these branches has reasonably well-defined areas of responsibility and authority.

Implicit is the concept that government is based on law and operates through the administration of laws, and policies developed within those laws, to serve the public interest. Since there is no organized system of principles, laws, and precedents in governmental bargaining, the system of collective bargaining that has developed in industry is being transferred to government and is having a number of effects:

1. Labor organizations more frequently than not attempt to insist that only one agent or agency negotiate and bargain for government on all matters, regardless of where the authority for decision on such matters rests under the law.

2. The unions and some of the negotiators for government insist on negotiations being handled behind closed doors rather than in a "fish bowl" situation, which is essential if the public is to be informed and to understand what is going on in government.

3. The unions more frequently than not are primarily concerned with the protection of the union, the expansion of its membership, and with commitments which will insure union security.

4. Many of the unions are attempting to negotiate on all phases, not only of personnel administration, but of operations. Attempts are regularly made, often successfully, to have provisions in contracts which place rigid controls on the assignment of personnel not only to work shifts and work locations, but also on the intrinsic nature of the duties. Successful attempts are frequently made to insure that promotions are based largely on seniority.

5. The broad areas on which unions seek to negotiate cover so many items that a considerable amount of time is required to discuss and/or negotiate on almost all personnel matters.

6. All knowledgeable personnel persons agree that in view of the large number of employees in almost any governmental organization, it is desirable to have a grievance procedure. Explicit in our system of government is the individual citizen's right of petition or redress against acts of his government. Explicit in most civil service laws are provisions which make it possible for employees

to appeal actions or decisions which adversely affect the welfare of the employee. With the advent of highly structured union relationships, one of the first items that is insisted upon by the unions is a formalized grievance procedure from three to five steps, including review by the first-line supervisor, division head, department head or his representative, some central agency, or some other form of review of the alleged grievance.

In large governmental organizations, as most of the statutes have been written, there tends to be a number of unions. Where there are several unions, each tries hard to demonstrate its power and relative desirability as an employee organization. In such situations there is a tendency for almost every act of a supervisor, public administrator, or manager to be grieved against. The result is that almost every supervisory employee at all levels, together with any departmental personnel officer or central personnel agency, is required to expend an unbelievable amount of time on trivia in many instances. However, one result is that each supervisor will tend to observe rules, regulations, and contract provisions more carefully. This is partly good, but it is partly bad in that the supervisor, in order to avoid the harassment of participating in an inordinate number of grievance conferences or procedures, may tend to ignore his responsibilities for maintaining positive discipline to insure that required services will be performed.

7. There has been a tendency to ignore the budget calendar, and even to enter into the area of budgetary decisions. The result, in effect, is that the budget is never closed. How, under these circumstances, can the elected representatives of the people be accountable to the public? If literally followed, such actions would make it impossible to determine a tax rate, to exercise meaningful authority over appropriations, or to control the quality and quantity of public service.

8. Decisions have been made which in effect mean that contracts supersede other statutory or charter provisions, ordinances, and rules and regulations of legally constituted rule making authorities, the impact of which tends to be the substitution of government by contract for government by law.

There is obviously room for union organization and representation of public employees. However, the late President John F. Kennedy's task force, which included such knowledgeable persons as Arthur Goldberg, Robert McNamara, Theodore Sorensen, Daniel Moynihan, and Ida Klaus, noted its conviction that there need be no conflict between a system of public employee representation, management relations, and the merit system, but the latter should remain the essential personnel policy of the Federal Government. The task force stated in its report to President Kennedy that

> the principle of entrance into the career service on the basis of open competition, selection on merit and fitness, and advancement on the same bases, together with the full range of principles and practices that make up the civil service, should govern the essential character of each individual's employment. Collective dealing cannot vary these principles. It must operate within their framework.

State statutes, particularly those of Michigan, tend to ignore such principles almost completely.

There can be no doubt that the growing strength of unionism among state and municipal employees across the nation can have sweeping implications in partisan political activity, and raises the possibility of serious limitation of government authority and the undermining of the merit system.

THE CHANGES IN THE SOCIO-ECONOMIC STATUS OF THE CENTRAL CITY, AND ITS PROBLEMS

The recent riots in the cities across our nation have cogently dramatized the deep-rooted and abiding ills which have contributed to what is referred to by many as the "urban crisis." While admittedly the tangible results of physical devastation are most apparent in the impacted ghetto areas of our populous urban centers, all Americans living in communities large and small—both rural and urban in character—are involved. According to Dr. Charles J. Hitch, the new president of the University of California, in his recent announcement to gear the resources of that institution to better focus on urban problems, "It is a moral, economic, and a racial crisis. It is also an educational crisis." Indeed, we are confronted with a crisis of many dimensions, including the financial. The exigencies of this crucial moment in our history demand that we act now in both a creative and courageous manner to effect, on a broad and massive scale, more efficacious solutions to these problems.

I would like to share with you some thoughts regarding the cities and their relationship to our present urban condition. At the same time, I would like to underscore the fact that the resultant social conflict which we are witnessing has world dimensions. This is evident to all.

Cities throughout history have functioned as self-contained socio-economic and political units. The cities served as the economic centers for the vast, sparsely populated surrounding countryside areas which relied on them for their lifeblood.

Today, instead, we witness a decline in the economic, social, and political significance of the city, which is likely to continue, especially with the recent growth of the metropolitan and regional area development concepts. Unless the cities are rebuilt and revitalized in a greatly accelerated manner, they will become but secondary, although complementary, governmental units in relation to the sprawling suburbs and centers of growth.

The proliferation of political jurisdictions is a major constraint to the solution of urban problems. The prospects are appalling when we consider that there are 18,000 municipalities, over 3,000 counties, over 17,000 townships, and almost 25,000 school districts in this nation of fifty states. And it becomes more amazing when you consider that today, 70 per cent of our people live on one per cent of the land, 30 per cent on all the rest. Dr. Jerome P. Pickard, author of *Dimensions of Metropolitanism,* states that "by the year 2,000, eighty-five per cent of the nation's population will live in urban areas of the United States."

What are some of the factors underlying the many complex problems that afflict the cities?

The displacement of the central city as the hub or nucleus of all economic and social activities is not entirely a recent phenomenon; only the extent and proportion of this displacement has accelerated in recent times. In fact, the exodus to the suburbs can be traced back to the 1920s, when the interurban trains provided for movement of both passengers and freight between urban centers. Today the trend continues, except that our network of expressways has replaced the interurban trains; and added impetus has been supplied by the automobile, which makes people more mobile and removes restrictions on their choice of home locations.

In the early 1950s, the advent of large suburban shopping centers gave further momentum to the decline of the cities as many business offices, service-type enterprises, and professional people followed the movement of population away from the core city. The central city, in other words, lost its franchise as the more or less exclusive purveyor of essential goods and services. However, the central city's existing facilities are increasingly geared to serving ever-expanding geographic areas.

With the growth of population, industry, and commercial activities, causing congestion, noise, and other deterrents, the upper-income people have fled the cities, followed by the middle-income families; and in their footsteps came the poor people from rural America, most of whom have been displaced from the countryside by the very agricultural technology that has produced the abundance of food and fiber to meet the needs of this country and of many foreign countries. In the main, the immigrants have been ill equipped to adjust to the urban environment, and this has led to many problems, such as social frustrations, unemployment, poverty, and slums, which aid and abet crime, disease, and ignorance. In addition, there are the problems of environmental health, recreation, education, mass transit, housing, and job opportunities.

These problems have become increasingly worse with the passage of years, since local governments in general made little effort to grapple with them.

Enormous financial resources, far beyond local governments' fiscal capacity, are needed to solve the problems facing the cities. According to the TEMPO (General Electric Company's center for advanced studies) study made for the National League of Cities, the total revenue gap for the 1966–1975 period will be 262 billion dollars. The total revenue gap is the difference between municipality revenue needs and actual revenues. Since local government cannot fill this gap, it is suggested that states be required to contribute, in the form of grants, 49 billion dollars; the Federal Government 125 billion dollars; that local government bonded debt be increased by 63 billion dollars; and nontax user fees and charges increased by 25 billion dollars. One billion dollars of Federal funds would be allocated to the municipalities the first year, rising during the next nine years, until in the tenth year the Federal grants would total 26 billion dollars. The study also recommends that existing Federal grant-in-aid programs to cities be continued and accelerated and that all Federal funds intended to aid localities be routed to the cities in accordance with their relative fiscal needs and capacities. This is in direct opposition to the National Governors' Conference, which favors state control.

It is estimated that present Federal tax rates will yield a total of 365 billion dollars from 1966 through 1975, provided that the gross national product increases at a rate of four per cent per year during the same period.

With few notable exceptions, state governments' recognition of the cities' problems has been quite belated, and little has been done. In fact, both the central cities and the states have been remiss in failing to recognize each other's problems. This failure of communication has been aggravated by the attitude of provincialism in the suburbs, and by the philosophies of the traditionally rural-dominated state legislatures. It is doubtful whether the Congress will accede to the requests of the big cities for vast sums of money to finance their rehabilitation programs. The *U.S. News and World Report* of May 13, 1968, reports that "In sixty-one cities of 200,000 or more population live 43 million people. Outside these concentrated areas, in suburbs, smaller cities, small towns, and rural areas, live 156.5 million people—nearly four times as many—with voters in about the same ratio."

The assistance so far rendered by the Federal Government has been primarily in the area of planning rather than in the construction of urgently needed low-income housing, capital improvements, and supporting facilities. Federally assisted planning programs have tended to deal with hospitals, mass transit, recreation, open lands, and public works (e.g., sewerage treatment plants). In the field of housing, efforts are usually directed in one of two channels: (1) to completely clear a blighted area and rebuild; (2) to attempt to preserve an existing community.

The central city can regain its strong economic position by concentrating on those services for which it is best suited, and by welcoming within its borders those people who work in those service occupations. It is impossible to have a metropolitan area without the city because of the key services it provides in the areas of government, banking, and selective or comparative retail shopping.

Each metropolitan area has its own complex of magnets that makes the central city what it is and gives it its unique flavor: New York, Chicago, San Francisco, and New Orleans, for example, each has its own personality and clusters of commercial enterprises.

Core banking services, governmental, and other specialized services can, by their very nature, be best rendered in the physical setting of the city. Further, entertainment and cultural activities will probably continue to be city-oriented. It should also be noted that the downtown stores have a "captive" market in the persons whose employment is downtown and who find it convenient to shop during their lunch hours and in the evening.

The future of the American city lies, perhaps, in the development of a balanced partnership between the central city and the suburbs, with the result that the two will rise together. Further, cities will make a "comeback" faster if an attempt is made to promote development along certain rather specific lines of economic and cultural services on a regional basis. Private enterprise, labor, and government must work together to help eliminate such problems as urban sprawl, the uneconomic use of existing facilities, the movement of industry to the suburbs in search of open space and a more favorable tax climate; and to provide the water, sewer, and highway facilities that are the framework within which urban development takes place. Also, not to be forgotten are the religious and civic organizations of our country.

What we must strive for in our endeavors is a "complete humanism"—the fully rounded development of the whole man and all men.

CROSSCURRENTS IN PUBLIC EMPLOYEE BARGAINING
by Eugene F. Berrodin

This article originally appeared in Public Personnel Review *in October 1968. Mr. Berrodin is manager of the Personnel and Services Division of the Michigan Municipal League. He has been engaged in public per-*

*sonnel administration for the past eighteen years, since
1960 as a consultant to units of local government. He
also serves as an instructor in personnel administration
for the International City Managers' Association.*

How shall we interpret the increased number and intensity of
public employee strikes? It is clear that public employer-employee
relations have undergone significant changes in the past decade.
These changes include the increased unionization and aggressive-
ness of public employees, new laws regulating public employee
bargaining, the trend toward more centralized or "integrated" public management and rejection of civil service systems, and efforts
to ease the restrictions on political activities of public employees.

The milieu out of which public employee militancy has grown
is a complex of economic, political, and social changes which have
taken place in varying degrees throughout society. While the
changes are rather easily identified, the reasons for them are more
subtle and complex. For example, in the United States today, one
in every six workers is employed by the government. Three-fourths
of this total, 7.7 million, are state and local employees. This is an
increase of 4.7 million over the past ten years.

In terms of social change, the general dissatisfaction of public
employees, particularly in large organizations, may be viewed as a
result of the bureaucratization resulting from the increased scale of
organizations. Other societal pressures, such as the growing density
and urbanization of the population, a sense of frustration with
large public and private institutions which are viewed as unrespon-
sive, and rapidly rising levels of aspiration, also contribute to the
current sense of restlessness. Urban life creates conflict. People are
close physically but remote socially. Crime rates and other measures of social disorganization increase with the growth in urbanization.

Frank Zeidler, former mayor of Milwaukee, has observed:

> Something in the public service has caused public
> employees to view the local government as an exploiting
> employer which must be fought even as a private employer.
> This attitude is in contrast with the conditions of thirty
> years ago when people struggled to get local public jobs
> under any conditions. It may be that working in a highly

structured and closely regulated bureaucracy as exists in many governments tends to stifle the spirit of many employees and creates in them a psychological dissatisfaction. The employee may feel that his talents, his instincts for workmanship, and his chances for advancement are stifled and he cannot advance under the civil service competition. Hence, the employer becomes a kind of exploiting enemy. . . .—"Remarks on Labor Law," Wayne State University, December 15, 1965.

One characteristic of public employee unions is their propensity to use political power to accomplish their objectives. This tendency is probably a direct result of the political environment which surrounds public employment. Organized public employees constitute potential voting blocks and politicians do not ignore them. Employee unions are frequently well informed on bond issues, charter referenda, and other local issues. With light voter turnouts in many local elections, public employees in cooperation with central labor councils may exercise decisive power.

Public employee union spokesmen have frequently declared that politics should be eliminated as a condition of public employment. However, organized public employees may be able to "eat their political cake and have it, too" through union-political activism combined with the job security created by civil service systems and collective bargaining contracts.

Much of the legislative support for public employee bargaining has been derived from the association of public employee unions with private employee unions. Industrial unions have acquired considerable influence with many state legislatures through their endorsement of candidates for public office. When elected, these candidates tend to be more responsive to demands for increasing the power of organized public employees through collective bargaining.

In recent years, the labor movement has exerted great effort in organizing public employees and in promoting legislation to establish the industrial style of collective bargaining in government. Stimulating this quest for new members is the fact that total union membership in the United States has been declining as a proportion of the total work force. Union membership declined from 33.7

per cent in 1953 to 28 per cent in 1966, expressed as a percentage of nonagricultural employment. This decline reflects a change in the composition of the American labor force, which now contains more white-collar than blue-collar workers.

The growing militancy of public employees requires that local legislative bodies, school boards, and public officials reexamine their views on the equity of their employment policies and on their procedures for employee negotiation and communication.

The older generation of public employees, many of whom were rather inactive and submissive, are being replaced in many instances by a new breed of activists who insist on their substantial involvement in the negotiation of wages, hours, and working conditions.

SOLUTIONS NEEDED

Dr. Harlan Hatcher, president emeritus of the University of Michigan, said in a lecture before the California State Bar (September 22, 1966):

> Now public employees and public service professions are turning to the labor union formula for relief from the tightening squeeze of a booming inflationary economy and lack of a satisfying identity within the society. It poses a question: Can we accept this as the ultimate achievement of American freedom and the pattern or model for its future growth? Or, like dueling in the eighteenth century, is this a primitivism we can outgrow? . . . Can't we find a better way, in a different context, to solve difficult professional questions that must be reasoned and analyzed and decided, but not "bargained" in this ritualistic sense?

The concept of "bargaining in good faith" as developed in modern industrial labor relations was, and is, quite persuasive as an ideal. However, even in the private sector, there are increasing demands that this concept be reexamined. "Bargain" is a delicate word. It means to negotiate, transact business; an advantageous mutual agreement. However, this connotation may stultify to "haggle," to "dispute," or to "wrangle." "Wrangle" suggests an angry dispute or noisy quarrel. What began as "bargaining in good faith" too often results in a tribal ritualism, irrational around-the-clock sessions to meet an artificial deadline, economic warfare, or a "public be damned" attitude.

The conduct of collective negotiations is in part a matter of gamesmanship. The game is played under elaborate, often unwritten rules and conducted with strong behavioral expectations. By definition, a game implies some degree of nonsense activity, or at the least, nonproductive activity. No one would argue that the outcome of negotiations is not serious. It is. But gamesmanship appears in the process.

A bargaining offer made at an inopportune time or place, or by the wrong person, may result in an impasse, whereas the same offer under other circumstances may be acceptable. Circumstances, such as timing, are critical in the bargaining process.

There may be limits upon the appropriateness of the bargaining process itself. For example, the *Report of the President's Commission on Technology and the American Economy* (February 1966) states:

> Basic issues such as the adjustment to technological change cannot be resolved by a small team of negotiators working themselves into a state of physical and mental exhaustion for a few months every two or three years. . . . These issues must be dealt with patiently, carefully, and, above all, continuously until satisfactory solutions emerge.

Alternative decision-making processes include the following:
1. The analytic-rational model: identified with the scientific method
2. Competition: rivalry, mediated by a third party—a commercial system.
3. Democratic process: rule of the majority with guarantees of minority rights—a political system.
4. Unilateralism: as the President says, "The buck stops here."
5. Bargaining: involves direct interaction of two or more parties—a process often used when goals are not shared.

SOLUTIONS ADVOCATED

A report of the American Bar Association, Committee on Labor Relations of Government Employees (1955) stated:

> Government which denies to its employees the right to strike against the people . . . owes to its public serv-

ants an obligation to provide working conditions and
standards which would make unnecessary and also unwarranted any need for such employees to resort to stoppage
of public business. . . .

The importance of full and equitable grievance procedures is
primary. Such procedures have both a remedial and a deterrent
effect.

Public officials and administrators must demonstrate a willingness to deal with individual and group presentations and petitions. These communication and negotiation procedures are vital
not only in handling grievances but in the discussion of general
policy questions. Experience has demonstrated that maladjustments
are far less likely to occur when employees, organized and unorganized, feel that they are able to contribute systematically to the
formulation and improvement of administrative policy and operations.

The Michigan Chapter of the Public Personnel Association in
1967 adopted a position statement on public employee labor relations. This statement indicates:

> The application of merit principles in public employ-
> ment whereby initial selection and advancement are based
> upon qualifications and fitness, is vital to the effective
> operations of government. Alternative systems in which ap-
> pointments are made on the basis of patronage, influence,
> seniority or other factors not related to successful job per-
> formance, have been demonstrated to be not only seri-
> ously defective but a threat to equal opportunity of em-
> ployment. . . .

The report of *President Kennedy's Task Force on Employee
Management Relations in the Federal Service* (1961) states in
part:

> The principle of entrance into the career service on
> the basis of open competition, selection on merit and fit-
> ness, and advancement on the same basis, together with a
> full range of principles and practices that make up the Civil
> Service System govern the essential character of each indi-
> vidual's employment. . . .

To some extent, the development of civil service and merit systems for public employees parallels the growth of industrial labor unions. The purpose of civil service and merit systems is to secure and retain competent and efficient employees in government and to guarantee employees certain rights and protections from discharge and other disciplinary action based upon political or other nonmerit considerations. Civil service and merit systems are quite common in the United States. They are found in the Federal service, in most states, and in the larger cities. Seventy-one per cent of U.S. cities over 10,000 population have a civil service or merit system for some portion of their employees. However, the application of merit principles varies widely as to coverage and adequacy.

Until rather recently, public employee unions have been staunch supporters of civil service systems. However, with the advent of public employee collective bargaining, an adversary relationship has developed; some public employee unions now viewing civil service commissions as an arm of management, rather than as impartial boards.

CRUCIAL DISTINCTIONS

The distinctions between public and private employment are crucial to an understanding of the role of collective bargaining in government. These differences include the following.

1. Governments are established by law to serve public needs and are not profit-oriented. They are charged with the maintenance of law and order, and must administer laws in the public interest.

2. Government is continuous. It does not cease to exist because of excessive labor or other costs or because of management decisions to discontinue operations.

3. Government officials are directly accountable to the public through the election process. Private management is not.

4. Governments have peculiar budget timetables and income limitations which place constraints upon demands for continuous or open-ended bargaining.

5. Public employees now have a number of avenues for resolving labor disputes, short of strikes, including direct appeals to legis-

lative bodies, the electorate, civil service, merit or tenure boards, and state or other mediation and factfinding processes.

In *Mugford* v. *Mayor and Council of Baltimore* (1944) the circuit court stated:

> Public officers do not have the same incentive to oppress the worker; and fair treatment, sought to be coerced by collective bargaining in the field of private employment, is, in the public field, to a large extent, compelled by law. Public officers, therefore, do not have the same freedom of action which private employers enjoy. Their authority is confided to them by law, and that law is limited. . . .

STRIKES

In democratic societies we must rely upon, enhance, assist, and support the joint decisions of elected and appointed officials of government who, for their specific jurisdictions, represent that intangible but vital condition known as the "will of the people."

While the threat or exercise of a strike may perform a useful function in the private sector, public employee strikes prevent the orderly processes of government. Public employee strikes create serious public crises. They subvert the quest for the uniform and equitable treatment of public employees and they generate more heat than light.

The report of the Governor's Advisory Committee in Illinois (1967) states in part:

> It has been suggested that some distinction could be made between critical and noncritical strikes in the public sector and that the strike prohibition be limited to the former. Supporting this proposal was the argument that certain strikes in the public sector may impose greater injury on the public than some strikes of public employees. The Commission is convinced that any attempt to draw a line between the critical and noncritical public strikes would bristle with unmanageable difficulties and would be likely to undermine the strike prohibition in those areas where the consequences of a strike might be intolerable.

Equitable procedures for the peaceful resolution of public employee disputes have been developed. These include mediation, public hearings, civil service or tenure board appeals, and fact-finding, with recommendations made public. Because these alternatives to strike action have been developed in the public service, realistic sanctions against public employee strikes are needed if they are to be deterred. These sanctions may include direct court action followed by fines and penalties (as in the New York Taylor Act), or by the withdrawal of recognition as in the Federal Executive Order and discontinuance of union dues checkoff, or both.

LOOK TO THE FUTURE

As Donald H. Wollett, chairman of the Committee on Law of Government Employee Relations of the American Bar Association, has said:

> Since I am persuaded that the established procedures and practices of private collective bargaining fit very badly in the public sector and can, indeed, do much mischief, I think we need to move very cautiously until we are much surer than I think we are now, that we know what we are doing. . . . The thing of which I am most certain is that the answers which we seek lie, not in the past, but in the future—in the ideas as yet undiscovered, and in experiments not yet undertaken, demanding fresh perspective and new approaches.

The issues of public employee collective bargaining must be dealt with patiently, carefully, and continuously until satisfactory solutions emerge.

FINANCIAL IMPLICATIONS OF EMPLOYEE BARGAINING IN THE PUBLIC SERVICE
by Kenneth O. Warner

This article first appeared in Municipal Finance *in August 1967. Mr. Warner is the executive director of the Public Personnel Association, a post he has held since 1949.*

Reprinted with the permission of the publisher from the August 1967 issue of *Municipal Finance Magazine.*

At the beginning let me make one point perfectly clear: when the municipal finance officer enters the world of collective bargaining, his job takes on new dimensions. Once concerned primarily with facts and figures, the finance man must now equate those facts and figures in terms of the wishes, desires, and demands of organized employees. Inevitably, under collective bargaining the finance man will become more deeply involved in human relations as they affect the service and productivity of people at the work place. This simply means that whether he likes it or not, the finance officer must add a new set of tools to his administrative kit. It means he must also learn to apply somewhat different techniques to his job of financial management.

Indeed, collective bargaining imposes on all public officials new and different duties. In fact, the 1960s may become known as the decade of revolution in public administration. I say "revolution" because application of the bargaining process to public business means that the entire content of public administration must be repackaged. Convincing documentation can be assembled to support the ideas that bargaining demands that all public officials perform different tasks than heretofore and that they conduct themselves in a different manner. We have developed this thesis in our book on *Public Management at the Bargaining Table* (Chicago: Public Personnel Assn., 1967).

This revolution in public administration is not an event that occurred overnight. It came into being gradually. It started in local government of the United States more than a decade ago, when New York City commenced bargaining as the result of an executive order. Gradually, the process expanded until now eight states have comprehensive collective bargaining laws that affect municipal governments. But of even greater significance, in many other states the practice has increased—even without legislative authorization—until now there are literally thousands of agreements between employee groups and various types of government units in all areas and at all levels.

In Canada, municipalities have been governed by provincial labor relations laws which authorized all-out bargaining for more than twenty years. Also in Canada the provinces themselves are experimenting with various arrangements for handling their government labor relations. At the federal level in Canada, Parliament this year enacted a comprehensive labor relations law that goes far beyond the U.S. Executive Order 10988 in applying the bargaining process to employees of the national government. Under certain circumstances, Federal employees are authorized to use the strike weapon, excluding of course, those whose duties are designated as necessary to public safety and security.

These general observations are pertinent to a consideration of how bargaining affects municipal finance for several reasons.

First, finance officers in the United States can profit a great deal by familiarity with the experience of their Canadian colleagues in this field. They have been through the mill and have learned the hard way. They now know some things to do and others to avoid.

Second, laws initially enacted by state legislatures regulated in detail the bargaining process in local government units and omitted state employees, or applied less stringent conditions to them. It is true that the more recent state laws extend bargaining arrangements to state as well as local government employees. But all local government officials must concern themselves with getting the kind of state legislation that assures local units of government sufficient authority and control over their own affairs to discharge their responsibilities to their own constituencies.

Third, bargaining is more likely than not to become the administrative way of life during the next decade. This is a prediction based on an assessment of current trends and recent social and economic developments. My personal belief is that whether through formal legislation or extra-legal developments, the bargaining process will become more common in the public service. Whether governments sign formal contracts with their employees, whether they enact ordinances or simply issue regulations on management-employee agreements on hours, wages and conditions of work—regardless of the form of the arrangement—in essence the process will be carried on bilaterally and not unilaterally as in the past. This means that the public official will make use of the bargaining process whether or not he has clear-cut legal authority.

Now we can direct attention more specifically to the financial implications of public employee bargaining. One impact of bargaining affects the finance officer in a personal way. It involves his attitude toward organized employees, his philosophy of management, and what he must do personally to discharge his newly acquired responsibilities. Another impact of bargaining relates more particularly to how the process affects the professional field of municipal finance.

IMPACT OF BARGAINING ON FINANCE

Let's briefly examine these two implications, looking first at the impact of bargaining on municipal finance—an extremely important aspect of public administration. To check my own thinking on this subject I sought the reactions of a score of finance officers and city managers in the United States and Canada on several points. I alone assume responsibility for what I am about to say, but among those contacted there was a surprising degree of agreement on a number of major points. In outline, here are some of the probable impacts of bargaining on municipal finance.

1. *Impact on the Budget Process.* Bargaining requires attention to gathering financial data, preparation and visual presentation of supporting financial information, and interpretation of public finances to the press, the public, and to employee organizations. Whether these aspects of budgeting differ under bargaining depends on what has been done in the past by a given jurisdiction. The result of applying such practices more assiduously might very well yield plus values for an agency. Bargaining will give finance men an impetus to shore up their budget process, and to be sure it's workable. And one thing is certain: You can expect that well-trained union representatives will carefully scrutinize budgets in their search for funds that can be allocated to wages and benefits.

Bargaining calls for development of a workable timetable for both officials and unions. Several considerations must be dovetailed:

   (a) the time for starting and stopping negotiations;

   (b) the length of the contract period;

   (c) the relation of contract period to fiscal years;

   (d) state legislation governing budget procedures of local governments; and

   (e) state legislation or constitutional arrangements regulating sources of municipal revenue.

Time does not permit elaboration of these points, but one illustration will throw light on them.

For example, unless a contract or agreement is reached before the budget is approved, a government agency faces a dilemma. It must set up a contingency fund to meet expected increases as a result of future bargaining, maintain an open-ended budget, or not make pay adjustments until the next budget period. None of these methods of dealing with the problem is completely satisfactory, although some municipalities have been forced into using contingency or reserve funds as a result of bargaining. As one observer told me, "this destroys much of effective budget projection."

Unquestionably, the budget process will be subjected to strains and stresses as a result of bargaining. In some jurisdictions under statutory bargaining these trends are already apparent. They include: A threat to legal restrictions that control the integrity of appropriations and tax limitations; demand for a municipal budget that is simple, understandable, and open for study by unions and the public; severe pressures on traditional budget and personnel techniques such as step increments; package deals in wages and benefits instead of cents-per-hour rates for given classifications.

2. *Impact on Amount of Expenditures.* This is a ticklish point to assess. It is difficult to decide whether expenditures for personal services increase more under bargaining than without it. A rise in the cost of living and general inflation unquestionably increase the cost of doing business. In my sampling of finance officers in the United States there was no agreement that bargaining in itself was the major cause of an increase of public expenditure but the respondents were almost unanimous that the cost of personal services was the major cause of higher budgets. Two Canadian finance officers in different provinces were less circumspect in their reactions, and much more explicit. In referring to wage hikes one said, "the increases granted for the fiscal year 1967 will have the effect of increasing the tax rate by approximately three per cent." The other said, in effect, "excessive wage demands from various unions in our city have raised our salaries above those in the private sector."

In a sense there is not much to be gained by arguing whether bargaining has resulted in greater pay increases and greater government costs than otherwise. The important point is: Can finance officers and their colleagues develop and maintain sound, well-structured pay plans?

3. *Impact on Taxes.* Again this is an "iffy" area of speculation. I know of no systematic factual studies on this point. It offers a good subject for research.

One general observation seems justified on the basis of common sense and the comments forwarded to me. Studies made for the National League of Cities indicate that municipalities in this country are in poor financial shape. Part of the problem is inadequate revenue, which may be another way of saying municipalities do not get their fair share of the total revenue pie. If this is true and bargaining pushes up the cost of personal services, it follows that the quest for shared taxes or new tax sources for municipalities will become acute. This situation may call for a careful analysis of municipal revenue sources. As one commentator put it

> . . . [My] city has little power to initiate new tax sources. Thus we are caught between mill limitations set by the state for property taxes and an inability to raise revenues from either a local sales or income tax. Should the economy falter, a cutback in services seems inevitable.

4. *Impact on Municipal Bonding Authority.* The extent of municipal bonding power generally rests on state statutes. There are instances over the country where voters have approved increased tax levies for policemen and firemen through referendum. Again it is conceivable that the quest for municipal income could lead to an expansion of bonding authority.

5. *Impact on Fringe Benefits.* There seems to be greater agreement that bargaining has resulted in vastly increased fringe benefits. One city cites an increase of 131 per cent in the benefit package over the last dozen years.

Here are a few ingredients of the more bountiful benefit package. Additional paid holidays, premium pay for certain specific holidays, new versions of standby pay, increased clothing allowances, increased vacation and sick leave, payment for unused sick leave on retirement or termination, lower or no public contributions to insurance and health programs, educational aids, more liberal pensions, increase in shift premiums, hazard pay, special compensation for such things as carrying guns and working weekends. As one official put it, "Under collective bargaining, fringe benefits may be limited only by the capacity of employee representatives to devise them."

6. *Impact on Capital Improvements.* I find no studies which try to show that bargaining has curtailed expenditures for capital improvements. In a few isolated cases officials may believe this has occurred. One official reported that last year an employee group made some headway in giving priority to pay and benefits over capital improvements. He views this as shortsighted, and states, "Benefits gained at the expense of capital improvements may come back to haunt employees as well as the public, for erosion of the physical plant makes what remains expensive to maintain and diffi-cult to use."

7. *Impact on Management Prerogatives.* Experienced nego-tiators advise one never to speak at the bargaining table of man-agement rights or management prerogatives. Regardless of this admonition it should be noted that the hard-bargaining school of unionists contend that *everything is bargainable.* This accounts for pressure to expand the benefit package. If everything is bargainable it follows that the area for independent management decision has been cut down. Therefore, in a sense, all-out bargaining decreases management prerogatives.

The generally accepted management view on this subject was well expressed by the chief finance officer of a large city. He said: "A grey area exists on the question of what is negotiable and what is reserved as a right of management. Serious questions exist on the rights to assign, to promote, to lay off, to plan, to budget, and to finance. They are undoubtedly subject to consultation but there is need for clarification and limitation of negotiable areas."

Bargaining impinges on the field of municipal finance in other ways, of course. Rightly or wrongly, some finance officers believe their official life is made more difficult by this process. Their posi-tion is epitomized by the official who said, "We can meet the obli-gations of our three-year labor contract only in a rising economy. The first demands were modest compared to those we will be faced with now that the precedent has been established."

On the other hand there are finance officers and city managers who see benefits in the bargaining process. They say: "It forces us into more economical operations. It makes us do what we should be doing anyway."

IMPACT OF BARGAINING ON FINANCE OFFICER

Now let's briefly examine another type of impact. This is the impact bargaining will exert on the personal role and training of the municipal finance officer. Here is a preview of what he can expect.

In order to operate in the new setting the finance officer must first become familiar with the history and practice of labor relations in the private sector. Although differences exist between labor relations in public and private sectors, without an understanding of the goals and techniques of industrial unionism, the public official will be afloat on an unfriendly and unpredictable administrative sea.

Second, the finance officer must face the stark realities that collective bargaining brings to the public service. At the same time he must develop a degree of objectivity and open-mindedness that will permit him to deal intellectually with notions that may have been repugnant to him in the past. Otherwise, the pressures created by application of bargaining concepts to the public service will produce frustration, conflicting emotions, and ruin his disposition at the office and at home.

Four points can be cited to illustrate the facts of administrative life brought about by bargaining.

1. No longer can the public official hide behind the legal concept of sovereignty as a bar to collective bargaining. Agreements reached through the give and take of bargaining now exist; they are now a fact of administrative life.

2. Strikes in the public service must also be reappraised in the public setting. They are illegal in the United States, but they still exist in point of fact. They are legal in some Canadian jurisdictions under certain circumstances. But, here again, the stark reality is that public officials have failed to prevent work stoppages, which are essentially the same whether they are called a strike, walkout, sit-in, or collective sickness. Realistically, the public services must either develop workable substitutes for the strike in every case, or experiment with approved strikes in certain cases

and under certain conditions. These are concepts that are indeed unpalatable to many public officials.

3. The traditional approach to pay plans may have to be tossed out the window. With bargaining there is a good chance that the tidy, systematic, integrated pay plan—designed to give equitable treatment to all employees in a given jurisdiction—will undergo considerable change. The 64-dollar question is how do you maintain fairness and equity when many unions bargain for wages in several different units of an organization. It should be noted that union representatives argue that anything would be an improvement over what now exists. The reason: Pay administration is not really scientific.

4. The final example of reality involves merit principles. Finance officers who support merit principles in municipal personnel administration must recognize that bargaining calls for a fresh look at how the concept of merit can be preserved within the bargaining framework.

Bargaining personally affects the municipal officer in another way. He must master the techniques, strategy, and practices of collective negotiation. This becomes a "must" because if he is not the principal negotiator, there is a strong likelihood that he will be a member of management's bargaining team. In the realm of techniques are included such matters as gathering, preparing, and presenting data; conduct at the bargaining table; preparation of the agreement; relations with union and management representatives; and a host of others. Suffice to say bargaining gives him new, additional, and exciting duties.

Let me conclude with these statements. Collective bargaining in the public service is here. For every public official it poses problems, headaches, and heartaches. But it also offers an opportunity to improve management practices and public services. The public treasury is not bottomless. That means the demands for higher salaries must be accompanied by better methods of performing services, even with fewer people.

The challenge to every municipal finance officer is to build a mature, stable relationship with employee organizations. This he can do only if he comes to the bargaining table well prepared and well disposed to render a high quality of professional service to his community.

RETHINKING THE PHILOSOPHY OF EMPLOYEE RELATIONS IN THE PUBLIC SERVICE
by Frank P. Zeidler

This article is from Public Employee Relations Library No. 1, 1968, of the Public Personnel Association. Mr. Zeidler is a municipal consultant and a former Mayor of Milwaukee, Wisconsin. He is also former director of the Wisconsin Department of Resource Development.

STRUGGLES IN EMPLOYEE-MANAGEMENT RELATIONS

After these many years of civil service practice and the development of advanced programs of public personnel administration, one is tempted to ask, "Is there any need for another reexamination of the fundamental philosophy of employee relations in the public service, or are the basic premises of past policies suitable?"

The answer to this question may be found in the accounts of the recent experience of the members of the Board of Supervisors of Milwaukee County who experienced a strike of the Milwaukee County hospitals and institutions last September. The fact that organized public employees would deliberately walk off the job in a large general hospital and its accompanying institutions without concern for the patients being served gave a shock to the officials that they had not felt before. A newspaper account of the reaction of some of these supervisors is interesting. The county executive, an elected officer equivalent to mayor, said, "I never thought they would pull a strike in a hospital. This is a sad reflection on trade unionism." The chairman of the county board said, "They'll never get anything out of me again." The union's best friend was reported as bitter, furious, and suffering from a sense of betrayal.[1]

In this case, as in other recent situations in public employment, the elected officials and the public itself have been forced to

Reprinted with the permission of the publisher.

rethink their own philosophy on employee relations in the public service. The officials and the public have arrived at this stage by the actions of employee organizations imbued with a sense of militancy toward government which is destroying the past concepts of paternal attitudes toward public employees so often held by officials and sections of the public.

THE SENSE OF MILITANCY

The year 1966 has revealed many sharp struggles in public employee-management relations in the United States and Canada. Canada was affected by a strike of railway employees, and in the United States governmental units in Toledo, Youngstown, Lansing, Duluth, Dayton, Atlanta, Detroit, Flint, Cook County, New York, and Milwaukee County have been affected. Strikes have been conducted by transit workers, public health nurses, hospital attendants, teachers, firemen, sanitation workers, and others.

A review of this recent history will cause any realist in government in the United States and Canada to realize that a considerable change has taken place in the attitude of public employees toward the government that employs them. This change in attitude has forced a basic review of the philosophy of employee relations by public management and the public.

To come directly to the issue, the shock of strike tactics and the new militancy of some public employee organizations are causing the rethinking of the philosophy of public employee relations. The militancy in public employee organizations in the United States is expressed in the demand for the right to strike. Jerry Wurf, president of the American Federation of State, County and Municipal Employees, expresses the view of many public employees: "Without the right to strike, there can be no true collective bargaining for public employees."[2] Another AFSCME leader has said that it is a mistake to expect "sweetness and light" in public employee-employer relations. He has said, "There has to be conflict: there is no other way."[3] A state mediator recently said,

> Even the most elaborate structures for direct negotiations, mediation and fact-finding surrounded by a wall of deterrents is not likely to deter strong unions of public

employees from striking if they feel they are not getting fair treatment.[4]

THE PURPOSE OF GOVERNMENT

In examining the new conditions compelling a rethinking of the philosophy of employee relations in the public service, it is well to consider the purpose of government. There has been attributed to Abraham Lincoln a statement which can be said to define a minimum condition for the purpose of government:

> The legitimate object of government is to do for a community of people whatever they need to have done, but cannot do at all, or cannot so well do for themselves, in their separate and individual capacities.

Under this philosophy people have established governments, and in the democracies the people elect officials to decide democratically what policies are desirable and to create the administrative structure to carry out those policies.

LABOR AND MANAGEMENT IN PUBLIC EMPLOYMENT

In recent times with the growth in the number of public employees and the consequent growth in the structure to administer the work of the employees, two major classes of public employees have appeared. These are the bulk of the employees, or "labor," and the supervisory employees, or "management." As in private employment, this division of employees tends to create classes and class action. The exclusion of the mass of employees from decision-making and management functions tends to create in the employees a tendency to regard government as something of an exploiter of labor. This attitude may be the main source of current employee militancy.

THE HISTORICAL VIEW

As one reviews the history of government and the concepts toward public employees, several distinct eras appear, each gradually evolving into the next era. The first era in public employment is that of the spoils system. Governments of the past have not had such lofty concern for the public good as Lincoln's statement might indicate. In the past, whoever controlled government received the economic benefits of society and the privileges; the reward of power and spoils went to those who gained control of government. We are not far removed from this ancient practice; indeed, in some places this concept holds today in various parts of the United States.

CIVIL SERVICE REFORM

The grave abuses of the spoils system culminating in the death of President James A. Garfield ushered in the era of civil service reform in the United States. Concerned citizens, in order to protect the public and to see that public service was properly rendered, sought to remove the control of public jobs from victorious politicians and to make public employment a matter of ability and merit.

The civil service movement had a considerable but not a total success. In many parts of Federal and local government, and to a lesser degree in state governments, effective civil service systems evolved with the result that public employees enjoyed a great amount of security and protection. Under civil service public employees often tended to enjoy larger incomes and benefits than did people in comparable private employment.

However, in some places the spoils system persists, and this condition gives rise to a powerful argument for employee unions to protect the employee and rid the government of an evil system.

PATERNALISM

The successful functioning of civil service in many places created a psychology in the minds of elected officials and employees of a paternalistic relationship that existed between them. The elected public official tended to take a fatherly view, protecting the public employees against the harsh demands of the taxpayer. Some elected officials sought to provide working conditions, wages, and other benefits superior to those of private employment. This kind of system still prevails in many places, including the Milwaukee County board until the recent hospital strike.

Under this system personal and warm relationships were

established between public officials and public employees. Many decisions were made on this personal basis of close public-family relationships.

THE GROWTH OF MASS EMPLOYEE ORGANIZATIONS

Within the last decade these earlier patterns have altered drastically. It has been a period of employee militancy, of organization, and of arm's-length dealing between public employees and public management. Without going into a lengthy account of why this has happened, I venture the opinion that the most important factor producing this change was the growth in the political and economic strength of organizations of private employees. The legislation which they secured to protect their own existence and strengthen their own economic power accrued to the benefit of public employees.

The same technology that produced mass production also produced mass employee organizations. These employee organizations, in order to gain and consolidate economic strength, had to pay much attention to political matters. The main weapon of the organized employee is his vote. By means of bloc voting and by helping in elections, the employee organizations in private employment were able to get favorable legislation at every level of government.

This favorable legislation for private employee organizations included the right to strike, an action forbidden to public employees. In addition elaborate legal machinery was set up for handling disputes, and a number of official agencies were created to facilitate the settlement of impasses before the strike was invoked. All these legal conditions resulted in considerable economic benefit.

Public employees tended to benefit from the economic power possessed by private employees who were organized. Gains won in the private sector of the economy tended to be adopted and even surpassed in the public sector through the action of sympathetic elected officials. From the point of view of economic benefits, then, the actual income and working conditions of many public employees was not grievous enough to give rise to the new militancy.

The new militancy has probably come about partly through psychological dissatisfaction. There was the dissatisfaction of the employee with his supervisor. There was the dissatisfaction of the employee who could not successfully compete for higher civil service positions. There was the dissatisfaction of the disciplined employee. There was the dissatisfaction of the employee bored with a secure, regular, and monotonous job.

Organizers of public employees, in order to cultivate this new field of organization successfully, have had to develop a new philosophy of employee relations as a form of "product differentiation." The civil service structures and philosophy of the past had to be rejected and discredited. The new model had to stress that economic gains had to be obtained outside of any previous framework, and this only through strong demands with the power to enforce the demands. The nearest model was that embodied in laws for employee-employer relations in the private sector which include the right to strike. Relying on the strength of private employee unions with legislatures, public employee organizations have made considerable headway. The public, which has accepted the philosophy of the right of employees to strike a private employer, understandably has been hesitant to extend this right to public employees to challenge itself; but it has in many states gone a long way toward this philosophy, and in Canada the ban on strikes in the public service has been lifted for many categories of employees.

Out of these circumstances, then, an era has been reached in which the public and public management have been forced unwillingly to accept the fact of employee militancy and employee strength and act as protagonists in the combat.

ECONOMIC NEGOTIATIONS AND THE PUBLIC INTEREST

Before one laments this new order of things, it is necessary to make a vital point here. This point is that in spite of all the disagreeableness that has and will occur in public employee relations, the process of economic negotiations between public management and public employees may in the long run be a more efficient method for accomplishing the public's business than the older system was. It appears as if there will be masses of public employees, especially in social welfare and education, as the nation becomes more of a social service state. Unless there is some kind of responsible employee organization, it may become an impossible task for public management to deal with the employees, or even to get a proper feedback on how public policies are operating.

Through the exchange of information that occurs in the negotiating process, public administration can gain useful information for the formulation of public policy. If the negotiating process continues over the years long enough for stable relations to develop between employees and administration, this condition, too, can accrue to the public benefit. Therefore it need not be a matter of unhappiness to accept the idea that large-scale mass operations of government entail negotiations between administration and employees.

However, once this principle is accepted it does not automatically follow that public management thereupon yields to every demand of the employees. On the contrary, what is then required is a competent administration that can realistically negotiate with public employees, and knock out the impossible demands that are bound to be brought forth.

NEW CONDITIONS IN EMPLOYEE-EMPLOYER RELATIONS

Apart from the condition of conflict built into the new laws on employee-employer relations in the public service, certain other new conditions must also be considered. One of these has already been mentioned; it is the concept that public employees must have the same powers that private employees have to enforce their demands which culminate in the right to strike or to exercise sanctions. Another concept one finds appearing is the concept that civil service is unneeded since the protective role of civil service for the employee is now to be assumed by his organization. Still another concept that tends to be expressed by employees is that government employment is not a privilege to serve the public, but an unhappy experience under an exploiting employer. Another and rather crudely voiced concept which affects the mental attitude of some employees is the idea that the taxing power of government produces an economic pie of which the employee demands his share.[5]

Naturally these conditions have shocked public management and the public itself. The relatively swift change in the attitude of public employees to militancy and the tendency to strike has caught public administration unprepared and has left the public with a sense of some helplessness when a vital public service is halted by a work stoppage.

It does not help the morale of public administration when the militant practices and demands of public employee organizations are reinforced by the observations of learned officials in the field of labor relations who insist that justice demands that public employees have the right to strike vital services if private employees can do so, and who can see little harm in the extension of the right to strike to public employees. Moreover, many of these observers note, there is little possibility of doing anything about strikes in the public service anyway.[6]

THE RESPONSE OF THE PUBLIC
AND PUBLIC ADMINISTRATORS

With this change in the philosophy of employee organizations, what ought to be the response of public administration and the public? The first step is to establish a clear differentiation between public administration and the public. The primary concern in employee-management relations in the public service is not that of the employee or of the public manager, but of the public; the philosophy of employee relations must be based on the concern for the total public and the public good. A structural pattern has emerged in the public service which indicates that there are three parties involved in the process of negotiations: the public employees, the public managers, and the public.

On occasion spokesmen for public employee organizations express the view that they and their clientele do not intend to be "second class citizens" at the bargaining table. They are in their own minds probably equating themselves with the administrative officials. Actually, however, by using this expression, they are in effect equating themselves with the public itself, whom the administrative officials are required to serve. This philosophy pressed to a further limit might imply that when a public employee challenged a public policy, it would be equating itself at the negotiations with the total public.[7]

From the point of view of the public, then, it is important that the public recognize that a power struggle for the control of government processes could develop. The power of government lies in its ability to tax, to set rates, and to enforce the collection of the taxes. In local government, and to some extent in state government, by acts of the state legislatures, this power to set rates is now shared through the process of negotiation and bargaining between elected representatives of government acting through administrative officials, and the leaders of employee organizations. What these two groups agree to is the enforceable rate. Thus cold realism would compel one to judge that governments have experienced a loss of sovereignty over their functions. This condition may be good or bad in the long run, depending on whether or not superior service is rendered by this arrangement. It is idle to state, however, that no loss of governmental sovereignty has occurred, or if it has, that it is a fact of little consequence.

It must be assumed also that, at least for a time, the excursions of public employee organizations into territory hitherto considered the exclusive domain of government will continue. At this stage each grant of new power tends to produce the pressure for additional grants; it is in the nature of things. For example, recent strikes by public employees resulted in considerable advances for the employees, and thereby other public employee groups have been encouraged to consider the strike as a weapon. The success of the militant American Federation of Teachers has compelled its rival, the National Education Association to revise its own tactics.[8]

In the new era of negotiation, it is likely also that the legislative policymaking agencies of government are probably going to be challenged not only on conditions of employment, but also on other policies, including the quality, kinds, and manner of service to be rendered to the public.

Some recognition must be given, too, to the current state of affairs inside unions and employee organizations. The legislative enactments that have permitted bargaining and negotiation bring about employee organizational rivalry, which results in conflict between competing organizations and competing and rival demands as they seek to outdo each other, especially in an attitude of militancy toward the public administrators. The American Federation of Teachers in its competitive situation intends to set up a strike fund.[9]

The public must also recognize that in many situations it is not able to cope with and to counter strikes in the public service. This condition exists for a number of reasons. In strikes of technical services, technicians are not available to carry on the service except for a limited number of supervisory employees. If a strike is called, few public officials want to be responsible for a court injunction for fear of losing the next election. Under some circumstances judges do not want to issue strike injunctions and will not even challenge contempt of court manifested toward their own court orders.

All these factors build up into a kind of grievance the public may have against public employee organizations which seem to now have the upper hand, but it must be recognized that in many states and many smaller communities where employee organizations are weak, public administrators exercise their power in an arbitrary, capricious, or malicious manner toward their employees, so that there is a need for employee organization to give protection.

If after an overview of the pluses and minuses of employee organization, it appears that they are here to stay and not only that but there is some just cause for their existence, then the new public philosophy toward this political phenomenon is clear. Since the rules of the new system call for arm's-length negotiation, the public has the duty to see to it that the public administration side of the bargaining process functions effectively in the public interest. The public administrator must be given the means and conditions to meet the skilled employee representative on equal terms if the public is to be protected. Incidentally this would be good for both sides.

ENABLING PUBLIC ADMINISTRATORS
TO NEGOTIATE SUCCESSFULLY

In strengthening the structure of public administration to provide for skilled negotiation for the public, a new set of actions must follow. Bargaining teams and chief negotiators must be developed. The administrators must master the laws concerning employee relations and the rules of bargaining. Staff services to provide up-to-date figures on wages and salaries and conditions of work must be supplied. The new negotiating pattern means that there must be better coordination between the agencies of a government so that the administrator of a department knows what is transpiring about his department at the bargaining table.

The new kind of employee relations means that the improvement of civil service and its related functions must occur to provide the basic expertise for the government in employee relations. Civil service must continue to recruit, to train, to examine, and to deal with grievances. It must develop a data bank on public employment conditions. It must protect the public from the spoils system, and the individual employee must have a forum in civil service for his individual needs. The public must not yield on the merit system of employment and advancement, and civil service must function to protect the employee from exploitation either by the public bureaucracy or by his own organization if it develops corruptly.

I therefore see no extinction of civil service unless public personnel people are insensitive to the changes and to the new opportunities opened to them for public service.

PUBLIC RESPONSIBILITY

In its new philosophy toward public employees, the public must recognize that the strike will be used, and the public must therefore develop a system which can absorb the force of this weapon. This is a subject much too new for anyone to comment on it expertly. Compulsory arbitration may be a legislative answer to the strike, for example; or if a strike does occur, limited services rendered by supervisory employees may be another kind of answer. From the public's point of view, I hope that the bitterness and frustration which develops over strikes does not lead to the policy of the governmental agency abandoning a service to private contractors to be quit of the business of negotiation. For reasons too lengthy to discuss here, I think this is a bad counter to the threat of the strike; but it is one being considered. The subject of a just counter to an unjust work stoppage needs to be much more thoroughly considered. Choking a man's windpipe is not a legitimate method of bargaining, and there are work stoppages in the public service that are akin to this.

In the new era, the public must also recognize that it must be alert about legislative developments, court actions, and administrative rulings and decisions so that all the things that happen in this expanding field do not lead to a corrosion of the public interest or to impossible weaknesses of the public in confrontation with public employees on economic or policy issues. This concern for what happens in legislatures and in government agencies must be a concern expressed apart from public administrators. Public administration officials are relatively powerless before legislatures in opposing the demands of organized public employees because the public administrators do not represent a bulk constituency or voting bloc. Therefore the public interest before legislatures must be presented by civic associations, municipal leagues, and other nonpartisan civic groups.

It may be in this area that the greatest weakness for the public lies, and that there may be truly a loss of democracy as some civic groups now fear because no group will consider it its business to protect the public interest in legislation dealing with employee-employer relations in the public service.

Parenthetically it should be noted that the concept of "the public" is sometimes attacked by theoreticians for special interests, public employees, or other interests. The argument goes that there is no such thing as "the public"—only many "publics" each with its special set of interests. Under this argument, it is advanced that public employees are also a "public" who have higher claims against the other "publics." This argument is a fundamental assault on the democratic process by attacking the notion that there is or can be a total community of interest as against special interests. It is the democratic process which through its parliaments seeks to find this total community interest for the people as against special group interests.

The public must also recognize that in the new relationships there is a psychological struggle between employee representatives and public administrators for public sympathy. To win popular support employee representatives advance the arguments already discussed here of second-class citizenship for public employees, unless they have co-equal bargaining powers and the right to strike, and the arguments that employee representatives represent the public as much as public officials since employees are also a "public." In addition to these arguments, a really powerful argument can be advanced, namely, that if there is strong employee organization, there will be an increased efficiency in government and an end to the spoils system. In this assertion there may be much merit especially in some of our boss-ridden cities.

Whatever the arguments advanced in this struggle for control of popular sympathy, it is apparent that strong communications must be developed between public management and the public as a whole, and between public management and public employees in order to give not management's side of an issue but the public interest side of an issue.

I make this distinction because the public must also seek to protect its own interest in the negotiating process. This is a touchy subject, because both employee representatives and public negotiators want bargaining in secrecy. Current practices of bargaining in secrecy result in the public and the taxpayer not having much influence on any immediate matter in negotiation. Once an agreement has been arrived at in secrecy, it is likely that the legislative body will accept the agreement. Any public hearing on the proposed agreement then becomes merely perfunctory and an expenditure of wasted breath for those who appear and choose to comment. Some change in this condition must occur. Perhaps a procedure could be devised in which any agreement arrived at by the public negotiators and employee representatives must be regarded only as tentative until after both sides have heard from the principals of the public negotiators in a public hearing.

NEW ADMINISTRATORS' ATTITUDES

The public management negotiator and even the elected public official must keep firmly in mind during the bargaining process that he is not representing his own interest, but the public interest. The moment the public negotiator begins to conceive of himself in terms of a boss or manager of a private business he is lost. The public administrator has no voting bloc to back him other than the public at large; his claim for management prerogatives vis-à-vis the public or the public employees is not enough to swing the political support necessary for him to survive in the long run. I realize that adopting this new attitude is going to be hard for some administrators. They have so long been used to authority and decisionmaking while shielded from the general public that they naturally drift into a proprietary concept over that section of government under their domain. This kind of public official is vulnerable to employee pressure under the new system of things.

THE PUBLIC'S NEGOTIATORS

It is for this reason that the public has to keep a watchful eye on its own negotiating officials in employee negotiations. There is a tendency for public employee organizations to try to sit on both sides of the bargaining table by exercising influence over the public negotiators through elected public officials under some obligation to the employee organizations for support. The public must ask of its negotiators not that they be implacably hostile to public employee demands, but that they be fair with the public interest.

NONINTERFERENCE IN EMPLOYEE ORGANIZATIONS

Another part of the new philosophy is that public managers and administrators must not meddle in the affairs of employee organizations. Employee organizations are undergoing and will continuously undergo much turmoil in forming bargaining units, getting representation, developing their own identity of interests, and formulating demands. There will be interorganization rivalries. There will be rivalry between professional associations and labor organizations. The temptation may exist for the public administrator to try to play these groups against each other. The public should not countenance any such action on the part of its administrators. All dealings must be at arm's length and the employee groups must settle between themselves their organizational policy within the framework of the law.

HANDLING GRIEVANCES

Finally, in this new era, if the public is not to be plagued by employee disputes, it is incumbent on public administrators to pay close attention to the day-to-day operations of the public service and see to it that grievances are promptly and fairly handled. Poor grievance handling causes many work stoppages. To handle grievances and problems well, supervisors must be competently trained.

DIFFERING CONDITIONS IN DIFFERENT SERVICES

This paper has not placed much stress on the different conditions that exist in employee relations in the Federal and state services and in municipal services within the states. Employees in the Federal and state service do not possess the power that employees of municipalities in the United States and Canada possess, but the trend is for all of them to possess the same powers. Hence, this paper has dealt with the most active situations which exist today, mostly in local or school government, and the philosophy that develops out of these experiences is valid for those situations which have not ripened into the stages of militancy backed by legislative authority for public employee organizations.

Note should be made of the fact that, in their current struggle to dislodge economic power from governmental agencies, the employee organizations are not fully successful in grasping this power for themselves. Instead the power is lodging in the hands of mediators and labor relations agencies. Thus a new power element is emerging in Canadian and United States governments.

SUMMARY

Concerning the new philosophy let me say in summary that it should be recognized that in the formation of public employee organizations there is value for effective administration of government under modern conditions. If this proposition is accepted, it should then be recognized that the current laws and conditions promote conflict situations in which employee organizations will tend to use the strike to make them equal with the total public power. To achieve a proper balance in this situation, public administration must be effectively structured to engage in bargaining and public administrators trained in the new processes. Day-to-day grievances must be competently handled.

The public must protect its legislative front with active interest in any legislation on the subject of employee-employer relations. The public must not allow the merit system of public employment to deteriorate, and it must protect the fundamental right of every citizen to have his voice heard in government. In exercise of this fundamental right, the public must give more thought to dealing with the problem of secrecy in bargaining as well as in other government matters. Finally the public must allow no doctrine or practice to be advanced in the debate over employee-employer relations which will be corrosive of the doctrines of democracy and the right of the total public interest to be paramount over any private or special interest.

REFERENCES

1. *Milwaukee Journal,* September 25, 1966.
2. *AFL–CIO News,* March 19, 1966.
3. *Milwaukee Journal,* March 13, 1966.
4. Allan Weisenfeld, "Collective Bargaining by Public Employees in the U.S.," in *Collective Bargaining in the Public Service,* Proceedings, 1966 Annual Spring Meeting, Industrial Relations Research Association, Milwaukee, May 6–7, 1966.
5. For the expression of some of these views see the discussions on "The American City and the Public Employee Unions," in *Collective Bargaining in the Public Service, op. cit.,* pp. 91 ff.
6. On this subject, see the discussion of Allan Weisenfeld, *op. cit.,* and Edward E. Herman, "Collective Bargaining by Civil Servants in Canada," in *Collective Bargaining in the Public Service, op. cit.,* pp. 1 ff.
7. See the discussion of Jesse Simons in "The American City and Its Public Employees Unions," in *Collective Bargaining in the Public Service, op. cit.,* pp. 104 ff.
8. See Edward E. Herman, *op. cit.*
9. *Milwaukee Sentinel,* August 23, 1966.

THE BOARD'S POSITIVE APPROACH
by Robert A. Jamieson

The following selection appeared in the American School Board Journal, *a publication of the National School Boards Association, in November 1967. Mr. Jamieson was then first vice president of the Illinois Association of School Boards and had been a member of the Peoria, Illinois, Board of Education for thirteen years.*

Whether it be in marriage, the second child, or even collective bargaining for teachers, major adjustment is always required by those who feel oppressed. Today many boards of education feel oppressed by increased teacher militancy which is viewed as another intrusion into their sphere of responsibility and another erosion of power.

The teacher also feels oppressed because his role in a modern society is not an easy one. In present day-to-day operations, teachers are asked to solve problems over which they have little if any control. The size and growth of districts from 130,000 down to 25,000 creates an impersonal relationship with problems of communication between teachers and decision-making personnel. Furthermore, schools have become the arena for issues such as federal aid, civil rights, and racial imbalance, and the separation of church and state, not to mention the war on poverty. Teachers have been given little protection in this crosscurrent, and their effectiveness has been reduced. Pressures for quality education are to be expected at a time when emphasis is on total education of all the children of all the people. There are technological pressures for new math, teaching machines, television, language labs, and computer programming. Finally there are financial pressures resulting from an archaic system of school financing, pressure to utilize the money available for new buildings to meet the population explosion, and the competition for the tax dollar by all governmental bodies.

The reason for the militancy of the teacher is decidedly encouraged and accelerated by the developing conflict between the two organizations representing the nation's teachers for dues income and large representative memberships for power. Boards have been led to believe that contract negotiations are needed because of universal dissatisfaction and the attempt to solve problems that exist in education. Most of those who have been involved in the day-to-day operations are aware that some problems of communications exist. However, throughout the land there are untold numbers of boards which have ideal working relationships without formalized collective agreements. Efficient and effective boards have always operated in this manner.

UNION POWER PLAY

The power play by competing unions has had a divisive effect on the total school effort. These unions have used boards of education as the catalyst for conflict, have ridiculed fiscal responsibility and conservative attitudes of boards, and have made many charges, demands, and promises beyond any basis of truth or accomplishment. This degree of immaturity, misinterpreted under these conditions as militancy, was destined to have serious results in the attempt to cultivate rapport between boards of education and teachers they employ. As Dr. Louis Pollak, the dean of Yale Law School, so aptly expressed it,

> Whether a teacher's organization is a union or is a professional association seems to be an important matter of mythology. The issue of whether an organization with which we deal calls itself a union or calls itself not a union, is not of sublime importance. Whether an organization represents people who regard themselves as professionals—as I think our teachers do and should do and should be— whether an organization can properly claim to be active in a professional way for persons who are professionals— seems to me not a matter of labeling. It is a matter of how maturely in fact people behave.

Boards of education are caught right in the middle in their attempt to effect a mutually beneficial settlement designed to reduce these pressures, keep teachers relatively happy, and at the same time, assume the responsibility delegated to them by law. For those who are attempting to maintain the status quo, the battle is fierce, and those who are attempting to influence the directions of the new challenge find difficulty in their legitimate desire for discretion and flexibility and the desire of the teachers for certainty.

What, then, is the school board's challenge and what is its role in meeting the challenge? The challenge is to find the delicate balance between the desires of teachers for more consideration in decisionmaking and the demands of constituents for the board to provide educational and social leadership in a modern society. After all, the major demands of teachers are objectives most board members share with them, and confrontation only takes place when priorities must be established in relation to the available funds for their implementation. This problem of delineation is a complicated task but in the solution is a major answer to the conflict.

POSITIVE BOARD ACTIONS

It may be difficult for some board members to accept, but in the arena in which they operate, the handwriting is on the wall for eventual legislation everywhere for either permissive or mandatory bargaining with public employees. Now is the time to refrain from opposing all legislation to permit collective bargaining with teachers and to actively influence, institute, and mold the kind of legislation the school board can support. If the legislation is not in the common interest, then oppose it with all the forces able to be mustered.

There are basic principles which can be applied to all legislation under consideration in many states and in those areas where future legislation is only a matter of time. These principles should place a heavy emphasis on informality, cooperative voluntarism in the local school district, avoidance of intervention of outside agencies or persons when possible, and minimization of costs in establishing and maintaining the formal relationship. By following these principles, school districts can evolve their own procedures without a complex, highly restrictive, formalized document which retards the opportunity or desire of the variety of districts within our nation to develop their own relationships.

Proposed legislation should: apply exclusively to teachers and boards of education and not incorporate them with other employees; operate within the framework of the state educational agency or any agency created for this purpose other than the department of labor; cover all certificated personnel actually engaged in full-time positions which are not administrative or supervisory in nature; provide for exclusive representation by one organization; permit exclusive representation by one organization; permit exclusive recognition by majority designation where no competing organization files in opposition; provide for negotiations on salaries, fringe benefits, procedures for processing complaints, and related economic matters; prohibit strikes and provide penalties for noncompliance; provide mediation and factfinding arbitration on nonbinding recommendations; require a waiting period following passage to allow boards of education to prepare for the assumption of the new responsibilities inherent in the legislation; provide a definite terminal date for salary negotiations; and finally, provide for a written agreement between the parties involved.

These criteria do not all meet acceptance by either teacher group, but in the desire to obtain legislation and to recognize the wisdom and right of teachers and professional staff to be heard on matters affecting the operation of schools, there must be some framework to begin the process. In the discussions that follow legislation, boards of education and teacher groups must assert and believe that school policies and programs and the solutions of school problems can best be accomplished by their working together in harmony and with respect for the roles of each.

MANAGEMENT RESPONSIBILITIES

Regardless of whether there is collective bargaining legislation or not, boards are responsible for creating a climate where good educational experiences both for the teacher and the child can take place. Management means more than mere authority—it also means leadership. How long the school board will maintain its ability to manage will depend on how effectively it displays courage, wisdom, vision, and understanding of the aspirations and feelings of those employed to carry out the affairs of the district. Keep in mind that no matter how well the board executes the agreement, it is not a substitute for the job of creating satisfactory relationships on a day-to-day basis, in every classroom in every building and from the central office. Only by exercise of sound management and human understanding does a system acquire the respect and confidence of its faculty. In all fairness, when school board members have an election within the school district to determine the bargaining representative for the teachers, the results of that election will be determined more by the record of the board's performance to date than by what it promises to do in the future.

Keep open the lines of communication without interfering with established lines of authority. Collective bargaining is the result of a situation, not the cause of it. Tolerance and patience are the order of the day. After the emotional fire and the ashes are left—when the teachers in the process have bared their aggrieved souls as to the real problems—only then can real bargaining take place. It is an effective medicine for an antiseptic beginning.

The grievance procedure is the core of the collective bargaining agreement. When handled properly it is an effective means for providing a safety valve for the utterances of employee problems. It is a protection not only for those in the bargaining unit but also for those on the board. For school districts which have failed to meet and confer with their community of scholars, the grievance procedure is a mandatory means of communication and a unique means of becoming informed of the district's problems. The board should never face a confrontation with teachers during the implementation of the grievance procedure. The board cannot abdicate its responsibility to be a source for a final decision, but to enter the process at an earlier stage reduces the effectiveness of the procedure and limits the scope of the authority involved.

SEMANTICS

In the area of board relationships and in the anatomy of negotiations, semantics play an important part. There is too much of a tendency to revert to industrial bargaining terms such as management rights, protective clauses, and others which do not properly reflect the relationships and which further induce antagonism. Board prerogatives are those rights or that authority which the school board must have in order to carry out successfully its function of managing the school system. This may be termed the functional, rather than legal, view of board prerogatives or sovereignty and is much more acceptable by teacher groups. A board has sounder arguments when it regards itself as being required to exercise functions in order to fulfill its responsibilities rather than as having a divine right to manage. Delineation of terms always is difficult to express. Board members must, however, be able to differentiate between terms of employment and educational policy. Without this distinction arguments rather than agreements will occur. Seeking for a middle ground requires compromise, the essence of collective bargaining.

Credence must be given to the "third party" to the agreement —the taxpayer and citizen who is ever vigilant to school board actions. He is never at the bargaining table except through the board as his representative. He is a very complex person. The teacher and the board member are only partial participants and have authority for only partial claims. The "third party" or community is also involved in the process of policy making. George W. Brown, superintendent at Webster Groves, Missouri, had an interesting comment. He said, "it may seem peculiar, and unfair, but the general public will only support education if it benefits their children. They do not object if it also benefits teachers, but they will not pay the bill just to benefit teachers." Some changes may be necessary to bring professional goals and the goals of society closer together.

Collective negotiations can be as effective for boards as for teachers. There is an opportunity during negotiations for boards to utilize these procedures to press for their own demands and obtain changes they have wanted for years. Some have even questioned the propriety of tenure laws under the new development. If a bargaining agent has been selected for the first time, what former practices are to be maintained? It might be an interesting experience in exploration.

SCALE OF VALUES

Morris E. Lasker, counsel for the New Rochelle Board of Education, in his article on "The Influence of Bargaining on the Quality of Education," comments on the favorable aspects of collective bargaining other than the improvement of teacher morale and the introduction of creative educational ideas. He says,

> the requirements that teachers through their representatives must, if they share power, share responsibilities for making choices, imposes on the teachers and their representatives the needs of the district as a whole. Collective bargaining should, and in my opinion, does force the parties to articulate a scale of values if for no other reason than the demands put forward almost inevitably exceed the resources available. The creation of such a scale of values is a maturing experience for those involved.

As Dr. Myron Lieberman has advocated, school boards must "tool up for action." Make proposals known and assume an offensive position. Do not sit idly back and wait for things to develop or boards will not be long disappointed in their lethargy. Abdicating responsibility in this regard is a violation of a public trust.

As in the grievance procedure, do not enter into direct contract negotiations. The superintendent or chief administrative officer of the district or anyone delegated by him is the school board's agent. Again the position of the board is weakened by participation at a level which violates sound administrative procedure. School boards must make quite clear that school administrators can no longer equivocate as to where they stand in relationship to their role as agents of the board. Failure to perform in this manner or to accept this responsibility should result in the early termination of their services.

OPPORTUNITY IN CRISIS

In the Chinese language there is a term Wai-Gi, which means "in crisis there is opportunity." Whether boards of education are in a period of crisis regarding teacher relationships is a matter for each board to determine. Opportunity has again been born out of conflict between boards and teacher groups, for as Doherty and Oberer declare in *Teachers, School Boards and Collective Bargaining,* "If teacher leaders and school officials learn to use this development wisely, it may prove to be the most therapeutic educational development of this century. If they do not, it may freeze into our system, more firmly than ever before, those personnel practices that can only lead to educational mediocrity." School boards should take careful stock of their past experiences. An unfortunate experience is not pleasant, of course, but it is even less so if boards fail to learn from it and use it to improve their future relationships. In this sense, then, the rapport between boards and teachers must be retained without reducing the flexibility and interaction necessary in a professional effort to a staid, restrictive formal agreement for collective negotiations. As Mrs. Fred Radke, past president of the NSBA remarked, "It is time for teachers to decide whether they are *calling for joint responsibility* with boards of education—or whether they are saying we have *joint concern* with boards of education and we want our opinions to be heard and our counsel to be carefully considered before decisions are reached by the board. If it is the latter, school boards can give their support."

DEALING WITH IMPASSE
by William E. Stiles, Jr., and Edward L. Robran

The following article appeared in the January 1969 edition of the National Education Association publication, Today's Education. *Mr. Stiles is a salary*

Reprinted with the permission of the authors and publisher.

and negotiation specialist with the NEA Division of Field Services. He has been directly involved in the negotiation of teacher-school board agreements in several states, including the first such agreements in Rhode Island, Ohio, Colorado, and Arizona. Mr. Robran is a salary and negotiation specialist in the Mountain Region Field Office of the NEA. He has been directly involved in the negotiation of contracts in Casper, Wyoming, and Denver and Colorado Springs, Colorado.

Despite the best efforts of the negotiators to achieve agreement, the parties are sometimes too far apart in their positions for them to reach agreement without outside help. *Mediation* is the term for the first step that is usually taken to resolve such persistent disagreement.

Mediation is the effort by a third and disinterested party to bring the two interested parties in bargaining to a voluntary agreement. The responsibility of the mediator is to reestablish negotiation on a productive basis—not, certainly, to decide who is right or wrong. Wisdom in selecting a mediator increases the probability of successful mediation of the disagreement.

In many states, the negotiation law provides for mediation through a state agency. In other states, a mediator may be chosen by whatever process the parties have agreed to use. The procedures of the American Arbitration Association (AAA) have proven to be quite satisfactory.

The AAA panel of arbitrators is made up of people with skill and experience in resolving disputes. Frequently, these are far more important qualifications than the mediator's knowledge of the public schools and education. The local association can avail itself of the experience of the NEA Division of Field Services when making a decision about a third-party intermediary.

Mediation is essentially a continuation of negotiation under the control and supervision of an impartial and experienced third party. The mediator tries to stimulate counterproposals, compromises, and concessions by bringing up new ideas, by suggesting new combinations of compromises and concessions, and by serving as a vehicle for communication regarding extremely delicate points. He may use a variety of techniques, but in almost every situation he will finally deal with the two negotiating teams by placing them in separate rooms and then serving as a go-between.

The mediator will look for signs of willingness to compromise —in any way, on any part of the issue—and may even suggest the basis for compromise. From time to time, he will try to ascertain how the association's team would respond if the board were willing to propose a new compromise. The likelihood is that he is dealing with the board's team in the same way.

If he is an experienced mediator, he will not violate either team's confidence but will use the data that he collected while meeting with one side to negotiate new compromises from the other.

When the mediator believes that he has arrived at either a partial or complete resolution of the difference between the parties, he will try to persuade one of the teams to make a formal proposal to the other and will bring the two teams together once again for this purpose. If the parties have been honest with the mediator and the mediator has been honest with both teams, this proposal will probably result in agreement or further meaningful negotiation between the two teams.

This description greatly oversimplifies the process of mediation. In truth, it may go on for several days, allowing only short intervals for participants to eat and sleep. A good mediator is very skilled in keeping the parties together until they have adjusted their positions to accommodate negotiation or until he feels that reaching an agreement is impossible.

Consideration of the above discussion should make one point very clear: The association that hopes for successful mediation must carefully choose the time for involving a mediator. Chances for success are far better if the mediator is involved when it first becomes apparent that continued negotiation between two parties will not produce agreement. When the relationship between the negotiating parties has degenerated to a sustained and hostile debate and the respective teams have assumed final hard-line positions, mediation holds little promise for resolving the dispute.

Currently, many people are confused about the difference between advisory arbitration or factfinding and binding arbitration. Also, some confuse the arbitration of a grievance problem with the arbitration of a negotiation dispute. While the NEA unequivocally advocates binding arbitration of grievances, that is not the topic of this discussion. The points that are made in this section do not necessarily apply in a like manner to grievance adjustment.

While it is entirely possible for the parties to agree to submit certain negotiation disputes for the binding decision of an arbitrator, as a general rule they do not do so. Advisory arbitration or factfinding, on the other hand, has proven to be a helpful means for resolving negotiation impasses.

In factfinding or advisory arbitration, each party presents its case to a disinterested third party or factfinder. This is done through a format which the factfinder establishes. Generally, in the course of a series of meetings or hearings each party presents whatever testimony and exhibits are deemed necessary to convince the factfinder that its position is more reasonable and correct than that of the other party. Once the factfinder has received all of the facts he believes to be pertinent, he stops communicating with the negotiating teams and writes his report. This will include his recommended settlement along with the findings of fact and the reasoning which led to the recommendation.

It is usually quite helpful for the association to prepare a statement of position for the consideration of the factfinder. Such a statement should set forth the question that is before the factfinder and a brief, logical, rational account of the reasoning that has led to the position the education association has finally decided to take.

The preparation of a position paper serves a twofold purpose. The association representatives will find that they are forced to get down to a kind of barebones examination of the real issues instead of relying upon emotionalism for their arguments. Once the issues have been reduced to their core, it is much easier to decide what evidence should be introduced to back up the arguments to be presented. The other purpose the preparation of a position paper serves is that of helping the factfinder write his report. If the reasonings are sound, they will often find their way into his work.

Many forms of factfinding are in current use. The most common of these are the three-man panel and the one-man factfinder. When using the three-man panel, the association appoints one representative, the board of education appoints one representative, and these appointees select a third person, who will serve as chairman for the factfinding panel.

Experience with negotiation in public employment has lessened the enthusiasm for the three-man panel approach to factfinding. When compared to a one-man factfinder, the three-man panel has many disadvantages but few demonstrable advantages. Therefore, local associations are well advised to press for an appeal procedure which calls for only one factfinder.

While the work of the factfinder may be less demanding and less delicate than that of the mediator, the issuance of a recommended settlement has enormous import to the local association. Therefore, extreme care must be exercised in selecting the factfinder. In the absence of an established state agency, the American Arbitration Association is a good source of qualified arbitrators. Each local leader should make himself familiar with the services available from the AAA.

If the local association was adequately prepared for negotiation, factfinding hearings will not necessitate extensive additional preparation. However, if the local association has not been working closely with affiliated state and national associations, it should immediately contact these organizations. They can be of great assistance in the selection of an arbitrator and in the organization of the presentation to the arbitrator.

The arbitration procedure is judicial in nature, and the proper presentation of evidence can make a significant difference. The advice of one experienced in the arbitration process—a representative from the state association or the NEA and/or a carefully chosen attorney—can greatly increase a local's opportunities for success.

The association representative is not supposed to be an objective student of a problem, but rather the prejudiced advocate for a point of view. The association's team will present all of the evidence which might serve to persuade a factfinder to rule in the association's favor. The fact that the association is involved in arbitration indicates that it has an adversary who opposes its effort. The association needs to take care not to introduce material that serves to the adversary's advantage.

8

THE STRIKE ISSUE

The question originally posed was: Can we remain a free society and still provide the great urban masses with the vital services they need?

The following seven selections deal with the issue of the strike by public workers. In the first article, a judge warns that civil rights demonstrations and the increasing militancy on the part of public employees can build up an atmosphere of lawlessness. In the second piece, leaders at a church conference warn against penning up explosive forces that can erupt in violence. The next two articles deal with reports made to legislators on the question of public employee strikes. Then a writer in the labor press presents the views of public employees. This is followed by the thoughts of a professor of economics who is also the director of a school of labor and industrial relations. The chapter concludes with an article by the president of the State Personnel Council of Minnesota.

STRIKES BY PUBLIC WORKERS
by Samuel M. Gold

Mr. Gold delivered the following address at a meeting of the New York County Lawyers' Association on November 16, 1967. The address was later published in the Bar Bulletin *of the association. Mr. Gold is a Justice of the Supreme Court of the State of New York, First Judicial District.*

Reprinted from *Bar Bulletin*, Vol. 25, No. 2, 1967, with the permission of the author and publisher.

The fundamental distinction between private and public employment is recognized in the provisions for enforcement contained in the Taft-Hartley Act and the Taylor Law.

By the terms of the Taft-Hartley Act, an injunction may be issued only when there is a finding that a national emergency exists. The Taylor Law makes it mandatory for the chief legal officer of the government involved immediately to apply for an injunction.

This is equivalent to an unqualified presumption of the threat of irreparable injury. What is the irreparable damage?

Unions contend that there is none: that what a pupil does not learn now, he will learn next week; that if trains don't run, people will somehow manage to get to their places of employment.

These contentions fallaciously assume that strikes of public employees will be short-lived, lasting a few days or a week.

Obviously, longer strikes will cause serious damage to health, public safety, and industry. But the greatest and most irreparable damage by far is the defiance of government authority as duly established by law.

Not so long ago, at a public celebration in Turkey, a group of peasants occupied seats that had been reserved for members of the Parliament.

They felt that, since they were present in person, they had no need of representatives. They probably felt that they could dismiss their chosen representatives at will and later rehire them. Obviously, effective democratic organization requires more than occasional acceptance of governmental structure and governmental authority.

At the very least, a government on any level must never appear powerless to enforce laws or guarantee continuation of important services.

For many years, people active in labor and sympathetic to labor have recognized that unions of government employees cannot always act like unions of industrial workers.

Examples are John L. Lewis, the very embodiment of labor belligerency, Philip Murray, and Justice Arthur Goldberg.

Justice Goldberg, as Secretary of Labor, speaking at a luncheon of the United Federation of Teachers, definitely and emphatically stated that public workers could not strike.

When the government took over the coal mines and placed

the then Secretary of the Interior, Ickes, in charge, John L. Lewis immediately recognized that the unions could no longer strike, because the employer·was now the United States Government.

Philip Murray likewise recognized this when the government took over the steel industry. You will remember that Justice Goldberg had been the attorney for the steelworkers union, as well as for the CIO, of which John L. Lewis was the president.

Historically, leading socialists, theoreticians, and politicians alike recognized that sacrificing the right to strike would be a consequence of government ownership.

Soon after the evolution of industrial society, labor unions learned that the general strike was a potent weapon for intimidating or overthrowing a government.

If you defy a government successfully, it may lead to its overthrow, and often that is its very purpose. It is sometimes stated, as though it were axiomatic, that collective bargaining is worthless without the implied threat of a strike.

This, no doubt, is true when dealing with private employers. It seems to me to have no validity when applied to public workers.

Franklin D. Roosevelt, to whom labor largely owes its legal right of collective bargaining under the Wagner Act, was emphatic in denying public workers the right to strike.

In a message to the Federation of Federal Employees on August 16, 1937, President Roosevelt stated:

> Since their own services have to do with the functioning of government, a strike of public employees manifests nothing less than an intent on their part to prevent or obstruct the operations of government until their demands are satisfied. Such action, looking toward the paralysis of government by those who have concern to support it, is unthinkable and intolerable.

Even under the National Labor Relations Act, governmental units do not have to bargain collectively. The city of New York and other local bodies have voluntarily granted collective bargaining rights to their employees, but they may legally withdraw them at any time.

If the claim is made that we are not keeping up with the times or with new social developments, the obvious answer is that the National Labor Relations Act has never been amended to include public bodies.

In my opinion, any attempt to change the National Labor Relations Act by making collective bargaining rights available to govermental employees would fail.

Yet the Social Security laws have been constantly amended to keep up with the times, and Federal employees who may not even threaten to strike and who do not even have the privilege of collective bargaining are about to receive their fifteenth pay rise in 22 years.

Why have there been so many and such widespread strikes of government workers, a group not hitherto distinguished by awareness of labor techniques or militancy?

It must be that because of the nature of their employment, with the advantages of tenure and security, they have heretofore appeared not to be concerned with the conflicts raging outside.

It was quite a surprise to the public to find that teachers, who seemed to have been living in a cloistered atmosphere, suddenly became "strike happy," so to speak. Obviously, they felt that the time had come when they must show their strength and muscle.

Undoubtedly, the history of the civil rights movement and the more than sizable gains made by many labor unions on behalf of their members have convinced large numbers of public employees that results are achieved only by direct action.

The success of the civil rights movement has also stimulated the militancy of labor organizations, including those of public workers.

This all builds up an atmosphere of lawlessness. Different groups now invade seats of government, such as the mayor's office in Milwaukee, the office of the president of the Board of Education in New York, and the office of the New York City Superintendent of Schools.

This is a new technique of which hundreds of other examples can be cited.

I realize full well that justice too long delayed does often invite extreme measures, ranging from civil disobedience to rebellion.

We delayed giving the Negroes their just rights and equality and, as a result, they have been resorting to violent measures.

The remedy, however, does not lie in prohibition and punishment exclusively. Complete reliance on punitive measures was what made the Condon-Wadlin Act unjust and unenforceable.

When the first strike of the United Federation of Teachers was ended after one day by the intercession of Harry Van Arsdale, president of the Central Labor Council, he assured the public that there would be no more strikes by teachers, implying by his tone and manner that it was just a temporary bit of mischief by a normally obedient child.

However, unions of public workers, particularly those containing large numbers of educated, articulate members, cannot be treated with such paternalism or condescension.

In return for surrendering the right to strike, they must be given satisfactory machinery and procedures for consideration of demands and redress of grievances.

Section 201 of the Civil Service Law, commonly referred to as the Taylor Law, makes an honest effort to do this.

This law creates a Public Employment Relations Board, which will appoint factfinding bodies and representatives of employee organizations and public employers to serve as technical advisers to these bodies.

The board has the power to resolve disputes as to the representation status of employee organizations or of employees of the state and state public authorities.

The law further grants to an employee organization which has been recognized the right to represent the employees in the negotiations and in the settlement of grievances and permits membership dues deductions.

Under the Taylor Law, an impasse is deemed to exist if the parties fail to achieve agreement at least sixty days prior to the budget submission date of the public employer.

On the request of either party, the board must grant assistance to the parties in effecting a voluntary resolution of the dispute.

The board will appoint a mediator or mediators representative of the public from a list of qualified persons. If the impasse continues, the board must appoint a factfinding body which shall have the power to make public recommendations for the resolution of the dispute.

If the dispute is not resolved at least fifteen days prior to the budget submission date, the factfinding board must immediately transmit its findings of fact and recommendations for resolution of the dispute to the chief executive officer of the government involved and to the employee organization involved and must simultaneously make public such findings and recommendations.

If, thereafter, the impasse continues, the Public Employment Relations Board has the power to take whatever steps it deems appropriate to resolve the dispute.

In the event that either the public employer or the employee organization refuses to accept, in whole or in part, the recommendation of the factfinding board, the chief executive officer of the government involved must, within five days, submit them to the legislative body of the government involved, together with his suggestions for settling the dispute; and the employee organization may likewise submit its recommendations.

The Taylor Law provides full protection, short of the right of public workers to strike, and it gives them a working substitute for it.

Having provided this comprehensive machinery for the resolution of labor disputes, the legislature solemnly announced that no public employee or employee organization shall engage in a strike and no employee organization shall cause, instigate, encourage, or condone a strike.

A public employee who violates this law is subject to the disciplinary penalties provided by law for misconduct.

Weaknesses exposed by actual experience in attempting to resolve labor disputes under this law could be corrected by additional legislation.

It is quite obvious from the reading of the law that public employees are not now left defenseless and that there is ample machinery for the redress of their grievances.

It would seem, therefore, that there is no further justification for them to be contemptuous of the law. In its first test, the recent teachers' strike, the Taylor Law has proved incapable of protecting the community from paralysis by a large union.

The 1967 school year began on Monday, September 11, 1967. The teachers had an agreement with the Board of Education which expired on June 30, 1967.

The union officers and the Board of Education had been negotiating a new contract for many months. The teachers executed resignations and contended before the court that they had given up their employment, hence they could not be charged with going out on strike.

Judge Nuñez found that this action of the teachers was merely an attempt to evade the provisions of the Civil Service Law, the common law, and the decisional law, all of which from time immemorial forbids and makes illegal a strike on the part of public employees.

The amazing solidarity of the teachers indicated that they considered union discipline a higher good than law and order. Apparently the sole concern of the teachers was to stick together and to save the union, without regard to considerations of lawlessness or the poor examples which they were setting for students.

That, to me, is the most ominous feature of the whole situation, that a group to whom discipline is of primary interest should have subordinated respect for law to union solidarity.

The safety of the streets, public places, the functioning of essential services, such as health, safety, education, transportation and the like, would be grievously impaired, if all groups followed their example.

I am not unmindful of the fact that the teachers have a most difficult task to perform and that they are working under the most trying conditions.

I know that the schools are the first to feel the impact of all social ills, such as slum conditions, unemployment, broken homes, hostility to parents, crime, and immorality, but I do not see, nevertheless, that these problems can be resolved by striking in defiance of existing law.

No one has a higher regard than I have for the sincere and highminded teachers who are struggling with oversized classes and disruptive children, and who are being wrongfully charged with the failure of some children to learn.

However, this does not seem to me to justify a strike by teachers. The Taylor Law is primarily an adjuration to public workers against striking: that is the main purpose of the law. Public workers are told that they may not defy the government.

It is my humble opinion, that, if regard for constituted authority were really to go out of fashion, life would become unsafe, unbearable, and probably impossible.

3 MAJOR FAITHS SOUND THEMES OF RACIAL JUSTICE, RIGHT TO STRIKE

On September 2, 1967, the AFL–CIO News *carried the following news story about the Labor Day messages of the three major faiths.*

Denial of the right to strike is justified only in the "rare cases when genuine damage to the general welfare clearly outweighs the values of freedom in labor-management relations," the National Council of Churches declared in its annual Labor Sunday message.

Even then, the council continued, "viable alternative methods must be found for securing freedom and justice" for the workers. Otherwise, the statement continued, "the right to strike remains a desirable element of our national labor policy."

"Public employees should not be denied the right to strike solely by virtue of their public employment," it declared. "In such areas as fire, police, or other services, where a strike would seriously endanger the public health or safety, other alternatives must be found."

The council noted that the strike "is a last resort of free workers in self-defense against what they believe to be unjust oppression."

"The way to industrial, as to international, peace is through endless persistence, responsible patience and goodwill, and an imaginative and cooperative search for alternatives to the strike," it added.

Citing the National Labor Relations Act's specific protection of the right to strike, the council noted the relatively small amount of time lost because of walkouts—"only one-tenth that lost from industrial accidents" in 1966—and called the right to strike "vital" to organized workers. "No man, no group of men, can be compelled to work without a loss of freedom," the statement declared.

Government intervention, the council pointed out, may lead to "undue reliance" on government and destroy free bargaining. Recent bargaining in the railroad industry, it added, "illustrates the dangers of such precedents."

The Social Welfare Department of the United States Catholic Conference, declaring that "labor relations in 1967 means race relations," keyed its Labor Day statement to the fact that the United States "has failed to preserve racial peace and to achieve racial justice."

"The more we build walls around the inner city," the statement declared, "the more we pen up explosive forces that will erupt in violence. Those who own or rent decent housing are not about to throw firebombs. But apparently some in rat-infested slums have concluded that no housing at all is better than the hovels they now inhabit."

To achieve racial peace and justice, the statement said, the first move should be "concerted efforts at every level of society to build bridges of communication between the races where today there are mostly barriers." It called for "strong steps" to restore or create understanding and trust, for intensive counseling and rehabilitative programs, and for supplemental education as well as training or retraining for school dropouts.

The department called on the country's religious bodies to "deepen their cooperation" in seeking racial justice and justice for the poor, seeking "to forge even stronger interreligious bonds," and urged organized economic groups, "particularly business and labor, to work for quick and effective solutions to the problems which confront us."

Confidence that the American labor movement will "play its noble part in bringing harmony where there is present disharmony, trust where there is now enmity, cooperation where there is now antagonism" in the quest for social and racial justice was voiced by the Synagogue Council of America.

The council declared in its Labor Day statement that "all Americans have a responsibility" when "inequities lay their ruthless hands upon a nation's life" and violence ensues.

"The time is now long since past when America can withhold a job from a man because of the color of his skin, or deprive him of the opportunity of a decent education or deny him the right of living in a house that will be for him a pride instead of a shame," the statement said.

> To right these egregious wrongs is surely our pre-eminent task, and we look particularly to the American labor movement because of its special awareness and concern, because of its dedicated responsibility to a fully realized America.
>
> The faith in labor's leadership, we are certain, will be justified in the critical days ahead.

The statement also reflected the traditional Jewish "deep respect and profound concern for the worker," recalling the ancient counsel that "learning uncoupled with work is learning which can ultimately bear no fruitful harvest."

THE RIGHT TO STRIKE

> *By order of the Massachusetts General Court (legislature), the Legislative Research Bureau was directed to prepare a report concerning collective bargaining and local government employees. The preparation of this report was the primary responsibility of attorney Samuel Brown. The following excerpt is taken from the Report of the Bureau to the General Court.*

In 1962 there were 28 strikes by public employees throughout the United States. In 1966 there were more than 150. In 1962 some 20,000 man-days were lost in these strikes; in 1966 that figure rose to 450,000 man-days lost. The American Federation of Teachers estimates that about 300 to 400 strikes or work stoppages by teachers alone will occur during the 1968–1969 school year.

The order for this study reflects the concern of the [Massachusetts] General Court in this area by its use of the following language: "a study relative to ways and means of resolving deadlocked disputes without resort to strikes or boycotts. . . ."

All the states which permit collective bargaining by public employees specifically forbid strikes, with the exception of California, whose statute is silent on this particular subject. Massachusetts follows the general rule in prohibiting strikes by either state employees or by local employees.

The reasoning behind the ban on strikes by public employees reflected the belief that a strike against the government, against the sovereign, was really—in a democracy—a strike against oneself, and thus a nullity.

A recent New York court decision [*Railway Mail Assn.* v. *Murphy,* 44 N.Y. Supp. (2nd) 601] reflected contemporary opinion in the statement that "collective bargaining has no place in government service." Certainly, therefore, public employee strikes, since they went far beyond bargaining, could not be condoned under any circumstances.

In 1919, at the time of the Boston police strike, Governor Calvin Coolidge said: "There is no right to strike against the public safety by anybody, anywhere, anytime." Since then there has been very little if any change in this philosophy about strikes against the public safety. But the philosophy about strikes not involving the public safety or health has undergone remarkable transformation.

FUTILITY OF STRIKE BAN

Events of recent years have clearly demonstrated the futility of a ban against strikes in the public sector. Such strikes have occurred in various states and metropolitan areas, particularly in New York City. Where the penalty is a prison term for strikes, it is simply impractical and impossible to jail thousands of persons. Usually, when such a strike has been settled, the terms of agreement provide that no penalties shall be imposed against the strikers. Heavy fines are of little consequence; they are quickly paid, without any dire effects upon union or members. When the penalty calls for dismissal from employment, it is completely impractical. Chaos would result before a major city like Boston could replace 4,000 qualified teachers or 2,500 policemen.

CHANGE IN RECENT THINKING

In any event, many political scientists have moderated their views on the right to strike. They intimate that a strike by city hall clerks may have less impact on the public than a strike of a milk drivers' union; that a work stoppage by schoolhouse custodians is not as serious as a strike by bus drivers on a privately owned transportation system. As a matter of fact, it is generally agreed by those concerned with this problem, including some in the field of government management, that, apart from a few areas involving the public safety and health, all government employees should be granted the right to strike.

It has been suggested, for instance, that public employees be classified into three categories—for strike purposes. Class I would consist of policemen, firefighters, prison guards, hospital employees, and similar personnel, who would not be allowed to strike under any conditions. Class II might embrace public welfare employees, teachers, rubbish collectors, and others, whose strikes might be condoned for relatively short periods of time. All other public employees would be identified as Class III personnel, who would have unrestricted rights to strike.

To illustrate the unions' policy on this issue, it is interesting to note that the most militant government employee union, the American Federation of State, County and Municipal Employees, will not take under its wing any police organization which reserves to itself the right to strike. On the other hand, the bylaws of the International Association of Fire Fighters for many years contained a "no-strike" clause, but this prohibition was removed at its 1968 national convention. Finally, both the National Education Association and the American Nurses Association have also modified their previous "no-strike" policies.

Many state and local governments are reviewing their laws concerning collective bargaining for public service employees, particularly their antistrike provisions. In Pennsylvania, a prestigious commission has recommended to the governor several changes in the state's "Public Employee Law," including one which would grant the right to strike to all public employees except those involved with the health, safety or welfare of the public [Governor's Commission to Revise the "Public Employee Law" of Pennsylvania. *Report and Recommendations*—June, 1968].

CONTRARY VIEWS

The fact that many experts favor the right to strike should not be construed as implying that government employee union leaders are eagerly awaiting the opportunity to lead their forces into such situations. On the contrary, union leaders, although wholeheartedly supporting the right, are unanimous in their reluctance to enforce it. To them the strike is a last, desperate resort —to be employed only if and when all other efforts have collapsed. However, they want this right because it is a powerful weapon at bargaining sessions. After all, when an employer knows that his employees cannot and will not strike, he is much more inclined to resist their demands no matter how legitimate they may be. Without the right to strike, the employees' representative at the bargaining table is seriously handicapped.

It is undoubtedly true, therefore, that the public employee is at a tremendous disadvantage in bargaining collectively because he has been deprived of the most powerful argument, the ultimate weapon—his right to strike.

By the same token, however, the government employer is likewise at a great disadvantage in disputes with his employees because he cannot use remedies which are available to his counterparts in the private sector.

Thus, the private employer can utilize a lockout, an option not available to the public employer. The former can stockpile in many cases. For instance, large buyers and users of steel can buy and store huge amounts of their products long before contract negotiations are slated to begin. The public employer is in no position to take this type of precaution. Private business may relocate and consolidate factories to avoid economic losses, provided this action does not amount to an "unfair labor practice" under Federal law. A city cannot move a school or firehouse out of the city or state. Finally, a private employer may close his plant and go out of business entirely if he is convinced that he cannot continue to operate at a profit. Government cannot close a necessary public facility.

Therefore it is quite possible that the loss to the public employee of his and labor's ultimate threat—the right to strike—may be offset by the unavailability to the public employer of bargaining weapons commonly used by his colleagues in the private sector.

Furthermore, the public employee has an approach which is rarely available to workers in the private sector. If dissatisfied with bargaining results, he can exert political pressure on the legislative or budget authorities, who are elective officials. If a mayor or a board of selectmen are unduly adamant and unyielding in their bargaining attitudes, public employees can mount a campaign to defeat such officials at the polls.

Yet it is argued that the opposite holds true. It may well be that mayors, selectmen, school committees, and law-making bodies would all be inclined to favor employee demands in order to avoid political repercussions. This, apparently, has not turned out to be the case. Officials charged by the statute to represent the cities and towns in collective bargaining with local employees have generally been surprisingly firm and fair in their dealings. This is one more reason why the relatively new law has proved to be so effective.

THE RIGHT TO STRIKE SHOULD BE STRICTLY LIMITED

In June 1968, the Pennsylvania Governor's Commission, appointed by Governor Raymond P. Shafer, issued a report on revising the state's Public Employee Law. The following excerpt deals with the commission's views on public employee strikes. The commission consisted of—among others—an industrialist, an educator, legislators, a clergyman, lawyers, and a general counsel to a labor union.

No one should have a right to strike until all collective bargaining procedures have been exhausted. If there is a strike before all collective bargaining procedures are exhausted, no other showing should be needed to cause the appropriate court to enjoin the strike.

Likewise there can be no right of public employees to strike if the health, safety, or welfare of the public is endangered. The rights of both public employer and public employee must necessarily be subordinated to the welfare, health, and safety of the general public. Consequently, the legislation we recommend will provide that if a strike is threatened or occurs after collective bargaining has been exhausted, it can begin or continue only so long as public health, safety, or welfare is not in danger. The appropriate courts should be empowered to enjoin any strike of public employees once that danger point has been reached. The court should be armed with authority to impose such penalties upon striking employees and the employee organization as will make most unlikely the beginning or the continuation of the strike once a court has determined that the public health, safety, or welfare is jeopardized.

But where collective bargaining procedures have been exhausted and public health, safety, or welfare is not endangered it is inequitable and unwise to prohibit strikes. The period that a strike can be permitted will vary from situation to situation. A strike of gardeners in a public park could be tolerated longer than a strike of garbage collectors. And a garbage strike might be permissible for a few days but not indefinitely, and for longer in one community than another, or in one season than another.

The collective bargaining process will be strengthened if this qualified right to strike is recognized. It will be some curb on the possible intransigence of an employer; and the limitations on the right to strike will serve notice on the employee that there are limits to the hardships that he can impose.

We also believe that the limitations on the right to strike which we propose, namely, that collective bargaining must first have been exhausted and that a strike cannot be permitted to endanger public health, safety, or welfare, will appeal to the general public as so much fairer than a general ban on strikes that the public will be less likely to tolerate strikes beyond these boundaries. Strikes can only be effective so long as they have public support. *In short, we look upon the limited and carefully defined right to strike as a safety valve that will in fact prevent strikes.*

We recommend severe penalties for the violation of an injunction against a strike for either of the reasons we have enumerated. We shall so provide in our recommended legislation. Basically these will take the form of fines or imprisonment or both against strikers or the organizations responsible for strikes.

MYTHS ABOUT PUBLIC EMPLOYEES
by Bernard Stephens

In an article in the Public Employee Press *of January 17, 1969, Mr. Stephens sought to correct the image of the public employee as having "one hand holding a picket sign and the other in the public's pocket" by refuting what he considers to be five myths. In the following excerpt from his article he discusses two of these myths: first, that "public employees are strike-happy," and second, that "power-mad union bosses call strikes whenever it suits them."*

Public employees are particularly conservative when it comes to striking. Just to cite one example of distortions in this area, the press and government officials have pointed over the years to the Transport Workers Union and its late leader, Mike Quill, as reckless exponents of the strike weapon—and yet the strike of 1966 was the only subway strike in the union's 30-year history.

For the locals of District Council 37, which bow to no one when it comes to militancy, there were no strikes during 1968, one brief stoppage in public works over a strong grievance in 1967—and then you must go back to 1965 for the welfare strike, and to 1962 for the Motor Vehicle Operators' strike.

For all government employees in this state [New York] during 1967 (latest available figures), man-days lost through strikes by government workers made up 22 per cent of the total. Since government employees in this state constitute 16.6 per cent of the total work force, it is a fact that government employees struck more often on a percentage basis than those in the private sector —but hardly enough to fit the description "strike-happy." Moreover, since government employees are now first tasting the fruits of unionism—and often meeting violent rebuffs from nineteenth-century-minded officials—it stands to reason that there will be strikes. Thus, as in the strike of state hospital workers last Novem-

Reprinted with the permission of the publisher.

ber, the *reason* why they struck must be deduced. Here was a classic example of a public official, Governor Nelson Rockefeller, presenting the state hospital employees with the choice of accepting serious violations of their rights and ability to improve their pay and conditions—or striking.

In any assessment of responsibility, that strike should be listed: "Cause: Incredible arrogance of Governor . . ." and not "strike-happy workers."

Workers in the mass industries of auto, steel, rubber, etc., were forced to strike in the mid-1930s, the days of the CIO— but who would deny today the justice of their struggles?

Union leaders in any area, public or private, know very well the cost and peril of a strike—the ultimate union weapon. But often it is the only resort left open to the workers and their leaders, since the *employer* may well be taking positions that can be met only with a strike. In many cases the public official feels that he "needs" a strike in order to show he *had* to give a raise. Of course the public employees are always blamed.

The fact is that strikes are rarely, if ever, "called" by a leader over the opposition of the employees involved. It would be a pretty stupid leader who did that, since the strike's effectiveness would be severely limited or destroyed.

A strike is a traumatic experience in the life of anyone who has experienced it; a strike is not taken lightly.

There are occasions when a union leader opposes strike action but is overruled by the employees. This has happened on several occasions in New York City in recent months, and is in itself graphic evidence of the absurdity of the charge that "union bosses" call strikes. But now we have a new twist in editorial comment, with the workers described as "grasping," "irresponsible," and "undisciplined." Now the "union boss" theory is dropped, and instead there is a demand that "some other way" be found—a way other than having the workers vote a contract up or down, that is.

In other words, let's have a little less democracy, they say. Unions aren't buying this—not this union, anyway. This land of ours must accept the discomfitures that come with democracy, as well as the blessings, and it must learn to assess the responsibility properly. Too often the real bosses—the employers and government officials who cause strikes through arrogance or political need—are the "good guys," while blame is heaped on the convenient scapegoats—the employees and their union leaders.

A NEW APPROACH TO STRIKES
IN PUBLIC EMPLOYMENT
by Jack Stieber

> *The following article is an address that was delivered at a Conference on Challenges to Collective Bargaining held on August 11, 1967, at the University of Hawaii, sponsored by the university's Industrial Relations Center. The speech was published in 1968 in the* Proceedings *of the conference edited by Benjamin C. Sigal.*
>
> *Mr. Stieber is professor of economics and director of the School of Labor and Industrial Relations at Michigan State University. He has served as executive secretary to the President's Advisory Committee on Labor-Management Policy and as research consultant to the International Labor Organization. He also acts as a consultant for public and private agencies.*

The U.S. Department of Labor reported 142 work stoppages in public employment last year [1966], involving 105,000 workers who were idled for 455,000 days. This made 1966 the biggest year, by far, for strikes in government. There were more than three times as many strikes as in 1965 and more than twice as many as in the previous peak year of 1952 during the Korean war. All but nine of the strikes in 1966 were in local government, with schools, sanitation, protection services, and hospitals and other health services, in that order, accounting for close to 90 per cent of the total. There were only two stoppages in public transportation, including the celebrated New York City transit strike in January, but they caused more than half of all time lost due to government strikes in 1966. In addition to reported stoppages, which include

Reprinted with the permission of the author.

only those involving six or more workers and lasting at least one day or shift, there were undoubtedly others of a few hours duration, not to mention mass resignations by teachers and nurses, "reporting sick," "work-ins," and other strike substitutes. This article will deal primarily with the strike problem at the local level where it is most pressing.

While still insignificant in number of strikes, workers involved, and days lost, as compared with any other industry, strikes in public employment pose a major problem in labor-management relations in the United States today. There are several reasons why so few strikes should occasion so much concern.

First, all strikes in government are in violation of the law. They are specifically prohibited by the Taft-Hartley Act, by all states which have public employment relations laws, and by numerous court decisions. The willingness of so many otherwise law-abiding citizens to violate and defy the law poses a moral issue as well as a practical problem of how to deal with such stoppages.

Second, many government services are vital to the normal functioning of the community. Strikes by policemen, firefighters, and prison guards are intolerable and even the organizations to which these employees belong do not assert the right to strike. Strikes in hospitals, sanitation, and public utilities may present a threat to health or safety if they last more than a few days. Public transit, especially in a few large cities, is so important to the convenience and economic well-being of the people that many would classify it as an essential service. And strikes which close schools disrupt the social, economic, and emotional lives of more people than almost any other kind of work stoppage.

Third, strikes in public employment are bound to increase because government is the largest and fastest growing industry in the United States and public employees are joining unions at a rapid rate. In October 1966 there were 11½ million government employees—2.9 million Federal, 2.2 million state and 6.4 million local. This total is expected to grow to 15 million by 1975 when one out of every five employees will be working in government. In the AFL–CIO, almost the only unions which are growing rapidly are those operating in government. The American Federation of Government Employees, which organizes Federal employees, claims 250,000 members; the State, County and Municipal Employees, 350,000; and the Teachers' Union, 132,000; increases of 300 to 500 per cent for each union over the last decade. Equally important are professional associations which, under pressure from union competition, act more and more like unions. The largest and most powerful of these is the million-member National Education Association and its state and local affiliates. To most people, employee organization and strike go together and there is nothing in the record of recent years to dissuade them of this belief.

Actually, concern over the strike issue has overshadowed the great progress that has been made in public employee-management relations in the last few years. The 1960s have already earned a place in labor relations history as the decade of the public employee. Executive Order 10988 signed by President John F. Kennedy in 1962; comprehensive state laws in Wisconsin, Michigan, New York, Connecticut, Massachusetts, Delaware, and Minnesota, and more limited laws in other states; and municipal ordinances in a number of the largest cities, including New York, Philadelphia, and Cincinnati, have finally given government employees rights accorded to private employees thirty years ago: the right to join unions, to have their organizations recognized by employers, and to negotiate over wages, hours, and conditions of employment. All the state laws have been passed or substantially liberalized since 1960 and every year finds additional states added to the roster of those with public employment relations laws. However, most states still have no statutes dealing specifically with public employees and a number of others expressly prohibit collective bargaining in government or have declared negotiated agreements to be unenforceable.

Because strikes are prohibited, the states with public employment relations laws have recognized a special responsibility to develop procedures to resolve impasses in negotiations. The principal methods used are mediation and, if that fails, factfinding with public recommendations. Wisconsin has had the most experience with factfinding. Between 1962 and 1966, factfinders were appointed in 38 disputes and their recommendations served as the basis for settlement in 70 per cent of the cases. Michigan, whose law was passed in 1965, has resorted to factfinding in some 50 disputes, with salutary results. Arbitration is provided in most states only at the request of the parties, although a few prescribe compulsory arbitration for disputes involving policemen, fire-fighters, and public utilities.

Most negotiations in public as in private employment are resolved by the parties with or without the assistance of government mediators. The use of factfinding—a procedure which is reserved for emergency disputes in private industry but is available in even the smallest and most inconsequential public dispute under most state laws—will result in settlement of all but a few really hard-core disputes. But what about impasses after all efforts to resolve the dispute have failed? Should public employee organizations be denied the ultimate weapon which is available to unions in private industry? What should be done about employees who strike in violation of the law? These questions have aroused great passions among some public employee unions and have led to considerable disagreement among impartial experts in the industrial relations field.

With respect to the second question, the trend is away from laws calling for automatic dismissal or other severe penalties, including reemployment only under extremely harsh conditions, for striking public employees. Experience has shown such laws to be ineffective because elected public officials will almost never invoke them. This was the case in New York under the Condon-Wadlin Act and in Michigan under the old Hutchinson Act. Most states with statutes governing labor relations in public employment do not specify automatic penalties for employees who violate the law by striking. However, the 1965 Michigan law states that a public employer may discipline a striking employee up to and including discharge, and the New York State law, passed in 1967 over bitter union opposition, provides penalties against unions rather than employees. The New York law calls for injunctions to halt public employee strikes and prescribes fines against unions that disobey such court orders, equal to one week's membership dues or $10,000, whichever is less, for each day that the strike continues.

Some of those who oppose a blanket prohibition on strikes in government argue that there cannot be genuine collective bargaining without the right to strike. Take away the strike threat, and employers, public and private alike, will realize that they have the upper hand and not engage in real collective bargaining.

Unions can cite case after case in which a government employer contended he could not negotiate certain issues but changed his tune quickly when a strike was threatened or actually called. Then apparently unsurmountable obstacles to negotiation seemed to fade away and an agreement was reached in short order.

Others consider it illogical and inequitable to deny the right to strike to government employees when it is not denied to employees in private industry doing the same work. Thus, the government, at one level or another, owns and operates printing plants, electric utilities, transit facilities, hospitals, cafeterias, liquor stores, and other establishments which are indistinguishable in almost every way from similar facilities in the private sector. In some cases, direct public employment shades over into government-owned but privately operated enterprises. In atomic installations, for example, collective bargaining modeled on the private sector has been permitted, including strikes, although the operation is wholly financed with public funds. Looking at the problem in another way, one may ask why clerks and office workers in the state capitol or in the highway authority should be prohibited from striking, while electric utility, transit, or even hospital employees may strike as long as they work for private employers. Surely, the services supplied by the first group of public employees are less essential to the community than those furnished by the second group of private employees.

Those who support the prohibition against all government strikes do so primarily on three grounds: (1) the fear that the principle of sovereignty will be imperilled by legalizing any strikes in government, (2) a difficulty in differentiating between essential and nonessential activities, and (3) the belief that the strike is an economic weapon which, in government, is not matched by countervailing power normally available in private industry.

The sovereignty doctrine holds that any strike of public employees is an attack upon the state and a challenge to government authority. It has been used for many years and is still cited in some states to deny government employees the right to bargain collectively. However meaningful state sovereignty may be to political scientists, it carries little weight with government employees when it comes to their relationship to the state as employer. Secretary of Labor W. Willard Wirtz put it succinctly when he said:

"This doctrine is wrong in theory; what's more, it won't work." It is interesting to note that other countries do not regard all strikes by government employees as a threat to state sovereignty. Most West European countries limit but do not prohibit all public employee strikes and in 1966, Canada passed a law which expressly permits Federal employees to strike. The Canadian statute gives unions of government employees a choice between compulsory arbitration or strike action in the event of an impasse in negotiations. The union must indicate which course it will follow at the beginning of each negotiation and may not alter its choice throughout that negotiation.

The essential versus nonessential services approach to government employee stoppages has usually been rejected because of the difficulty of classifying activities in each category. Furthermore, this approach would have to take into account the distribution of employment at the local level, where almost all government strikes have occurred. Of the 6.4 million local government employees, more than 3½ million are employed in schools—2.3 million as teachers and 1.2 million in noninstructional activities. An additional 1.6 million are employed in police and fire protection, public welfare, hospitals and health, sanitation, correctional institutions, and public utilities. Only 1.3 million are engaged in activities that are clearly nonessential in the sense that interruption of service could be endured for an extended period without posing a threat to the health, safety, or welfare of the populace. The employment distribution will, of course, vary from one community to another. It is clear from these statistics that, if it is to be meaningful, any law which limits the prohibition of strikes to essential government services would have to be narrowly construed and would certainly have to exclude schools, where more than half of all local government employees are concentrated. A law which extended the right to strike only to a small minority of all public employees, most of them unorganized and without the power to carry out a successful strike, would be a hoax.

While the classification of essential and nonessential services would be difficult, I am not convinced that it represents an insurmountable obstacle to legislation which would distinguish between prohibited and permissible stoppages in government employment. This is an administrative problem no more difficult than many others handled by government agencies, and particularly by the National Labor Relations Board in its day-to-day administration of the Taft-Hartley Act.

The third argument against relaxing the prohibition on government strikes is that public employers cannot long withstand stoppages which victimize the community. It is argued that private employers may resort to a variety of weapons to combat strikes: they may lock out their employees; try to operate with other workers; suspend operations, secure in the knowledge that pent-up demands or strike insurance will mitigate economic losses; or even go out of business entirely. The knowledge that potent weapons are available to the opposing sides exerts reciprocal pressures upon the parties to modify their positions to the extent necessary to bring about a settlement. Both unions and employers know from experience that jobs can and have been lost and markets seriously depleted as a result of strikes or settlements leading to noncompetitive price increases.

The government employer is in an entirely different position. He cannot lock out his employees or decide to go out of business. Extended suspension of government services is not politically feasible. While government may, in an emergency, call upon the National Guard or the Army to perform certain essential services, this solution does not lend itself, even on a temporary basis, to such public services as education and hospital care. Besides, such action involves political risks which elected officials would be reluctant to take.

The economic and market pressures which operate upon unions and private employers do not usually exist in the public sector. Competitors will not teach children, write relief checks, or provide case work services to welfare clients; consumers will not find ready substitutes or learn to do without garbage collection or medical care; excessive settlements will not price most government services out of the market, although the resulting tax increase may drive elected officials out of office.

Certainly there are important differences between strikes in government and work stoppages in private industry. At the same time, strikes by public and private employees have the same economic objectives—the improvement of wages, hours, and working conditions. Given the low salaries and poor conditions which often characterize employment in our schools, hospitals, social agencies, and other public services, one is loath to deprive these employees of any legitimate weapon to improve their situation, unless it is clear that irreparable injury may result to the community at large.

The United States has come a long way in dealing with public employee-management relations during the last few years. Future progress will depend, in part, upon how we handle the difficult problem of public employee strikes. What are the lessons of past experience for future policy on this issue?

1. The right to join employee organizations and to negotiate with their employers through representatives of their own choosing should be guaranteed to all public employees at all levels of government, by Federal legislation, if necessary. Government employees in backward states should not be denied these fundamental rights.

2. Governments have a responsibility to promote settlements without interruption of public services. This includes provision for mediation and factfinding with recommendations in all disputes in which an impasse has been reached in negotiations.

3. Employee organizations and public employers in all government services should be encouraged to develop their own procedures to resolve disputes without interruption of work, including the use of voluntary arbitration. Long experience in private industry has demonstrated that the parties are usually better satisfied with their own solutions than with those imposed from the outside.

4. Regardless of preventive measures or prohibitions and penalties provided by law, strikes in government will occur. Government policy towards such stoppages should take into account the nature of the service provided and the impact upon the public. There is no more reason to treat all strikes in government alike than there is to apply the same yardstick to all stoppages in private industry. Just as a work stoppage on the railroads or waterfront is handled differently from a strike in a widget factory, so should a strike of policemen or firefighters be regarded differently from an interruption of service in state liquor stores.

5. Public services should be classified into three categories: those which cannot be given up for even the shortest period of time, those which can be interrupted for a limited period but not indefinitely, and those services in which work stoppages can be

sustained for extended periods without serious effects on the community.

With respect to the first category, which in my opinion would include only police and fire protection and prisons, compulsory arbitration should be used to resolve negotiation impasses but only after all other methods have failed.

Strikes in the second group of services, which would include hospitals, public utilities, sanitation, and schools, should not be prohibited but should be made subject to injunctive relief through the courts when they begin to threaten the health, safety, or welfare of the community. The courts, in deciding whether or not to issue injunctions, should consider the total equities in the particular case and should utilize their traditional right to adapt sanctions against those violating injunctions to the particular situation, as recommended in the report of the Advisory Committee on Public Employee Relations to Michigan Governor George Romney. The term "total equities" includes not only the impact of a strike on the public but also the extent to which employee organizations and public employers have met their statutory obligations.

Work stoppages in government activities which do not fall into either of the above classifications should be permitted on the same basis as in private industry.

These changes in public policy will come slowly, if at all. Experimentation with different approaches in the states is desirable and should be encouraged. Eventually, however, I believe that laws dealing with employee-management relations in government will tend towards greater uniformity because the nature of public employment differs little among states, and employee organizations, which are national in scope, will insist on equality of treatment for all government employees.

THE STRIKE IN THE PUBLIC SECTOR
by John Bloedorn

This article originally appeared in the Labor Law Journal *of March 1969. Mr. Bloedorn is the personnel*

Reprinted with the permission of the author and publisher.

director of the Minnesota State Department of Taxation and president of the State Personnel Council.

To strike or not to strike—that is the question that once was applicable only to employees in the private sector. Now a critical development in current government-employee relations is that public employees are making use of the strike to an increasing degree even though the right to do so is not allowed in any state. The states are responding to this development by passing new laws through which public employees are gaining the right to share in the decisionmaking process affecting their wages and working conditions. Ten states have passed comprehensive laws dealing with employee relations. Twenty other states have passed laws that are less comprehensive or that apply only to selected groups of employees, such as nurses, teachers, or firemen.[1]

For the most part the new legislation being adopted covers all or some of these seven topics: (1) the right to organize and join labor organizations, (2) the right to present proposals, (3) the right to meet and confer with employers on matters relating to hours, wages, and working conditions, (4) the right to bargain collectively, (5) procedures for recognition, (6) provisions for dispute settlement, and (7) strike prohibition.

In Minnesota state employees are not allowed to bargain collectively but provisions for each of the other six topics are provided for by statute with the exception of the right to present proposals. This right exists de facto since the right to meet and confer is legally authorized. It is expected that public employees in Minnesota will be granted the right to bargain collectively this next session. The basis for this prediction is:

1. That Governor Harold LeVander voted in favor of a resolution adopted by the Midwest Governors' Conference on July 2, 1968, which called for the right to bargain collectively by public employees.

2. The Minnesota State Civil Service Department has gone on record favoring adoption of collective bargaining procedures.

3. The Governor appointed an *Ad Hoc* Committee of seven leading state administrators this past spring to study state employee relations generally and the use of collective bargaining in the classified service specifically.

4. All members of the State Personnel Council attended a one-day seminar pertaining to collective bargaining in the public sector on June 27, 1968.

5. The director of the Minnesota State Civil Service Department appointed an *Ad Hoc* Committee to study state employee relations this past spring. The committee's membership includes the Civil Service Director, five Personnel Directors of the largest state agencies, and the executive director and assistant executive director of Council 6 AFSCME (American Federation of State, County and Municipal Employees).

Each of these developments points to the fact that in Minnesota the question is not whether collective bargaining in the public sector should be authorized, but more specifically, what its structure, scope, and procedures should be. As a corollary to these considerations the strike issue becomes one of increasing relevance.

THEORY

For the most part almost all of the literature on collective bargaining in the public sector carries a post-1960 publishing date. President John F. Kennedy's Executive Order 10988, issued in 1962, may be considered the catalyst for the great interest in the subject. As an example, the July 1968 issue of the *Public Personnel Review* contains eight featured articles, three of which are on collective bargaining in the public sector. The issue also contains a special section listing the literature available on the scope of collective bargaining in public agencies. Of the 34 references listed, 31 of them were published subsequent to Executive Order 10988. The issue's editorial is also on public collective bargaining.[2]

In most of the current literature the strike issue is a primary consideration. The views expressed on it are many. Some discuss the issue but do not take a stand, but many others stand squarely on one side of the coin or the other. The following discussion enunciates these viewpoints.

HEADS UP

In general, those who favor lifting the ban argue that the strike must be granted if collective bargaining is to be effective. They claim that a no-strike policy enables public agencies to refrain from negotiating in good faith or from assuming responsibility for finding necessary funds for proper pay and working conditions. This seems to be the current view of most employee organizations. Previously many employee organizations disclaimed the right to strike, but now they vigorously claim that such a right must be granted. As an example, the position of the AFSCME has become more militant on the issue as is vividly displayed in the following statements.

In 1962, Arnold S. Zander, then the international president of the AFSCME stated:

> The strike, the basic union weapon in union negotiations in private employment, is the most questioned and most controversial device in labor relations in public employment. We oppose strikes: they should not be necessary. To outlaw strikes will not eliminate them, bona fide negotiations will.[3]

Five years later, Jerry Wurf, the present international president of AFSCME stated:

> Strike prohibitions are not simply ineffectual, though they are undeniably that. What is far more serious, they warp the vital process of collective bargaining. They bring employees to the bargaining table, but as inferiors. Simultaneously, they provide false reassurance to management representatives and induce less than genuine negotiations. Ironically, they create the very tensions, exacerbate the very situations, provoke the very strikes they were allegedly formulated to prevent.[4]

The employee organizations have support for their contentions from a number of high-ranking government officials. Raymond F. Male, the Commissioner of Labor and Industry in New Jersey, is one of those who feels the right to strike can be imperative:

> Oh the cries of the wounded when somebody strikes against government. "Of the people, by the people, for the people. You can't strike against us. When you took this job, you understood that didn't you?" . . . I submit to you that critical as it may be to head off a strike in a hospital, it

may be more critical not to have the weapon available to workers to alert management, government, the customers of government, and the public that they must do something; that they cannot go on ignoring the problem.[5]

Dr. O. Glenn Stahl, director of the Bureau of Programs and Standards of the U.S. Civil Service Commission, in his book, *Public Personnel Administration,* concluded that, ". . . striking on the part of public workers does not seem to be a hazard to the public welfare as a practical matter, nor does legal prohibition appear to be justified on a theoretical basis."[6]

Leonard D. White, in his now classic study on the issue, argued that only those strikes posing a serious threat to the public interest should be prohibited by law:

> The true criterion of distinction should be based on the nature and gravity of the consequences involved in a strike, whether by persons employed by government, by a government corporation, by a public trustee, by a mixed enterprise, by a private corporation affected with a public interest, or by a privately owned and operated industry or enterprise. The rule may be stated in some such terms as these: A strike that would bring direct, immediate, certain, and serious danger to a primary interest of the community should be prohibited by law, with adequate sanctions, but also with adequate means to secure full public consideration and solution of the issues involved. In other cases the law should remain silent. The criterion of distinction is therefore the consequence of a strike upon the public interest, not the status of the employer.[7]

This argument is further elaborated on by Sterling Spero, whose thinking on the strike issue also was one of the forerunners of the contemporary views of public employee organizations:

> When the state denies its own employees the right to strike merely because they are its employees, it defines ordinary labor disputes as attacks upon public authority and makes the use of drastic remedies, and even armed forces the only method for handling what otherwise might be simple employment relations.[8]

These arguments lead William B. Vosloo in his outstanding book, *Collective Bargaining in the U.S. Federal Civil Service* to state:

> We conclude then, that the democratic ideology does support the rights of all citizens, whether government employees or not, to play reasonably full roles as citizens. . . . Furthermore, in the absence of the strike weapon or the right to resort to arbitration, public employee organizations would be virtually helpless in the face of adamant management, were they not to have recourse to the weapons of "pressure politics." Consequently, there are both theoretical and practical reasons for granting to civil servants a citizen's role similar to that afforded those who do not happen to be on the payroll of the government.[9]

TAILS DOWN

On the other side of the coin stand fifty state laws, court decisions, or attorney general opinions, and one Federal statute banning the use of the strike as well as a host of government officials and knowledgeable experts on labor relations. Simply stated, they feel that the strike is not an appropriate weapon in the public service and should be prohibited. They argue that government services are essential and cannot be dispensed with. They contend that while the strike is valid in the private sector where economic resources are distributed by the action of market forces, it is not appropriate where resources are raised and distributed by government. They argue that strikes are attempts to substitute the private and personal interest of the employees for the public interest, and that the authority of administrators is so limited that they do not necessarily have the power to commit the government to the demands requested in lieu of a strike. One of the most forceful arguments against the strike has been made by W. D. Heisel and J. D. Hallihan, city officials in Cincinnati, when they state:

> A strike is fundamentally an economic contest. Strikes are called when a union believes it has greater economic strength than a company and that the company must modify its negotiating position to an acceptable point

or be put out of business. In government, this basic assumption simply does not exist. No state, county or city government is going out of business. Public services are essential and must be maintained.[10]

Many of those who favor the use of the strike feel that a distinction should be made between those government employees who perform essential services and those who perform nonessential services. They argue that there is no justifiable reason why those who perform nonessential duties should not be allowed the right to strike. On the other hand, the New York Governor's Committee on Public Employee Relations, in their report, point out that definitions of what constitutes nonessential services would surely be so controversial as to be administratively impossible. The committee's chairman uses the example of a state park ski instructor in defense of this stand when he states: "Many would doubtless argue that the unavailability of ski instruction, because of a strike, would jeopardize, in a real way, their health and safety."[11] It is interesting to note that Jack Stieber, who was the chairman of the Governor's Task Force on Labor (Michigan), seems to reject this argument, but does oppose the use of strikes for political reasons: "The second, and in our view the more fundamental, argument against lifting the prohibition on the strike in public employment holds that the work stoppage does not serve the same purpose in public employment that it does in private industry. . . . The difference is that the threat is political rather than economic."[12]

Many others reject the strike because of this political threat. It is interesting to note that socialist Frank Zeidler, who served as the director of the Wisconsin Department of Resource Development and was formerly the mayor of Milwaukee for twelve years, forcefully states this position:

> There is, it seems to me, one issue that must be considered "settled" in this nebulous area of public management and official attitude of elected public officials toward employee organizations. This issue is the right to strike. In a democracy, with a truly representative government in office, it cannot be a prerogative of an employee organization to force a government to capitulate by striking a crucial service. If a strike can force a duly constituted, elected, demo-

cratic government to capitulate, this action signifies that the power of government has shifted from the people to employee organizations. A public employee organization cannot argue that it more fundamentally represents the people's interest than does a duly elected representative, democratic government, and that therefore it can strike that government.[13]

More simply stated, no single group can substitute its private interest for the public interest in a system of representative government.[14]

Arvid Anderson, who heads the New York City Office of Collective Bargaining and is a veteran public employee relations practitioner, argues that strikes challenge government sovereignty:

> The reasoning behind court decisions and statutory prohibitions of strikes in public employment is simply that government will not permit a challenge to its sovereignty by the use of the strike weapon. This viewpoint has been summarized: Those who work for governmental bodies are deemed to have a higher obligation to refrain from interfering with its operations than does the ordinary citizen. This explanation makes more sense than attempts to justify prohibitions against strikes by public employees on the grounds of health and safety factors alone.[15]

One final argument in opposition to the use of the strike is that often the management negotiator does not have the authority to accept a proposal which would avoid the threatened strike. He must bargain within the monies appropriated and is not in a position to commit the true source of authority, the legislative body, to an expenditure beyond that which is appropriated or might be appropriated. This point was vividly made by Franklin DeWald in a recent speech to AFSCME officials:

> The fact is that the critical point in public bargaining does not occur between the public executive and the union negotiators at the bargaining table, where they are expected to bargain in good faith according to sacred formula[e]. The critical point comes when the legislative branch appropriates funds from the taxpayers' pocketbooks to finance

the costs of the bargaining agreement. What is the worth of a public administrator's signature on an agreement when he cannot authorize or guarantee the money, or the changes in an ordinance or law to fulfill these agreements? The agreement may be used as a lever on an appropriating body, but it certainly is a far cry from the signature of Malcombe Denise on last year's Ford Contract.[16]

In conclusion, those who oppose the strike seem to base their stand on one or more of the following: the public sector differs from the private sector, a strike interferes with essential services, it would not be in the public interest, it threatens the sovereignty of government, and administrators lack authority to make certain binding commitments.

STRIKE PROHIBITIONS

Having presented both arguments it should be noted that strikes against the government are almost universally prohibited by the states. These prohibitions take the form of such legal measures as laws, court decisions, personnel rules, and attorney general opinions.

Jack Stieber, in his chapter "Collective Bargaining in the Public Sector," states that six states have what he terms comprehensive law pertaining to public employment including Minnesota. It is of interest to me that he singles out the Minnesota strike prohibition for special consideration:

> It is interesting to note that five of the six states with comprehensive laws, although expressly prohibiting strikes by public employees, do not spell out penalties for striking employees. Only Minnesota specifies such penalties, including termination of employment, and if reappointed employees may not be paid more than before the strike, must wait at least one year for any increase in compensation, serve a two-year probation period and lose tenure right. These penalties are similar to those contained in the Condon-Wadlin law of New York state and in other states which detail penalties for strikers.[17]

The Condon-Wadlin law of New York was recently repealed because it was proven ineffective by the New York City transit strike, as well as other strikes in New York. George Taylor states that this law not only imposed impractical penalties but showed the impotence of government when it is handicapped with unworkable laws.[18] It would seem that the New York experience may well cause the Minnesota law to be revised this next session, particularly if collective bargaining is to become a reality.

PROPOSING A SOLUTION

The problem with proposing a solution for the strike issue is that it is impossible at this point in time to validate a solution favoring the right to strike because no state has seen fit to put collective bargaining into practice without some kind of strike ban. It also is impossible to validate a solution which provides procedures for collective bargaining with a strike ban because these experiments are so new that an assessment at this time would be premature. Professor James Stern of the University of Wisconsin has analyzed the first three years of experience with factfinding in Wisconsin and concluded that, "The law has made a substantial contribution to the improvement of collective bargaining among public employees."[19] In contrast, union officials in Wisconsin are generally disappointed in the law because its scope is too narrow.

In Oregon the results to date have been disappointing according to the *Report of Task Force on State and Local Government Labor Relations* produced by the 1967 Executive Committee of the National Governors' Conference. The report also seems to suggest that the Wisconsin experience has been comparatively more successful because their law is well structured: "The experience of Oregon illustrates the kinds of problems that arise, when a state consents to collective bargaining with its own state employees. . . . In contrast to Oregon, Wisconsin state employees bargain under the provisions of a well-structured law."[20]

The Michigan experience also appears to be disappointing, according to Franklin DeWald:

> In Michigan in 1966, the first full year after our public employee relations act was amended to require collective bargaining by local units of government (but still prohibiting strikes), we had 23 strikes in public employment, more than in the previous 20 years. In 1967 we had

about twice that many, and friends in the State Labor Mediation Board are fearful of a further increase in number this year.[21]

The one experiment with collective bargaining with a strike ban which seems to be a success is that of Tennessee Valley Authority (TVA). Whether this experience is transferable to state governments in dealing with their employees is doubtful, though, because the TVA, a public corporation, has a uniquely different relationship with Congress than that of state agencies with their state legislatures. More specifically, the TVA negotiators have the necessary administrative authority to make binding agreements on almost all matters affecting employees. One instructive finding is made by Arthur Thompson and Irwin Weinstock who concluded:

> Managerial attitudes toward employee organizations may prove to be the most important factor influencing the success of collective bargaining in the public service. There can be little doubt that the attitudes of white-collar TVA employees toward unions and the obvious success of collective bargaining have mainly been the product of TVA management's affirmative willingness to share its decision-making powers with unions in matters affecting the employees.[22]

Thus it would seem too early to test the hypothesis of most scholars who, according to the above-cited Task Force Study, hold that positive labor legislation with procedures for dispute settlement is the best method of minimizing the number of strikes.[23]

I would like to propose a solution which at this point in time is purely speculative, since no state has seen fit to abolish its ban against strikes. The basis for the solution was derived from one sentence which appears in the *Report of Task Force on State and Local Government Labor Relations:*

> One of the most interesting developments to date is a clause in the 1967 Vermont law authorizing municipal employees to bargain collectively: No public employee may strike or recognize a picket line of a labor organization while performing his official duties, if the strike will endanger the health, safety, or welfare of the public.[24]

Solution. Assuming a collective bargaining act is adopted, the ban against strikes should be lifted so that effective collective bargaining could take place; but to protect the public health, welfare, and safety, a special procedure patterned after the Taft-Hartley national emergency clause should be included. Under such a provision the governor could direct the state attorney general to secure an injunction to prevent a strike, if the governor felt the state's health, welfare, or safety would be threatened by the strike. The court order could allow the state up to 45 days to conduct an election among employees on the employer's final offer and to settle the dispute.

Obviously, if such an approach were applied, procedures would be needed to make it work. Before suggesting a number of them, I would like to state that this solution is intended to be applicable to all negotiable items, but the procedures to be specified are intended to pertain only to those negotiable items which would apply to all state employees similarly such as: grievance procedures, state salary plan, fringe benefits, sick leave, vacation leave accrual, and transfers. Also, if factfinding steps would be used as would be expected on economic matters, they would be completed before negotiations would begin. Other items unique to individual departments such as: seniority rights, hours of work, application and interpretation of work rules, health and safety practices, promotions, layoff, discipline, and use of vacation leave would be negotiated at the department level and would necessitate different procedures.

Procedures. The contract period should be for two years, negotiations should be completed by January 1 of each year that the legislature would meet, and the agreement should take effect at the beginning of each biennium. The negotiated agreement should be submitted to the legislature at the beginning of the session. The legislature should be allowed to exercise a legislative veto power within 15 days after the proposal is submitted to it. The legislature should be able to veto the agreement in its entirety, or only objectionable portions. If the legislature did not exercise its veto power they would be expected to provide the necessary funds to implement it. If the legislature did exercise its veto, the proposal would be returned to the negotiators for reconsideration for up to 15 days. Then a revised agreement would be resubmitted to the legislature as before, which would become binding if not vetoed. If vetoed within 15 days, the legislature would explicitly specify what it expected in a final agreement. If this was objectionable to the employee representatives, they could declare a strike to commence another 15 days later.

If such were to take place, the governor could invoke the state strike emergency clause and direct an election to be held among employees on the employer's final offer. If the employees were to reject the final offer, a means of binding arbitration involving the appointment of two legislators, one member selected by the governor and the other selected by the employee organization; and a member, not being a legislator, selected by the other two appointees, would be used. The committee appointed would resolve the issue or issues before the end of the legislative session so that the necessary funds could be appropriated. The entire procedure, if all steps were needed, would be completed in 105 days or less, which is a shorter period of time than the 120-day legislative session.

I would submit that such an approach would successfully compromise the presently opposing positions held by those who favor a strike ban and those who oppose a strike ban. First of all, it would provide for the strike to be used as a weapon to insure effective collective bargaining. Employees would not be placed in an inferior position at the bargaining table. Thus, decisions pertaining to public employment would be bilateral rather than unilateral, and public employees would no longer have to consider themselves second-class citizens.

On the other hand, I would submit that this proposal adequately resolves each of the objectionable aspects of lifting the strike ban as enunciated by those who oppose the use of the strike. First of all, through the use of the governor's state emergency strike clause, the public's health, welfare, and safety would be protected because essential services would always be provided. Secondly, it recognizes that the public sector is different than the private sector, and that private sector strikes are economic threats, whereas public sector strikes are political threats. It provides a political means of resolution within which both the sovereignty of the state and the public interest, no matter how defined, are protected. Even if an issue were taken to the final step, two of the three arbitrators would be legislators and the matter would be resolved while all of the democratically elected decisionmakers would be under one roof. Finally, management negotiators would have the authority to negotiate effectively without the fear that they would be committing the state to something beyond which its constituency would accept, for the legislature would continue to authorize whatever was agreed upon through the use of a legislative veto or by having binding arbitration with two of the three arbitrators being legislators. While the legislative veto as used by congressional committees has been the subject of much criticism in the literature pertaining to legislatures, it would seem to have great potential for involving the legislature in the determination of public labor contracts as outlined above.

Viewed optimistically, such a proposal would provide the ultimate weapon to employee organizations, which they feel is essential to effective collective bargaining. Yet that ultimate weapon would never have to be actually used—only its threat of use.

CONCLUSION

In conclusion, I feel that the enactment of a collective bargaining act this next session, even with a strike ban, will be an important step toward improved public employee relations. Not because drastic changes will take place, for the Minnesota merit system presently provides adequately for almost all negotiable matters, but because the adoption of collective bargaining procedures will provide a great psychological lift to the AFSCME in the state service. It will give them a rallying point and something which they can take to prospective members to get them to join. With added membership will come greater security, and the union will be able to use its energies for improving employee relations rather than merely attempting to survive.

I firmly believe the TVA philosophy that unions should be viewed as essentially constructive forces rather than as necessary evils. As the personnel director of a state agency with a payroll of 1,200 employees during peak seasons, I am faced with a total union membership of less than 60 employees. In arguing for strong unions and not denying recognition, W. D. Heisel and J. P. Santa-Emma state some of the possible problems which occur when a union is weak:

(1) It will be smaller numerically and therefore not necessarily representative, just as a small statistical sample of anything is not likely to be representative of the whole; and (2) it will possibly be of poorer quality, and therefore inclined to be obstreperous, irresponsible, demagogic, extremist, or incompatible with management. If you express disapproval, the better employees may well stay away from unions. Or, if they do join, they may stay out of leadership positions. Thus, by default, its leadership goes to the malcontent.[25]

To a certain extent, both of the above enumerated circumstances exist in a number of state departments in Minnesota. The advent of collective bargaining may well change such situations to the betterment of both union and managements' goal-effective employee relations.

REFERENCES

1. 1967 Executive Committee-National Governors' Conference, *Report of Task Force on State and Local Government Labor Relations,* published by the Public Personnel Association on behalf of the 1967 Executive Committee of the National Governors' Conference, Chicago, 1967, p. 3.
2. See Kenneth O. Warner et al. (eds.), *Public Personnel Review,* Public Personnel Association, Chicago, 1968, vol. 29.
3. Arnold S. Zander, "A Union View of Collective Bargaining in the Public Service," *Management Relations with Organized Public Employees,* Public Personnel Association, Chicago, 1963, p. 38.
4. Jerry Wurf, "The Case for Collective Bargaining in the Public Sector," *Public Services International Bulletin,* Public Services International, London, 1967, p. 11.
5. Raymond F. Male, "Labor Crises and the Role of Management," *Developments in Public Employee Relations: Legislative-Judicial-Administrative,* Public Personnel Association, Chicago, 1965, pp. 104, 109.
6. Robert E. Catlin, "Should Public Employees Have the Right to Strike?" *Public Personnel Review,* vol. 29 (1968), p. 4.
7. Leonard White, "Strikes in the Public Service," *Public Personnel Review,* vol. 10 (1949), p. 6.
8. Sterling Spero, *The Government as Employer,* Remsen Press, New York, 1948, p. 16.
9. William B. Vosloo, *Collective Bargaining in the United States Fed-*

eral Civil Service, Public Personnel Association, Chicago, 1966, p. 35.
10. W. D. Heisel and J. D. Hallihan, *Questions and Answers on Public Employee Negotiations,* Public Personnel Association, Chicago, 1967, p. 193.
11. George W. Taylor, "Public Employment: Strikes or Procedures?" *Report of Task Force on State and Local Government Labor Relations,* published by the Public Personnel Association on behalf of the 1967 Executive Committee of the National Governors' Conference, Chicago, 1967, p. 42.
12. Jack Stieber, "Collective Bargaining in the Public Sector," *Challenges to Collective Bargaining,* Prentice-Hall, Englewood Cliffs, New Jersey, 1967, pp. 82–83.
13. Frank P. Zeidler, "Adjusting to New Public Personnel Policies," *Developments in Public Employee Relations: Legislative-Judicial-Administrative, op. cit.,* pp. 121–122.
14. Charles A. Meyer, "The Detroit Employee Relations Story," *Management Relations with Organized Public Employees, op. cit.,* p. 87.
15. Arvid Anderson, "Legal Aspects of Collective Bargaining in Public Employment," *Developments in Public Employee Relations: Legislative-Judicial-Administrative, op. cit.,* p. 147.
16. See "Public Management Views Public Employee Unionism," a speech by Franklin K. DeWald, Michigan State Personnel Director, at the AFSCME Conference, College Park, Maryland, March 1968.
17. Stieber, *op. cit.,* p. 74.
18. Taylor, *op. cit.,* p. 37.
19. Stieber, *op. cit.,* p. 75.
20. 1967 Executive Committee-National Governors' Conference, *op. cit.,* pp. 30–31.
21. See "Public Management Views Public Employee Unionism," *op. cit.*
22. Arthur Thompson and Irwin Weinstock, "White-Collar Employees and the Unions at TVA," *Personnel Journal,* vol. 46 (1967), p. 21.
23. 1967 Executive Committee-National Governors' Conference, *op. cit.,* pp. 33–34.
24. *Ibid.,* p. 89.
25. W. D. Heisel and J. P. Santa-Emma, "Unions in Cincinnati Government," *Management Relations with Organized Public Employees, op. cit.,* p. 119.

9

COMPULSORY UNIONISM OR
UNION SECURITY?

In collective bargaining contracts, labor unions seek security clauses called union or agency shops or maintenance-of-membership clauses. These clauses are essential, the unions insist, if they are to remain responsible parties to the contracts, particularly in situations where there is employee turnover.

In 1955 a single-purpose organization called the National Right to Work Committee was formed to promote right to work laws which called for the elimination of these union security clauses, branding them as compulsory unionism and a denial of worker rights. This committee has conducted a running fight against union shops while labor unions, in rebuttal, have called it an open shop organization campaigning for "Right to Wreck Laws." This conflict, which has been going on in the private sector, is now moving into the public sector.

In the following article, Reed Larson discusses the National Right to Work Committee's feeling on unions among public employees. The second article, from a labor publication, states the union side of the argument.

PUBLIC EMPLOYEES AND THEIR
"RIGHT TO WORK"
by Reed Larson

Mr. Larson is the executive vice president of the National Right to Work Committee, which he describes as a single-purpose organization concerned only with

Used by permission of the author.

266

> *opposing compulsory unionism. The motto of the com-*
> *mittee is: "Americans must have the right but not be*
> *compelled to join labor unions."*

Most Americans are puzzled, frustrated, and confused by the mounting waves of strikes and even violence in disputes affecting public employees: firemen, teachers, hospital employees, garbage collectors, and many more. Behind these disputes are a variety of issues, some of them undoubtedly involving legitimate employee grievances. But underlying much of the unrest is the agitation of union organizers seeking new fields to conquer.

With union membership among manufacturing and service industries having topped out in the last ten years, and in fact, declining as a percentage of the work force, union pros have looked for new fields to conquer. They found government unionism holds the most lucrative potential of all. There are twelve million government workers; three million Federal employees and nine million state, county, and municipal employees—and their number is growing by leaps and bounds. Now unions are in the process of turning this potential into membership. And with the help of some politicians who received campaign support from union treasuries they are making rapid strides.

In a column written last summer, syndicated labor columnist Victor Riesel, writing out of Bal Harbour, Florida, where the American Federation of State, County and Municipal Employees AFL–CIO was holding its annual convention, said, "There is talk of spending $2 million annually for unique deficit funding or organizing drives to put a union label on all state and local governments in the United States—to organize not just a million, not just two million, but soon to speak for literally 10 million public employees."

Riesel pointed out that the 1500 delegates who cheered their fiery leader, Jerry Wurf, when he demanded the right to strike every municipal and state service except the police and firefighters are deceptive in appearance. "They are neat, low-key people—the representatives of police, state troopers, grainweighers, port authority and highway workers, campus employees, garbage collectors, zookeepers, museum guards—the lifeblood of the block you live on." Yes, they are low-key, but as Riesel added,

they are conscious of their power and the most conscious of them
all is Wurf, who says his 400,000 followers—growing by 1,000 a
week, three times faster than any other union—will "argue at first,
then bargain but if necessary strike the city and state halls and
executive mansions."

Riesel continued,

> They sound quiet. But this is a tough union—ready to para-
> lyze any community from upper Michigan to Mobile. . . .
> They cheered Wurf again when he said AFSCME
> can be the number one union in all America. Because they
> know he means it. They know what the field is, explosive
> like some supernova on earth, what with six out of every 10
> new jobs in this country now developing in the "public
> sector."
> The old days of wheedling and begging, of pleading
> with civil service executives or mayors or governors or
> councils are on the way out. Done! Obsolescent! So Wurf
> says.

"They cheer," Riesel concluded, "and a world waiting for
news of wayward hurricanes and political storm doesn't seem to
hear this voice of the future."

Yes, the general public seems only to take notice when their
garbage piles up.

As strife and unrest spread among government workers
around the country early last year, the National Right to Work
Committee launched a study of the extent to which compulsory
unionism was involved. Here are some of the things we found.

—In Pennsylvania, garbage piled high in the streets of
Scranton as union bosses tried to blackjack city officials into a
compulsory agency fee contract for sanitation workers.

—More than 60 Michigan municipalities have contracts
which impose some form of compulsory unionism as a condition
of working for the government.

—There are now more than 125 unionized police departments across the nation; many of them require membership as a
condition of employment, and the first steps to form a single,
national policeman's union are being taken. Forced-joining is now
the "law" for policemen in Carlsbad, New Mexico; Oakland

County, Michigan; Waterville, Maine, and many more. A year ago the New Hampshire State Supreme Court ruled that the City Marshal and two brother officers in the small town of Berlin had to join a union in order to hold their police jobs.

—Demands of union officials for a compulsory agency shop were described by press reports as "a striking point" in last fall's New York City teachers' strike which kept more than one million children from classes as the fall school term was to begin. And just a few weeks ago the *New York Times,* in a lengthy analysis of the New York school strike, said, "Shanker had also sought an agency shop which would require all teachers to pay dues to the union whether or not they were members, and the Board of Education believes that the strike was called more to enforce that demand than for any other reason."

—The *Times* went on to say "No union of municipal employees has such a clause in its contract—though it is an open secret in the labor movement that the City expects to begin granting agency shops in 1969." Quite prophetic. Just last February, Mayor John Lindsay appealed to the state legislature for approval of a bill which would allow the agency shop. He needed this action to legalize contracts he has already signed which would compel 90,000 of New York City's public employees to pay union dues as a condition of continued employment!

The National Right to Work Committee immediately raised a strong objection to the proposed "agency shop" law which, we felt, would compel thousands of New York City's public employees to finance an incumbent mayor's bid for reelection.

In an open letter to Governor Rockefeller we said,

> Approval of the "agency shop" bill would empower labor union officials allied politically with the Mayor to collect the equivalent of union dues from approximately 90,000 municipal employees. These employees have declined to join and support unions presumably because they believe union representation is more harmful than beneficial.
>
> It is a well-established fact that Mayor Lindsay's previous campaigns for public office have produced substantial contributions from union treasuries. Approval of the "agency shop" legislation he seeks would pave the way for the extraction from every City employee's paycheck of

money which would be used by union officials to underwrite Mayor Lindsay's campaign for reelection.

Our opinion was echoed in a blistering editorial in the *New
York Daily News,* February 26, 1969, titled "Windfall for the
Unions." The editorial said,

> Under agreements now being signed and sealed, city
> workers will be delivered to the unions via the "agency
> fee." This is the device used to force nonunion employees
> to cough up sums equal to those paid as dues by union
> members.
>
> The agency shop—which is compulsory unionism in
> everything but name—most likely will be applied first to
> 47,000 city hospital workers in Victor Gotbaum's State,
> County and Municipal Employes union.
>
> The Lindsay-Gotbaum deal is a blatant betrayal of
> the rights of nonunion city workers. It will also swell the
> war chests of the labor nabobs, practically guaranteeing
> they will be even more sassy, defiant and demanding in
> future negotiations.

—The final example is at the Federal level. The evidence was
strong that a political deal between former President Lyndon
Johnson and union officials to pave the way for the forced unionization of three million Federal employees had been made early
last year. Fortunately, the public outcry which followed the disclosure forced union bosses and administration officials into a
hasty retreat. As the *St. Louis Globe-Democrat* said in an editorial,

> . . . Freedom of choice and freedom of association are
> historic American rights. The thought of compelling any-
> one to join an organization against his will is thoroughly
> repugnant. In this case of government employees it is also
> objectionable on the grounds that it would tend to trans-
> fer an employee's primary loyalty from the government to
> the union—a situation that could lead to chaos.

It is easy to figure out why union officials put compulsory
membership at the top of their "want list" when negotiating with
public agencies. There are more than twelve million public em-

ployees, including nearly three million Federal employees. If every public employee were under compulsion to pay union dues of $5 a month, the take would amount to $700 million a year—not counting millions in initiation fees!

The stakes are enormous and the union bosses are at work. As Jerry Wurf said, "Our potential is nothing less than fantastic . . . right now six out of every ten new jobs being created are jobs in government." He added that his union would have a million members now instead of just 400,000 if all his contracts called for compulsory unionism!

It is obvious to us that union officials, with the help of some politicians, who receive campaign support from union treasuries, are making fantastic progress in a massive, coast-to-coast, community-by-community program aimed ultimately at locking every public employee into a contract forcing him to pay dues into a union treasury in order to keep his job.

To us the real threat in the compulsory unionization of government workers lies in the fact that it provides a thinly disguised pipeline diverting enforced salary deductions in the form of union dues to provide campaign funds for union-controlled politicians—politicians who as public officials are the government employee's bosses, and who are the very persons who forced him to pay the union in the first place.

The action of Mayor Lindsay is an excellent example of this problem and graphically illustrates why the AFL–CIO recently made an unprecedented decision at the national level to participate fully in campaigns for mayors and other local officials. In the past this has always been left to the local unions, some of which are effective and some of which are not. Our interpretation of this new emphasis is that it is part of an overall program aimed at obtaining union-controlled public officials at the local level who will—to put it bluntly—roll over and play dead whenever they are confronted by a union organizer representing a handful of militant employees.

The crux of the problem here is the inordinate influence of union political power on public officials charged with the responsibility of setting employee policies. In private industry, the interests of union officials are being served primarily on one side of the bargaining table. But in public employee bargaining we can see what amounts to an agent of union power representing both the employer and the organized employees. The solution, as we see it, is to make compulsory unionism illegal; to take the choice of membership or nonmembership in an employee union out of the hands of the politician and the union professionals, and keep it where it belongs—with the individual employee.

It is the widespread practice of compulsory unionism in private industry that frees union officials from the normal responsibilities of operating a voluntary organization. It is compulsory unionism that releases a major percentage of union resources directly for political action rather than for selling and maintaining membership. According to union spokesmen, retention and expansion of compulsory membership is essential if they are to continue and expand the political activity which they consider necessary and desirable.

Union representative Walter H. Barnes, of the Teamsters Local 636 in New Jersey, let the cat out of the bag last fall after the New Jersey legislature, over the veto of Governor Richard Hughes, passed a Right to Work law covering the state's public employees. Barnes said, "Since we can't get the union shop I have orders from the President of our local to stop trying to organize the Department of Public Works in Englewood because it just isn't worthwhile."

The late President John F. Kennedy clearly recognized the danger involved in the forced unionization of public employees when he insisted that his 1962 Executive Order 10988, authorizing the unionization of Federal employees, also protect the right *not* to join. That order reads: "Employees of the Federal government shall have, and shall be protected in the exercise of the right, freely and without fear of penalty or reprisal, to form, join and assist any employee organization or to refrain from such activity." That part of the Kennedy Executive Order can properly be called the Federal employees' Right to Work law. And as long as it remains in existence compulsory unionism cannot exist for Federal employees.

President Kennedy's Secretary of Labor, Arthur Goldberg, in explaining the order in a speech to members of the American Federation of Government Employees AFL–CIO said,

> I know you will agree with me that the union shop and the closed shop are inappropriate to the Federal government.

And because of this, there is a larger responsibility for enlightenment on the part of the government union. In your own organization you have to win acceptance by your own conduct, your own action, your own wisdom, your own responsibility and your own achievements. . . . So you have an opportunity to bring into your organization people who come in because they want to come in and who will participate, therefore, in the full activity of your organization.

As I mentioned earlier, a suspected "deal" to revise the order and put Federal employees under some form of compulsory unionism was dropped last year as a result of public protest. The National Committee disclosed early in the year that a Presidential compulsory membership Review Committee, set up by President Johnson in late 1967 to recommend changes in the Executive Order covering labor-management relations for Federal employees, was considering compulsory unionism. While the flood of public protest forced the Johnson administration to drop their plans, the threat of compulsory unionism will continue to hang like the sword of Damocles over the head of every Federal worker, so long as the issue is subject to the whim of whomever might occupy the White House.

Fortunately there are members of Congress aware of and working to correct the problem. The leader in the House is the dynamic, young Georgia Congressman, Ben Blackburn, who introduced a Federal Employees Freedom of Choice Act last year and reintroduced it early this year. This legislation features the exact language of the 1962 Kennedy Executive Order. The right of Federal employees to join or to refrain from joining employee unions was also endorsed in the platform adopted by the Republican National Convention last August. The platform statement pledged, "We pledge to protect Federal employees in the exercise of their right freely and without fear of penalty or reprisal to form, join or assist any employee organization or to refrain from any such activities."

In reintroducing his bill Congressman Blackburn said,

I am hopeful for some action this year. Implementation of a GOP platform pledge supporting a "Right to Refrain" law was embodied in President Nixon's late September position paper on labor management relations for Federal employees. This bill should be passed, and quickly. Not only to protect the Federal employees but to act as a model for state legislation—such as enacted in New Jersey last year protecting the rights of millions of public employees throughout the nation.

The Senate counterpart of the Blackburn bill has been introduced by Senator Wallace Bennett of Utah and cosponsored by 17 other Senators.

There is a large number of Senators and Congressmen—representing a cross section of political philosophy—that indicated their support of Congressman Blackburn's proposal.

A National Committee survey during the 1968 political campaign revealed that congressional candidates, who responded overwhelmingly, favored the Federal employees Right to Work law. The count was 177–8, and not one of the incumbents favoring it was defeated. Senator Edward Brooke of Massachusetts said, "You can be sure that I am against compulsory unionization." Congressman William Moorhead of Pennsylvania said, "I certainly agree that an individual should have the right to determine whether or not he wishes to join a union." Senator Charles Percy of Illinois said, "I would not support legislation for a closed shop in government service," and Senator George McGovern of South Dakota said, "I believe firmly that the decision whether or not to join a union should be a matter of free choice."

Practically speaking, however, it is unlikely that Congressman Blackburn or Senator Bennett will get favorable, if any, action on their bills. Ironically it is the Committee seniority system—the favorite whipping boy of the union bosses for years, but now a way of insuring that union-dominated politicians control key Committees—that probably will block constructive legislation in favor of the individual worker.

However, union professionals will still have to contend with an Administration bound by the language of the Republican platform and led by President Nixon, who pledged on October 21, 1968, to press for legislation that would "recognize the right of a Federal employee to join an employee organization if he chooses to do so."

What state legislatures and the Federal Government do in the next few years in terms of labor relations for their own employees is a crucial question. One can only hope that the direction is not that taken by the Federal Government in handling industrial labor relations.

The few laws enacted which attempt to restrain union excesses through government regulation of internal union affairs have been eroded through application of union political power. The problem is basically one of union power—power concentrated in the hands of a few top union officials and used to elect and control public officials. For the past 30 years Congress has piled legislation upon legislation for the express purpose of enhancing the power of labor unions without providing the restraining influence of voluntary union membership. Syndicated columnist James J. Kilpatrick summarized it quite well when he said, "At the bottom of this whole business is the vice of compulsory unionism."

There is one other aspect of public employee labor-management relations that should be touched upon—the matter of exclusive representation. When you talk to most people about granting organizing rights to public employees, you automatically mean giving the majority the privilege of speaking for all, including the unwilling minority. Perhaps it is time to challenge that concept. Perhaps this idea—one of the fundamental assumptions in our present system of labor law—is erroneous.

Congressman Ben Blackburn was one of the first to raise this question of the validity of granting public employee unions exclusive representation rights. On September 25, 1968, he introduced a comprehensive bill to provide for improved employee management relations in the Federal services. The bill—H.R. 19983—includes the following language,

> When an employee organization has been recognized as the exclusive representative of employees of an appropriate unit it shall be responsible to represent only those employees who are members of that organization and shall be entitled to ask for their negotiation agreements covering

employees who are members of the Government employees union only.

The importance of exclusive representation will never be discounted by some 1500 teachers in the Florida school system. Ten months ago the Florida Education Association called for "a mass resignation" of their members—the first statewide teachers' strike in the nation's history. Nowhere was the strike more bitterly contested than in Miami's Dade County. There the Dade Classroom Teachers Association, the largest local of the FEA, led the walkout. However, members of the much smaller Dade County Education Association, opposed in principle to a teachers' strike, struggled along with outraged parents to keep Miami schools open. The strike finally ended with what can only be called a "lulu" of an agreement between the CTA and the Dade County Board of Public Instruction.

Under the agreement the CTA, which represents about 6,300 of Miami's 9,000 teachers, is to have exclusive bargaining powers with the Dade County board. These powers extend not only to wages and working conditions, but to professional matters as well. Only the CTA would have the privilege of payroll deductions. The CTA would name members of the Professional Policies Committee. It would have exclusive privileges of union meetings on school property, days off with pay for teacher conferences, use of the interschool mails, and *even* exclusive use of school bulletin boards. In every school building, the CTA would appoint one teacher as union agent or shop steward in charge of grievance negotiations. Jimmy Hoffa could not have drafted a contract with more clout.

Under the agreement, those teachers who did not go out on strike, the guys with the white hats, the guys that kept the public schools open—those guys were left out in the cold. They could not so much as post a notice, solicit members on school property, or call a meeting of its own members after school hours. An independent teacher could not even work out a grievance privately with school authorities; a "written copy of the disposition of the grievance" would have to be given to the CTA.

As Jack Kilpatrick said, "There you have it . . . They can join the CTA and pay $60 a year in dues to a union they despise, or they can remain aloof and be denied any effective voice in the formation of professional policies. Such dilemmas may be familiar in industrial employment; they are novel, and they are damned ugly in the classrooms of our public schools."

Since then a state court has ruled the agreement null and void since "the public policy of Florida does not permit collective bargaining of public employees." But as Jack Kilpatrick concluded, "A heavy-handed precedent has been set in the nation's seventh largest school system. What now distinguishes the teacher from the longshoreman? Anything at all?"

In the coming months as we delve further into the morass of determining what is a fair and just way to deal with public employee unions, it may well be that the concept of exclusive representation should be carefully studied. The "sweetheart" deal consummated in Dade County late last year is, in fact, the pattern already being legislated in state after state. It seems that now is the time to challenge or at least question this approach.

As a single-purpose organization the National Right to Work Committee is concerned only with compulsory versus voluntary unionism. We believe the drive for compulsory dues underlies most of the current turmoil in public employee-management relations. And we believe strongly that any meaningful labor legislation—for industrial as well as public employees—must have as its foundation the elimination of compulsory unionism. It is our firm belief that the record shows that voluntarism will go far to provide the checks and balances necessary to keeping union leadership responsive to the individual member.

WHY UNION SECURITY?

The following article that was provided by Francis E. Lavigne of the Massachusetts State Labor Council AFL–CIO shows why organized labor is opposed to the work of the Right to Work Committee. This material was prepared by the various departments of the AFL–CIO in Washington.

Roughly 80 per cent of all union members work under some type of union security clause.

What is union security?

It is a provision in a labor-management contract that says, substantially, that every worker who gets a job at the plant must join the union.

Many of the largest and most efficient industries in the country operate almost totally under union security provisions. In automobile, steel, construction, aviation, clothing, printing, and a host of others, employers and unions have agreed on union security clauses. Union security is popular with workers, unions, and employers.

During its first years, the Taft-Hartley Act provided that no union security contract could be signed unless it had been specifically authorized by a government-conducted secret ballot vote. That Taft-Hartley provision was dropped when it became apparent that workers, by secret ballot, were 85 per cent to 95 per cent in favor of union security.

Workers like union security because it helps all the workers, as "citizens" of their industry or trade, to share the responsibilities of the union which has helped to bring them economic and social benefits.

Union leaders like union security because it eliminates the threat that their organizations may be undermined through outside or illegal interference. Union security promotes industrial stability and permits the union, on the basis of its accepted status, to work constructively with management in a more cooperative relationship.

Employers have found that union security improves morale among the workers—because every worker knows that responsibility is equally shared and that the union, his collective bargaining instrument, has protection and status.

On the other hand, certain groups have been promoting legislation in the various states to outlaw union security. In 19 states, antiunion security statutes—popularly but mistakenly known as "right to work laws"—have prevented even employers and unions who want union security to include it in their collective bargaining contracts. The argument for these so-called "right to work laws" is that it gives workers an alleged "freedom of choice," whether to join the union or stay out.

But industrial experience proves this to be an illusory right that bears no relationship to the realities of life in the factories, shops, and mills.

Under the Taft-Hartley law, a union, when chosen by the body of workers, is the sole bargaining agent for all employees in the production unit. It has a responsibility to all workers; the benefits it wins apply equally to union member and nonunion member. The nonunion member, thus, is a "free rider" who takes the advantages and benefits of the collective bargaining process but refuses to assume his share of the responsibilities.

The states in which laws to outlaw union security have been passed are, for the most part, the least industrialized states. The effort of the sponsors of this type of legislation is less to prevent union security per se than to weaken or jeopardize the status of unions and to make the organizing of unions among unorganized workers more difficult.

In the states with the most industrial experience, so-called "right to work laws" have received little support. In Massachusetts, for example, both the Democratic and Republican parties joined together in the state legislature to defeat a "right to work law" proposal by a vote of 190–2.

The policy of the United States Government, as voiced by the Congress, is to encourage free and constructive collective bargaining. "Right to work laws" in 19 states hamper the collective bargaining process and hamper good industrial relations.

A number of religious groups have spoken out on the question of state laws to prohibit union security (the so-called right to work laws):

The Executive Board, Division of Christian Life and Work, National Council of Churches of Christ in the USA, June 1956, said: "It is [our] opinion that union membership as a basis of continued employment should be neither required nor forbidden by law: the decision should be left to agreement by management and labor through the process of collective bargaining."

The Rev. Dr. Walter G. Muelder, dean and professor of social ethics, Boston University School of Theology, Boston, Massachusetts said:

> The right-to-work laws are a virtual conspiracy of the crafty, the ignorant, or the misguided to subvert industrial

peace, exploit men's need to work, and deluge the community with industrial irresponsibility. Right-to-work laws do not create jobs; they only victimize the worker and make his organization ineffective.

Dr. Israel Goldstein, rabbi of Congregation B'nai Jeshurun in New York, and president of the American Jewish Congress since 1951 spoke out: "Since unions are required by law to represent all workers equally and without discrimination, a requirement which is proper, the states should not be permitted to prohibit fair and equal contributions to those same unions by workers who reap the benefits of such representations."

The Rev. William J. Kelley, O.M.I., L.L.D., a lecturer at Catholic University, Washington, D.C., and one of the nation's authorities on labor legislation said: "Right-to-work laws are immoral according to Catholic social teaching. . . . All good men and women, Protestants, Jews, and Catholics, should seek by every just means to get such right-to-work laws repealed and should oppose them whenever they are proposed."

The Rev. John F. Cronin, S.S., assistant director, Social Action Department, National Catholic Welfare Conference, has said:

> It should also be noted that the pressure for such legislation does not arise from workers seeking their "rights." Proponents of these measures are uniformly employers' organizations and related groups. Often such laws are part of a program by under-developed states, seeking to attract industry by the lure of a docile and low-paid labor force. Campaigns of this nature have been carried on in recent years with little or no attempt at concealment . . .
>
> Our conclusion, then, is that on political, social, and economic grounds the case for right-to-work laws is not sound. On the contrary, the employer groups who espouse them are acting shortsightedly, even in terms of their most selfish interests.

THE UNIONS' ANSWER

Under the headline: "Right Wing combines racism, open shop to provide 'friendly protection' for labor," the following article appeared in the Service Union Reporter *of March 1969. This is a monthly publication of the Service Employees International Union which represents thousands of workers in the public employee field. This article is fairly representative of anti-right to work articles found in the labor press.*

The National Right to Work Committee, the creature of anti-union employers intent on weakening and ultimately destroying the trade union movement, has reached a cynical low as the "friend and protector" of the worker's rights.

Over the years it has paraded across the country with high-blown rhetoric about freedom and liberty to the point where the public disbelief was nearly complete and total.

For the simple facts quickly surfaced—that the aim was freedom to exploit workers through low wages, company-dictated working conditions, and a complete lack of job security.

Keeping unions weak would produce these results in the minds of the right-to-workers, who dreamed of an earlier century when employers ruled as absolute monarchs.

DISCREDITED CAMPAIGNS

Its campaigns discredited and voted down wherever they surfaced, the Right to Work Committee revised its blatant approach, updated its public relations, and tried the "reasonable" approach, this time with ads and other materials that on examination were found to be filled with distortions, quotes ripped out of context, vague or nonexistent attributions of statements and all the rest of the pitchman's bag of tricks.

Now it has reached what can only be described as the bottom rung of a descent into abject cynicism.

It has rounded up a few men who typify the most exploited groups in the nation—workers who have been exploited by the antiunion, ultra-conservative forces over the years—and declared that these workers demonstrate the need for right-to-work laws.

The way to this protection is to join forces with a phony strikebreaker who is traveling the country trying to break the farm workers' strike and the boycott of the gallant men and women in the United Farm Workers Organizing Committee against the table-grape growers of California.

BADLY MISGUIDED

It is to join forces also with those badly misguided workers in the Negro community who have opted for black separatism, who in their turn to a racist approach would help weaken the trade union movement—the force that has helped bring human dignity and an end to exploitation to black and white workers alike by the millions.

And the right-to-workers have reached out also to the large area of poorly paid government employees to try and break a surging tide of unionism and organization among public workers —again black and white alike.

To use the poorest and the most exploited to insure that they will remain both poor and exploited by weakening the strength of the unions that can best give them aid and protection is an approach that no decent, self-respecting American citizen can tolerate.

There is inherent, perhaps, in this latest affront to conscience the final gasps of an organization that cannot by its very nature make a contribution to American society except to defile it.

But it is vital that the National Right to Work Committee be kept under relentless exposure so that its attempts to further exploit the current ills of our society are stymied, and reasonable and civilized men can go about the task of providing decent living standards, good jobs at good pay for the farm worker, the public worker, and the most cruelly exploited of all, the black worker.

10

OTHER VIEWPOINTS

In the following selections, a U.S. Senator, a Federal official, and a professor of public administration give their views on the challenges of collective bargaining in the public sector and discuss why the citizen should be concerned.

THE CHALLENGE OF PUBLIC
EMPLOYEE BARGAINING
by Robert P. Griffin

United States Senator Robert P. Griffin (R.-Mich.) delivered the following address at the National Conference of State Legislative Leaders on December 5, 1968.

Even the most casual observer of the contemporary scene is aware that something dramatic and revolutionary is going on in the ranks of government employees.

In 1966, there were 142 strikes involving state and local employees—exceeding the total for the four previous years combined. Such statistics have been on the rise since then.

Several days ago, policemen and firemen in Newark, New Jersey, called in "sick" and refused to go back to work until ordered to do so by a court.

School children are picketing now in New York City to protest longer classroom hours which have been scheduled to make up for the many weeks their teachers were out on strike this year.

A spokesman for the American Federation of Teachers has

Reprinted with the permission of the author.

written: "What American schools need most is more teachers strikes."[1]

On all sides there are growing signs, not only that more and more government workers are joining labor unions, but that they are becoming more and more militant in their attitudes toward government employers.

In June 1967, New York City welfare workers reported for work but then refused to perform their duties. Union instructions to their members read in part:

> Do not answer phones. Do not pick up pen or pencil. . . . Do not go into the field. . . . It is preferred that people be in groups since it will be difficult to determine who is working and who is not. . . . Clean out your desk. . . . Go to the bathroom. You cannot be denied your legal right to do so.[2]

Within a few days this "work-in" developed into a full-fledged strike which lasted for nearly six weeks and involved about two-thirds of the city's welfare workers.

Michigan officials are conscious of the fact that New York City is not the only place experiencing serious labor problems in government employment. Last year Detroit's policemen climaxed a dispute over wages by calling the station house to say they were "sick." It was the worst case of "blue flu" in the city's history. And, unfortunately, Michigan has been a "leader" as far as the number of teacher strikes is concerned.

In part, the quickening pace of organization in the public sector is the result of Executive Order 10988, issued in January 1962, by President John F. Kennedy. For the first time that order formally granted to Federal workers the right to organize and required government employers to bargain with employee representatives.

Although postal employees and Federal workers in a number of categories have belonged to employee organizations for many years, until then there had been no clear statement by the Federal Government of bargaining policy with respect to its own employees.

In the eyes of some, the 1962 Executive Order served not only to clear up some gray legal questions, but as indicated by the then Undersecretary of Labor, James J. Reynolds, it pointed to public employment as "a tremendous untapped area [for unions]—like opening a new oil field for them."[3] In the eyes of others, the 1962 Executive Order has opened up a Pandora's box.

According to Professor Kassalow of the University of Wisconsin, the United States is the first major industrial nation in the world to achieve the status of having more white collar than blue collar employees in the total work force.[4] In the face of a declining blue collar union membership, it is no wonder that some national labor organizations are focusing now on white collar government employees as a means of maintaining their relative strength.

According to the Department of Labor, union membership in this country dropped from 33.7 per cent of the work force in 1953 to 29.5 per cent in 1965. On the other hand, union membership among public employees, estimated now at about 1.5 million, reflects a gain of nearly 60 per cent during the last ten years.

Jerry Wurf, president of the American Federation of State, County and Municipal Employees, claims that the membership of his union has increased nearly 30 per cent in the last three years, making it the fastest growing union in the AFL–CIO.

Prompted by the 1962 Federal Executive Order applicable to Federal workers, a number of states have followed suit by enacting legislation which spells out organizing rights for local government employees and imposes an obligation to bargain upon local government employers.

Most noteworthy are the statutes or constitutional provisions in effect in Connecticut, Delaware, Massachusetts, Michigan, Minnesota, Missouri, New York, Oregon, Rhode Island, Washington, and Wisconsin.

Without purporting to provide a comprehensive analysis, I should like to focus special attention on the Wisconsin statute enacted in 1958 and 1962 and the Michigan statute enacted in 1965.

Generally speaking, under these two acts all public employees other than state employees are covered, and they are guaranteed the right to join labor organizations, to be free from certain unfair practices, and to bargain collectively with their public employers.

The Wisconsin act grants employees a wide degree of self-determination in fixing their own bargaining units which, in some cases, has resulted in considerable fragmentation and a multiplicity of unions with which public employers must deal. The Michigan statute, on the other hand, vests in the state agency (the Labor Mediation Board) much more discretion and authority in determining the appropriate bargaining unit.

Under both statutes, public employer representatives and recognized public employee representatives are required to bargain in good faith until they reach an agreement or an impasse.

Without going into more detail, the attempt is apparent throughout such legislation to lift many of the principles and concepts developed during the last thirty years in the private sector and make them applicable to labor-management relationships in the public sector.

Union spokesmen not only applaud the limited legislative efforts made to date, but they vigorously contend, in effect, that there are no essential, material differences between public and private employment which justify any significant limitations on the rights of government employees.

But many spokesmen for public employers contend just as vigorously that there are fundamental differences between the two types of employment which require that new and different concepts be developed to fit characteristics and limitations peculiar to public employment.

For example, the principles of collective bargaining which have been developed in the private sector have been premised on the right of employees to use the strike as the ultimate economic weapon. But strikes by public employees are universally condemned and are illegal in almost every jurisdiction.

Despite current efforts by some union leaders to bring about legislative changes, the general attitude toward government employee strikes is deeply imbedded in the body politic.

Governor Calvin Coolidge hit a responsive chord when he reacted to the Boston police strike in 1919 with the words: "There is no right to strike against the public safety by anybody, anywhere, anytime."

After championing enactment of labor's Magna Carta, the Wagner Act, President Franklin D. Roosevelt expressed the strong view in 1937 that, "Militant tactics have no place in the functions of any organization of government employees." He asserted that a strike against the government would be "unthinkable and intolerable."[5]

Even Walter Reuther has said, "Society cannot tolerate strikes that endanger the very survival of society. I don't think we ought to have strikes in public service industries."[6]

In 1947, the Taft-Hartley Act included a provision to the effect that any individual employed by the U.S. Government ". . . who strikes shall be discharged immediately . . . and shall forfeit his civil service status, if any, and shall not be eligible for reemployment for three years."

In 1955, Congress went further and provided that any person employed by the United States ". . . who participates in any strike or asserts the right to strike against the Government of the United States shall be guilty of a felony, punishable by a year in jail or a fine of $1,000, or both."

In contrast to developments in other areas of public employment, it is interesting to note that no significant work stoppages by employees of the Federal Government have been recorded in recent years.

Underlying any consideration of the pattern of illegal strikes and work stoppages among local government employees, one must take into account these questions: (1) Is it realistic to give government employees the right to bargain collectively and then to deny them the right to strike? (2) Is there any acceptable and workable alternative to the strike?

With regard to the first question, one writer has commented: "Granting the right to engage in collective bargaining to public employees and denying them the right to strike is like inviting a child to a candy parlor without allowing the child to taste the candy."[7]

Perhaps it is not surprising that Jerry Wurf takes the position that, "Without the right to strike, there can be no true collective bargaining for public employees."[8]

From time to time, various alternatives or substitutes for the strike have been proposed. Those most frequently mentioned involve (a) compulsory arbitration or (b) factfinding with public recommendations for settlement.

Any suggestion of compulsory arbitration runs headlong into a series of obstacles. For example, in a report by the Public Personnel Association the following comment by Arvid Anderson poses this practical consideration: "Based upon Wisconsin's two-year experience with a compulsory utility arbitration statute . . . *compulsory arbitration will mean the end of collective bargaining.* The parties simply do not try seriously to resolve their own disputes."[9]

Furthermore, compulsory arbitration raises substantial legal arguments which have to be considered. The main constitutional problem involves the doctrine that representatives of the people may not delegate to others the exercise of authority vested in them by law. The early cases consistently held that governmental authority may not be delegated to others.[10]

Despite such obstacles, some inroads have been detected. For example, Minnesota has a statute applicable to state, county, and municipal hospitals providing for compulsory arbitration to resolve any unsettled issues of hours or wages. Rhode Island is experimenting with a similar approach on a limited basis. In addition, one circuit judge in Michigan has held that a provision in a public employer collective bargaining contract calling for binding arbitration of grievances is "specifically enforcible."[11]

However, the principal proposed substitute for the strike is illustrated by an approach embodied in the Wisconsin and Michigan laws. In the event of a bargaining impasse, these statutes provide for factfinding with public recommendations, which are nonbinding.

In an evaluation of the Wisconsin experience, James A. Belasco has provided this interesting commentary:

> . . . the arbitrator keeps one eye on the possible public reaction and the other on the facts in the case. One might even speculate that the effective arbitrator first discovers the recommendations which will be accepted by the general public and then justifies his decision on one or the other of criteria mentioned above. In short, in advisory arbitration, which relies heavily upon public approval and support, acceptability is a crucial consideration, far more potent than specific facts and figures. . . . Thus it is not uncommon for the same arbitrator to employ different criteria in different cases involving the same issues.[12]

One important difference between the Wisconsin and Michigan statutes is this: Under the Michigan law a Mediation Board hearing officer, paid by the state, is assigned to find the facts and make recommendations. Under the Wisconsin act, the state board makes the assignment from a list of arbitrators and the costs involved are borne equally by the union and the public employer. It is contended that the cost in Wisconsin is a significant economic incentive which operates to encourage settlement without resort to this procedure.

In summarizing experience under the Wisconsin act, commentator Arvid Anderson said this:

> It is too early to say conclusively either that fact-finding will not work or that it is the ideal solution for resolving public employee disputes.
>
> Probably a decade of factfinding should be experienced before any serious attempt is made to resort to compulsory arbitration or consideration given to legalizing the strike weapon as a means of resolving public employee disputes.[13]

Obviously, public employee bargaining is a new frontier in labor-management relations. A great deal needs to be discovered, and we are fortunate, in a way, that there are 51 laboratories (the states and the Federal government) available for experimentation.

In conclusion, I believe these points deserve to be stressed:

1. The challenge of public employee bargaining does involve fundamental differences which distinguish it from bargaining in private industry, and no amount of rhetoric can brush them aside.

2. New concepts will have to be fashioned to accommodate such differences as this: A government manager generally lacks authority to make binding commitments whereas in private industry management has the power to make commitments as well as the power to back them up.

3. Settlement of a public employee dispute often involves political considerations rather than simply economic considerations.

4. A law prohibiting strikes must be enforced or it should be taken off the books. When government cannot, or will not, invoke

the penalties it threatens, strikes are not only encouraged but respect for the government is undermined.

Although the road ahead looks bumpy, I am confident that we will be able, in time, to forge the appropriate concepts and principles which will make it possible both to protect the public interest and to provide government employees with economic treatment which is roughly comparable to that accorded their private sector counterparts.

REFERENCES

1. David Selden, *Saturday Review of Literature,* May 15, 1969.
2. *The New York Times,* June 20, 1967.
3. *Ibid.,* April 2, 1967.
4. Kassalow, *American Labor,* June 1967.
5. Letter to the president of the National Federation of Federal Employees, August 16, 1937.
6. *National Civic Review,* July 1967, p. 394.
7. Clery, *Labor Law Journal,* July 1967, p. 408.
8. *AFL–CIO News,* March 19, 1966.
9. Report on Wisconsin Employment Board, p. 7.
10. For example, see *Mann* v. *Richardson,* 66 Ill. 481 (1873) and *Mugford* v. *Baltimore,* 8 L.C. 62, 137 (1944).
11. *Local 953* v. *School District of Benton Harbor, Berrien County,* 1967.
12. Report of Public Personnel Association on Wisconsin Employment Board, p. 12.
13. *Ibid.,* p. 7.

PUBLIC EMPLOYEE COLLECTIVE BARGAINING
by Richard P. McLaughlin

This address was delivered at a meeting of the National School Boards Association on December 12, 1968. Mr. McLaughlin is general counsel of the Federal Mediation and Conciliation Service.

Public employee collective bargaining is one of the more important public domestic issues of our time. In the area of labor-management relations, it is *the* issue of today. Lending to the importance of the issue is the urban context in which the public employment problem often appears. The disturbing crises in our big cities are pressing down upon us. We have seen several recent public employee disputes take on added meaning when it became apparent that the underlying social problems were the genuine causes of the dispute. I need only mention the sanitation workers' strike in Memphis last April or the recent teachers' disputes in New York to verify that proposition.

In a much broader sense, the current demands of public employees for representation and collective bargaining are illustrative of the mood of many Americans. People today want a "piece of the action." This is seen in the erosion of many of the old institutional forms and concepts. As *The New York Times* stated in its lead editorial on December 8, 1968, the roots of confrontation are found in "a deep social malaise that is expressed in an attack on all authority and institutions—from the power structure of local boards of education to the Vatican."

The *universities* are under great pressures today from students who want a voice in determining administrative and curriculum changes, among other things.

The *organized religions,* particularly the Catholic Church, are undergoing massive assaults against old ideas or doctrines which some people think are no longer responsive to today's needs.

An impatient generation of young and bright Americans is searching for a more individualized existence than they now see in an affluent, computerized society. They are largely skeptical of the established political machinery as an effective means for achieving it.

And, as the presidential election demonstrated, the old *political* forms and coalitions are no longer relevant. The primary system, the unit rule, the electoral college, and even the political convention itself are all in jeopardy because the voters now want to be involved—they want their voices to be heard and their vote to count. In this sense, we are rapidly moving to the arena of "participatory politics."

Fred Harris is a 37-year-old Senator from Oklahoma. He is an able and articulate spokesman for this new generation. As the dominant member of the Kerner Commission (the National Advisory Commission on Civil Disorders), he said it was the "frustration of powerlessness" that finally caused many Negroes to express their frustration in violent and destructive ways.

I believe that a frustration of a similar kind now exists for many public employees. They want to be involved, they want their voices heard, they want a "piece of the action" in deciding their terms and conditions of employment. In short, they want something like their brethren in the private sector now enjoy.

Yet, in many states, they are rebuffed by the esoteric legal doctrine that their employer is sovereign—the King Can Do No Wrong—and that collective bargaining, and even more so the strike, are unavailable to them. It seems that these old ideas, like the other causes of frustration, must accommodate to today's needs.

Public employees want, need, and I think are entitled to their fair share of the economic pie. More importantly, they are entitled to be heard.

Let me briefly give you my personal ideas and thoughts on how we can make some progress in this direction. Incidentally, I do speak for myself today, and not necessarily the Mediation Service or its director. I will make no comment on any state law covering public employment, except to recognize that such laws exist—and they provide a variety of measures which may or may not be effective. My comments are directed not to the way things are, but to the way they ought to be.

REPRESENTATION

First consider the matter of representation. I don't think anyone disagrees with the idea that employees, public or private, should have the right to express for themselves whether they wish to be represented by a particular organization. Where this right does not now exist it should be provided, preferably by legislation.

That legislation should also create an impartial board or agency to decide questions incidental to representation. For example, the matters of the "appropriate unit," or who should vote, standards for electioneering, and procedures for the actual elections are items that should be resolved by an impartial board other than the public employer.

The National Labor Relations Board, which administers the

basic labor law covering private employers, has set forth a very thorough set of procedures and rules in connection with unions organizing drives and elections. The Public Employment Board should be guided, to the extent that it is practical, by the NLRB rules and standards.

In those states where there is no public employment law, the parties may wish to agree, *by private contract,* to be bound by the NLRB rules and standards. Then, at least, the parties will have some guidelines to follow in determining these questions of representation. Here again, though, there is a definite need for an impartial board or agency to ultimately resolve disputes over the mechanics of representation.

I would also suggest that, in the event there is no impartial board or agency to resolve these disputes, the parties may wish to agree upon a third person, probably an arbitrator, to sit as the impartial party on these representation matters.

There are many public employers confronted with competing demands for recognition. In these cases, the employer is invariably charged with favoritism or giving assistance to the union which eventually prevails. Rather than assuming the hazardous role of deciding these tricky questions, it might be more sensible for the employer, if he does not wish to be bound by the rulings of a third party, to make a declaration that he will be guided in the course of the organizational campaign and election by published standards similar to those of the NLRB.

Several years ago, the governor of California invited Professor Ronald W. Haughton of Detroit's Wayne State University, who is also director of Michigan's Institute of Industrial Relations, to come to California to help resolve the labor dispute then affecting several large California grape growers, the Teamsters Union, and the Farm Workers Union. The major question was what union, if any, would represent the agricultural workers. Professor Haughton persuaded all parties involved to agree, by private contract, to be bound by procedures and standards of the NLRB. Only through this agreement were the thorny questions of representation decided.

Obviously, farm workers are not teachers; it is an entirely different situation except in one respect: like many public employees, these farm workers were not covered by any legislation. Yet these parties agreed to adopt and implement, by private agreement, a preexisting body of law.

To me, the imagination employed in this situation demonstrates that where the parties are in good faith and willing to work together, there are ways and means to resolve a mutual problem.

In short, it makes sense and is fair that the employees have the right to express their wishes through the election process. We have ample evidence to show that if employees are denied this basic and fundamental right, laws prohibiting the strike are meaningless.

MINOR DISPUTES

The Railway Labor Act, which covers employers in the railroad and airline industries, classifies labor disputes as "minor" and "major," and a separate procedure is provided for the resolution of each.

Simply stated, a "minor" dispute is one that involves a question about the interpretation or application of a collective bargaining agreement. Typically, such problems in the private sector arise with some regularity and are normally resolved through what is called "grievance machinery." This calls for the parties to attempt resolution of the matter according to a set procedure through escalating levels of responsibility. In the event no solution is reached, the matter is ultimately referred to an impartial arbitrator for his final and binding decision.

This system of "industrial jurisprudence" works very well in the private sector. About 95 per cent of all collective bargaining agreements provide for this private dispute-settling machinery. I can think of no reason why it could not be equally successful in the public sector.

The Federal Mediation and Conciliation Service, which I represent, maintains a roster of some 1200 qualified and experienced arbitrators who are available to hear such disputes. Many of these arbitrators are skilled and experienced in the area of public employment problems. Upon the request of the parties to a dispute, this agency furnishes a panel of arbitrators from which you may select one to hear and decide your dispute. Or, if desired, it directly appoints an arbitrator to hear and resolve the problem.

THE MAJOR IMPASSE

There is no recent subject which has generated more heat and less light than the questions of whether public employees should have the right to strike or whether public disputes should be settled by compulsory arbitration.

The current weight of opinion appears to be against the strike; it is, I believe, now illegal in almost every jurisdiction. Yet unions insist that collective bargaining is a meaningless gesture unless that right to strike is ultimately available.

On the other hand, compulsory arbitration is equally unsatisfactory since it is inconsistent with the concept of living in a free society. All employee organizations and virtually all employer groups oppose it. Labor relations professionals oppose it, as do most politicians. The prospect of a general compulsory arbitration law for public employment is indeed remote.

We are thus apparently in a position that our southern friends would describe as "between a rock and a hard place."

This should not be the case. All the speeches and articles on the subject have polarized the public and have supported this "either-or" logic. The problem is now phrased in such absolute alternatives as "we have compulsory arbitration or we don't," or "public employees should have the right to strike or they should not."

The efforts so far have been intended to find a substitute for the strike, or to bring finality to a labor dispute without calling it compulsory arbitration. These efforts have largely taken the form of blending together, in various mixes with various degrees of intensity, the procedures of factfinding and mediation. These devices, however worthwhile, are only part and parcel of the collective bargaining process. Both mediation and objective factfinding are essential tools in the resolution of labor disputes. But, they are not and cannot be made into *substitutes* for either of the ultimate alternatives of the right to strike or compulsory arbitration.

I firmly believe that *we should begin to think about these two ultimate alternatives in less than absolute terms.*

The strike, for example, is not an absolute right, even in the private sector. It has been limited by Congress and the courts for many years. We should at least begin to think about whether a limited or narrowly defined right to strike, provided certain other factors apply, could be developed to protect the interests of all parties, including the general public.

On the other hand, arbitration of labor disputes is not all bad. If the parties agree to use it, that is voluntary arbitration; only the award is compulsory. Here, too, then, we must consider another form of arbitration, limited, for example, to scope and duration, and available only when certain other conditions have been satisfied.

We must think about two new procedures or arrangements: one, that is a little bit less than the right to strike; second, an arrangement that is a little bit less than compulsory arbitration.

In this connection, consider an overall procedure that might be used in the event of a major impasse in collective bargaining. Ideally, this procedure would be set forth in a state law, just like the National Emergency Procedures are set forth in the Taft-Hartley Act. Although I have some ideas, I don't propose to set down in any exact order the precise steps or timing to follow to resolve such a major impasse.

On the contrary, such an effort would violate what should be the principal characteristic of the impasse procedure: flexibility. It must be flexible enough to be adapted to the particular circumstances of the case: the nature of the dispute, the kind of service performed and so on.

Second, the parties should be able to draw upon the skills and assistance of experienced mediators. Indeed, intensive mediation will normally and in most cases help produce a settlement. This has been the experience of the FMCS.

Third, objective factfinding should be used. Here, I speak not only of facts and evidence presented by the parties to a third person, but of data collected independently. The third person should be paid to do this. Perhaps the parties would agree in advance to accept his findings as accurate.

Fourth, pressures of various kinds must be built into the procedure to bear upon the parties. In the past, for example, these pressures have included fines, loss of certification, loss of checkoff, and even jail sentences. Frankly, I doubt that this kind of pressure is particularly effective, except perhaps in the most extreme cases. Recent experience should bear us out on this.

Rather, there might be pressures like objective and *final*

factfinding, first made privately and, if no settlement results, to the general public. Each side might be required, either at a public hearing or if applicable, before the legislative committee which appropriates funds, to explain and justify their last position and to explain why they have not accepted any recommendations made by the objective factfinder.

Another form of pressure on both sides would be present if the employees could vote, by secret ballot, on the employer's last offer. In the event of rejection, they could then immediately vote again, by secret ballot, on what further steps might be taken: for example, limited or general arbitration in some form, a limited strike, replacement of the bargaining committee, a counterproposal to the employer, or any other alternative the mediator might suggest. In short, the pressure is created here by placing the decision-making in the hands of the membership after they have a chance to vote on the last offer. Both parties would think long and hard before relinquishing this decision to a secret vote of the members.

The limited strike I mentioned above could be limited in several ways. First, it would always be subject to an injunction upon a judicial finding that it threatened the "public health, safety, or welfare." This is roughly the same standard used in the National Emergency Procedures except that it would apply on a local, not a national framework. This would obviously be the finding in the event of a strike of firemen, nurses, or policemen.

Next, the strike could be limited by placing a time limit, for example, 10, 30, or 60 days. Not much, you may say; I say it's better than nothing. You may say the public can't take such a strike; I say let a judge make that decision. Perhaps with this strike of limited duration would be combined the requirement of full arbitration if there was no settlement during the term of the strike.

The strike could also be limited, when realistic, by allowing the employer to contract out the work performed by the strikers.

The fifth characteristic of our impasse procedure is public exposure. It *is* the public who ultimately pays the bills, and determines the relative value of public service; they also have some voice in electing or appointing public officials. Once this procedure reaches the factfinding stage, the public should be equipped to form its own opinion so it can bring appropriate pressures to bear.

Sixth, there should be uncertainty of outcome. By building in contingencies, transferring the power of decisionmaking, and employing courses of action which are automatically triggered, each side will be kept off balance; they will not be able to predict the ultimate outcome of the dispute.

These six factors, combined together in varying degrees and blends, should pressure the negotiating parties into making a settlement short of the ultimate weapons. Remember, in most cases those alternatives will not be used; it is simply the therapeutic effect of their availability which improves the bargaining process.

Basically, all that has been suggested is that imaginative and creative persons, mindful of the public interest and the needs of the employees involved, should be able to develop procedures that are workable and realistic. We should stop thinking that the only alternatives in a public employee dispute are the unlimited right to strike or compulsory arbitration of the entire contract.

JOINT STUDY APPROACH

Those who have engaged in contract negotiations know how the tensions and pressures build up as the strike deadline approaches. This is hardly the climate in which parties can take a cool dispassionate look at emotional, particularly difficult, or long-range problems. Yet, it is in this crisis atmosphere that such problems arise.

I feel that the parties should establish procedures for the continuing study and discussion of their problems away from the bargaining table. This makes contract negotiations much easier.

The joint study group is not suggested as an easy device to avoid or indefinitely postpone decisions—far from it. The group I have in mind would be composed of representatives of each side, preferably at the highest level, who would confer on a regular basis and conduct their meetings according to very definite procedural ground rules. They might even choose to include informed neutrals in the group.

First, day-to-day disputes arising under the agreement would *not* be discussed. Other machinery should hear and decide those issues.

Second, the parties should have freedom of study and discussion without commitment. This permits a candid exploration of the issues without which accommodation and better understanding cannot occur.

Third, there should be no deadlines. It goes without saying that you cannot place a timetable on inventiveness.

Fourth, there should be no publicity or "leaks to the press" in connection with these meetings. This avoids the creation of false fears or expectations in anyone's mind and the attendant pressures that would ordinarily develop. Nothing is released until full agreement is reached.

Obviously, there might be other safeguards and procedural rules the parties might wish to follow, depending on the particular circumstances. The principal merit in this arrangement is that the parties are free to discuss, without commitment and inhibitions, their mutual problems.

This joint study approach is not new or novel. It has been successfully used by companies and unions in many other industries—notably, steel, longshoremen, meat packing, and construction—where the parties dealt with the emotion-packed issues of automation and job security. There is no reason why such a procedure should not be employed in the public sector.

FACTFINDING

Too often, in the past, factfinding has resulted in two competing sets of conclusions. If done by an outsider, one side will normally reject his findings. I think this kind of in-fighting can, and should, be eliminated.

It should be conceded that there is a paucity of information —cold, hard facts—upon which employees, unions, and public employers can base their future relationship. Without this information, particularly in the course of contract negotiations, the parties must rely on old wives' tales about tax levies, budgetary problems, comparative wages and skills of certain employees, unions and union leaders, and the real or imagined differences between the private and public sectors.

True and intensive factfinding has distinct advantages for all parties in a labor dispute. Placing the union's economic proposals in the proper perspective may actually persuade the public employer; it helps the employees themselves to understand what is a realistic, just, and attainable goal. And, perhaps most critically, once the agreement is made, the parties together may then convince the public that the agreement is a sensible and fair one.

This intensive factfinding could be done unilaterally, but preferably by the parties together. To achieve maximum effectiveness, however, the findings, to the extent possible, should be put in a form fully acceptable to both sides before negotiations actually commence.

This task is one that very naturally could be included on the agenda of the joint study group that was mentioned.

The basic findings should come from an objective, but expert source, and could include surveys of wage rates and benefits for persons in different localities engaged in comparable situations. These could be analyzed in light of the cost of living, productivity,, and similar data. Public sentiment could be explored on the relative value scale of the services performed by different kinds of public employees.

In short, public employers and public employee groups, together or individually, should begin to develop the factual reserve upon which realistic agreements can be made. A group like yours could even serve as a clearing house for this kind of information for school boards throughout the country.

THE NEW ADMINISTRATION

Before concluding, I would like to make three specific suggestions on what the new Administration might consider regarding the problem of public employment generally.

First, I would hope that our new President will give prompt attention to the Task Force Report on Executive Order 10988. As you know, this covers employee relations for workers in the Federal civil service. This report, which has been completed for some months and which was preceded by extensive hearings, should be high on the list of "things to do." The Federal Government should lead the way in adopting sound and workable procedures for its employees.

Second, there is a vital need for making skilled and experienced mediators available in the event of threatened or actual strikes of local and municipal employees. There are pathetically few states and cities which now have this capability. Where this assistance is not available, the parties simply go without. I would hope that President Nixon will recommend to the new Congress that funds be appropriated so that the FMCS can adequately furnish the same assistance to local public groups that it now provides for private employers, in cases where no other mediation services are available.

Third, the entire problem of collective bargaining in the local public service is becoming larger every day. I fear we have seen only the beginning. Accordingly, I hope the new Administration will encourage and assist those states and municipalities which are now making efforts to put their house in order. A cooperative Federal-state venture of this sort, involving officials at the highest level, would go a long way in providing the direction and leadership we so sorely need.

CITIZENS' CONCERN WITH MUNICIPAL COLLECTIVE BARGAINING
by John M. Capozzola

This concluding selection was originally an address delivered at the National Conference on Government sponsored by the National Municipal League in New Orleans, Louisiana, on December 2, 1968.

Mr. Capozzola, is an associate professor of public administration at New York University. He is also the co-author of a forthcoming book on the subject of municipal collective bargaining.

In considering this subject, some preliminary observations seem appropriate. The problems that confront city officials, employee organizations, and the public are not likely to be temporary. Specific trends which shall be mentioned later are likely to continue over the coming decades. Nor are the problems unique to large cities such as New York, Philadelphia, and Detroit. Furthermore, there is no need for elaboration on my part that the plight of the city is not confined to labor relations, which is properly considered as only one aspect of the so-called urban crisis.

Reprinted with the permission of the author and the National Municipal League.

Throughout we should keep in mind that an almost infinite number of variables tend to make easy generalizations regarding collective bargaining deceptive. As Justice Oliver W. Holmes simply but accurately observed, "General principles don't always decide concrete cases." Certainly it is misstating the problem—despite the incantations of some editorial writers—to charge that public employee groups are formed solely to use muscle to grab power to satisfy selfish desires, just as it is inaccurate for some union leaders to define collective bargaining as "pure muscle."

Basically it is erroneous to look upon public employee groups as other than one more pressure group in the democratic process; and while collective bargaining admittedly is based on a "power principle," power can be exercised within the general framework of law without eliminating reason. There are no definitive answers to all the questions that can be posed, and when the dialogue is carried to extreme positions, we are constrained to utter those bland generalities that mutual restraint and responsibility are necessary, and that there can be neither absolute sovereignty for government nor complete liberty for employee organizations to do as they wish.

Another preliminary observation is that in certain instances a host of other problems have aggravated and complicated the confrontations between employee organizations and city officials. Racial issues, the civil rights movement, demands for community control and decentralization, welfare problems, skyrocketing budgets, the special problems of professional unions and associations—all these and many more add to the difficulties in an era when protests, demands for power, and greater participation permeate most aspects of our lives.

Three final points should be briefly stated. First, the idea of a trade union as an object of opprobrium should be cast aside, even by a few supercilious columnists who exclaim "Thank God, we are not a nation of AFL–CIO plumbers." Secondly, we must keep in mind that public sector bargaining is immature—that there is an exuberance of youth and zeal which will mellow with time, just as the private sector has attained a general sense of stability. Finally, we need a reexamination of some of our long-established principles such as the absolute, total ban on all public employee strikes irrespective of employee group involved and the circumstances under which a strike takes place. Perhaps that often-quoted dictum of President Calvin Coolidge—when governor of Massachusetts—that "There is no right to strike against the public safety by anybody, anywhere, anytime" might be changed to "There should be a right to strike against the government as an *'employer,'* depending upon the circumstances."

A Frenchman observed decades ago, "A strike is not a matter of right, but a brutal and spontaneous fact precipitated by events." While there is a total legal ban on public employee strikes in the United States, strikes and strike threats have occurred with unprecedented frequency. Only a few statistics are needed to make the point.

1. From 1958 through 1967, at least 567 public employee ↑toppages took place.

2. More teacher strikes occurred in 1966 than during the previous five years. In 1967 the number of teacher strikes almost doubled, and during the first 10 months of 1968 schoolteachers have been the occupational group most prone to strike.

3. Until 1966 sanitation workers were the public employee group most likely to strike. During 1967 and 1968 the same group still held a second position after teachers.

4. Only 2 hospital and other health service strikes were recorded from 1958 through 1965. In 1966, 17 strikes were called, and the number increased to 19 in 1967.

5. During the first 10 months of 1968, police and firefighters engaged in stoppages, slowdowns, or job actions on 25 occasions.

6. Recognizing that there are often multiple causes involved in work stoppages, during the first 10 months of 1968 at least 14 stoppages were due to unmet demands for recognition or representation.

The public obviously has reason to be concerned with the increase in the number of strikes that have occurred during the past three years. This is especially the case where there has been an overemphasis on the "right" to strike, with recent events indicating a predisposition to use the strike as a weapon of first rather than of last resort. Simultaneously, on the part of government too much emphasis is centered on "strike prohibition" rather than strike prevention. No legal ban can prevent all strikes any more than one can legally abolish crime. The immediate need is for a change in the context in which labor relations are carried out, and a modification of specific concepts which have traditionally governed municipal labor relations. Slowly but inexorably there has been a change in the climate of labor relations in many cities and states.

Perhaps the most striking way to illustrate the change in the climate of municipal labor relations is to recount an actual happening in a midwestern city during the mid-thirties. A union leader and two of his business representatives tried for several months to obtain an appointment with the members of a city council. Having finally secured an appointment, the union members entered the council chambers. The councilmen seated behind a long table refused to look in the direction of the union leaders, staring at the walls or continuing to examine their papers. After a moment of tension and quiet, the attorney for the Common Council rose and said, "May the record show that the Council does not recognize the presence of the union representatives as this would be an invasion of their sovereignty."

Now the word sovereignty has been defined as supreme, indivisible temporal power, or, in less weighty words, as the right of the state to make public policy decisions, including the manner and modes of making such decisions. Public employers, however, have traditionally made use of the doctrine to oppose collective bargaining on the grounds that the government as the custodian of sovereignty, i.e., ultimate authority in the community, *must* exercise the right of final decision in *all* matters affecting its relations with its employees.

The obvious corollary is that the government as a sovereign employer asserts that its relationship to its employees is different from the relationship of private employers to their employees. From this basic premise stems the belief that the methods used by workers in private employ to bring pressure to bear upon their employers, including the strike weapon, have no place in the public service, as their use represents a derogation of sovereignty and an attack on the sovereignty of the state.

The incident described had close parallels in the year 1968, with some state and city governments claiming that their position as sovereigns entitled them to rights and privileges to which no other employer could lay claim, insisting that government's role as the maintainer of law and order compelled it to demand implicit obedience. For example, in March 1968, the attorney general of Nevada stated that collective bargaining and strikes by public employees in Nevada were illegal. The opinion also declared that public employers may adopt regulations preventing employees from belonging to an organization seeking to represent employees for the purpose of collective bargaining.

In Memphis, the failure to implement the bargaining process successfully had tragic consequences. Yet, vestiges of the long-established resistance to collective bargaining are not confined to state and municipal governments. During the 1968 session of Congress, several bills were introduced in both houses to prevent union security pacts at the Federal level. The much-heralded Kennedy Executive Order 10988 continues to vest final decisions on bargainable issues in the employing authority or central personnel agency. Indeed, to date, less than one-quarter of the states mandate collective bargaining for most municipal employees.

Some state courts have shown no reluctance to issue injunctions against public employee strikes irrespective of the circumstances or the category of employees involved in the dispute. A few diehard public officials show no inhibitions, describing the ultimate purposes of the AFT–AFL–CIO as "illegal activities."

But, despite these examples, the trend towards state mandated municipal bargaining continues. Municipal employment is by far the most rapidly growing segment of the American labor force; the AFL–CIO has staked it out as the most fertile field for organizing efforts, and the growth of union membership has resulted in the expansion of collective bargaining as a method of determining employment relations. As of June 1968, nine states (Wisconsin, Connecticut, Massachusetts, Michigan, Missouri, New York, Oregon, Rhode Island, and Washington) had passed comprehensive labor statutes mandating municipal bargaining, and most of these statutes were passed after 1965. In October, 1968, New Jersey enacted a statute providing for collective bargaining. Four additional states (Alaska, Delaware, New Hampshire, and Vermont) authorized municipal employers to engage in collective bargaining at their discretion. Some statutes continue to reflect the traditional hostility towards bargaining and underscore the necessity of a clear legal prescription that both sides of the table must bargain in good faith with the intent to reach a mutually satisfactory decision.

There are many reasons for citizen concern with the bargaining process as it now operates beyond the fact that it inevitably assumes the coloration of municipal politics. Some employee organizations persist in resorting to the "end run" technique in its various forms, attempting to gain from the legislature what they failed to achieve from the executive branch. The desires of some employee unions to "leapfrog" economic packages gained by other unions force cities to negotiate while looking over their shoulders at forthcoming bargaining sessions with other groups. The cries of "Me, too" inevitably tend to disturb the delicate balance of the municipal finance structure. Although there have been attempts at a single set of negotiations—and some cities have already moved in this direction—the broad problem of intra-union as well as inter-union competition complicates efforts to achieve a breakthrough in this area.

Space does not permit more than a brief reference to that fascinating subject of the script or ritual by which the bargaining process is in some cases acted out. The initial exorbitant demands, the threatening statements of doom and gloom, the role-playing, and the histrionics and table-pounding are considered by some an essential part of the process, which has been likened to a rain dance. In some instances the whole psychology of bargaining is further complicated by the sensitivities and egos of the participants. Surely the new leader is under a compulsion "to do better" than his predecessor, just as it is considered part of the game to test the resistance and capabilities of new political or administrative chieftains. One point is clear: Those who do not understand the internal problems of a union leader fail utterly in their assessment of the situation; likewise histrionics and table-pounding are no substitute for concrete gains for the membership.

There are a host of technical bargaining problems confronting the administrators that concern the citizen but are largely the worry and responsibility of the representatives of the city. Unit determination, certification, employee organization demands for a modified union shop, agency shop, or maintenance or membership clauses—all these are facets of union security wherein the decision of the city negotiator has implications for the citizenry at large. The general lack of experienced negotiators, mediators, factfinders, and arbitrators to resolve impasses over these and other issues points to a stormy future.

I have touched briefly on some of the issues without raising the question of the public's right to know what takes place during the actual bargaining. A number of states have "open meeting" or "antisecrecy" statutes designed to prevent decisionmaking in private, wherein such decisions are perfunctorily ratified in public without discussion. The trend of court decisions, while upholding the public's right to have final and binding decisions by its representatives made in public, appear to be realistic in recognizing that without the use of executive sessions, it is less likely that settlements will be quickly negotiated.

There are a number of fine points, not easily settled, on the role of the press, which does have an obligation to keep the public informed. But there have been occasions in which the press has served more as an advocate of one position rather than an "impartial" reporter of the news.

There is one area where no one would deny that the public is concerned, i.e., the extent to which budgets have increased, and, as a result, the increase in our taxes. The extent, however, to which collective bargaining per se has caused the increased costs is a moot point. Generalizations are easy, and statistics can be amassed to show that since personnel costs are the largest segment of a city budget, the bargaining process inexorably contributes to higher expenditures.

The amount of significant research in this area is sparse, but some tendencies may be summarized. 1. The cost of contract settlements has risen, but even the figures released do not reveal the true fiscal impact of the settlements. 2. The actions of public employee unions have tended to preempt certain areas traditionally considered the sole prerogative of the politically elected representatives of the people. 3. The revenue patterns of municipalities have already been reexamined and we may expect more of the same. 4. Fringe benefits of an amazing variety are being negotiated and extended to most classes of city employees. 5. The role, functions, and methods of municipal finance officers will undergo further changes.

There are other administrative implications of concern to citizens beyond the fiscal aspects, such as maintaining stability in the pay structure and coordinating the bargaining process with budgetary timetables. Bureaucracy has a tendency to perpetuate outdated methods as it grows and becomes complex. Operating in alliance with the "managerial bureaucracy," the employer will attempt to man the barricades against further encroachments into areas traditionally considered management's prerogative. Organized employees, especially in the professions, have long sought to influence policy and limit managerial discretion in pursuit of professional autonomy. The merit principle, in the view of many, has come under attack, and civil service commissions are regarded by some union leaders as little more than "tools of the employer."

As of November 11, 1968, New York City was deeply involved in a school strike that was an amalgam of problems including decentralization, demands for community control, due process, union security, and law and order. The conflicting charges and countercharges have produced an explosive situation in which the education of 1.1 million school children has been disrupted, and the hate literature being circulated can only inflame the situation further. In this case the conflicting aspirations of the participants make a total victory for either side a virtual impossibility. Frustrated and embittered local groups demand greater community control. The city administration remains committed to decentralization. Too much decentralization, however, would not only be a threat to the union's bargaining power but also a threat to civil service laws, procedures, and the merit principle itself. These fears have tended to fuse teachers, school custodians, supervisory personnel, and some parents into a solid bloc.

On the other hand the proponents of local control see the civil service structure as an impediment to searching for the special talents needed to cope with the problems of the ghetto. Some people recite the charge that the Central School Board heads a "pathological bureaucracy." More extreme individuals charge teachers with the "programmed mental retardation" of black children. Whether true or not, the belief that a white power structure is the intolerable obstacle to gains by the culturally deprived adds up to a combustible situation. When one considers the magnitude of education (with some 60 million of our population involved as pupils, teachers, or administrators) it is obvious that citizens had better become more concerned. We have already had statewide action by teacher organizations, and in the text of his tentative proposal for teacher unity one person has stated that the new organization would seek state and national agreements on "basic conditions and school funds." I quote one of his reasons for proposing the "merger" of the AFT and the NEA: "Neither organization could conduct a successful statewide or national work stoppage if necessary in order to win added funds" [*GERR,* No. 268, B–11, October 28, 1968].

In summary form, several trends have developed warranting greater citizen interest in public service bargaining. As of 1968, more than 12 million employees, approximately one-sixth of the nation's labor force, earn their livelihood working for the government. By sheer numbers this constitutes an effective political bloc, and an increased proportion of these employees now comes from minority groups. This tendency is in line with proposals that government should be the employer of last resort, and perhaps even the employer of first resort, to help in the solution of ghetto problems.

The militancy of public employees, while not new, has changed in form and degree. Militancy is contagious and the activism is not confined to public employees, with a variety of societal groups demanding more participation and more power. There has been a transformation in the role of professional associations. Having always sought to influence and even control policy, these associations now talk and act much more like trade unions to demonstrate their virility and protect their organizations.

Another trend has been the increase in factionalism within unions. While it may be argued that this is in the interest of democratic trade unionism, it must be noted that rebellious rank-and-filers have made the ratification of contracts more difficult, causing several strikes.

The most significant trend, of course, has been the number of states which have introduced collective bargaining through comprehensive statutes. This is decidedly evidence of the erosion of the view that the doctrine of sovereignty *commands* a unilateral mode of personnel administration. Even a few court decisions relating to strikes or the issuance of court injunctions have made a first step towards elimination of the blanket strike prohibition. The Governor's Study Commission in Pennsylvania in June 1968 proposed a limited right to strike which was quickly rejected by the governor and not included in proposed legislation.

In some ways, the most interesting trend is the politicalization of the public employee movement, where the parties engage in what is primarily a political contest. Unions, with the support of the general labor movement, counter the efforts of management by demonstrations and mass picketing of city hall, exert pressure on the top political echelon, and lobby at the state and city legislative level.

The movement from pure "Gomperism" to "Gomperism plus political power" has been accompanied by a relaxation of the restrictions on the political activities of public employees. Furthermore, the role of the Central Trades Council remains a powerful factor on the municipal scene, sometimes as a restraining hand.

When all the chips are counted, however, perhaps Alistair Cooke raises a fundamental issue worth pondering. He states, "Nobody feels an obligation to the city anymore. The only obligation is to one's family. The breakdown in society comes when people can't recognize any public obligation beyond their family." With all due respect to Mr. Cooke, Pericles said it much more forcefully over 2,000 years ago in his Funeral Oration, in which he characterized citizenship as the Athenian's proudest glory.

> An Athenian citizen does not neglect the state because he takes care of his own household; and even those of us who are engaged in business have a very fair idea of politics. We alone regard a man who takes no interest in public affairs, not as harmless, but as a useless character; and if few of us are originators, we are all sound judges of policy.

GLOSSARY OF LABOR RELATIONS TERMS

Agency shop. A place of employment where nonunion members are required to pay a fee usually equal to union dues. Under the law, employee organizations have to negotiate for everyone in the bargaining unit and the fee is charged for negotiating and servicing the contract.

Appropriate unit. A group of employees entitled to vote for and be represented in collective bargaining by an organization. Before the election takes place the unit is fixed by the national or state board through the establishment of community of interest of employees and the exclusion of supervisory personnel who are to be considered management.

Arbitration. A process used to bring about a settlement of a dispute through a third party. Usually both sides agree to accept the decision of an arbitrator or a three-man board of arbitration. Compulsory arbitration means parties to a dispute must use a third party rather than resort to a strike or lockout.

Central body. A group, council, or federation of labor unions in one city, all belonging to the same parent body such as the AFL–CIO. They may be affiliated with different international unions such as the Teachers Union and the Bricklayers and still be united in an AFL–CIO Central Labor Council.

Certification. Official notification, usually following an election, that an employee organization has been recognized as the bargaining agent of an appropriate unit.

Checkoff. An agreement whereby the employer deducts the union dues for the union from the pay of the employees.

Closed shop. A place of employment where an employee must be a member of the union before he can be hired.

Employee election. Voting by employees to determine which organization should represent them in bargaining with an employer.

Factfinding. A process whereby an individual or a board is chosen to make a study of facts in a dispute and make recommendations for a settlement of the dispute. Recommendations may be made public.

Free riders. A term used to describe employees who do not pay dues or fees but receive benefits won by the union.

Good-faith bargaining. As set out in the Taft-Hartley law, both parties must meet at a reasonable time and discuss or confer on issues. The law does not require that either side must make a proposal or a concession.

Grievance. A complaint by either the employee or the employer that there has been a violation of the contract. Some contracts call for the settlement of difficult grievances by arbitration.

Independent union. An association, organization or group which is not affiliated with a national organization or a federation of unions such as the AFL–CIO.

Lockout. The shutting-down of a place of employment to put pressure on employees during a dispute. An example of this would be a union in one department striking and the employer closing down the entire plant and putting the other employees out of work.

Maintenance-of-membership. An agreement to preserve the security of the union requiring that employees who are members of the union on a certain date will remain members while the contract runs.

Mediation. Using the neutral offices of a third party to bring both sides in a dispute together.

Open shop. A place of employment in which the employee may or may not join the union.

Unfair labor practices. Procedures which are forbidden by the National Labor Relations Board or certain state boards. In the field of public employee bargaining these vary from state to state. The laws of Connecticut and Illinois cover them fairly extensively. Examples of unfair labor practices by an employer would be:
   a) refusing to negotiate in good faith.
   b) discriminating between union and nonunion members.
   c) attempting to control or dominate an employee organization.
   d) punishing or discriminating against an employee who attempts to organize or who files an unfair labor practice.

Some examples of an unfair labor practice by an employee organization would be:

    a) refusing to negotiate in good faith.

    b) coercion of employees in matters of their rights.

    c) inducing an employer to commit an unfair labor practice.

Union shop. A place of employment where an employee agrees to join the union within a specified time after being hired, usually 30 days.

INDEX

315